Falling in Love with Your Self

The Principles and Practice of Self-Love

by Michael R. Kent

Paulist Press   New York   Mahwah, N.J.

Some of the affirmations that begin on page 241 originally appeared in the book *Shame Faced* by Stephanie E., copyright 1986 by Hazelden Foundation, Center City, MN and are reprinted by permission.

Library of Congress Cataloging-in-Publication Data

Kent, Michael R., 1939-
    Falling in love with your self: the principles and practice of self-love / by Michael R. Kent.
      p.   cm.
    Includes bibliographical references.
    ISBN 0-8091-3389-X (pbk.)
    1. Self-acceptance. 2. Self-esteem. 3. Inferiority complex. I. Title.
BF575.S37K46   1994
158'.1—dc20   93-42477
                                                           CIP

Published by Paulist Press
997 Macarthur Boulevard
Mahwah, New Jersey 07430

Printed and bound in the
United States of America

Contents

Introduction 1
        The Ugly Duckling 1
        "Ugly" Americans 2
        Shame and Self-Esteem 3
        The Cult of Narcissism 4
        Self-Love Is Learned 6
        Why This Book? 7

PART ONE: *Before You Can Fall In Love*

CHAPTER ONE: In the Absence of Love 15
        Shyness 15
        Loneliness 16
        Chronic Dissatisfaction 18
        Depression/Fear/Anxiety 20
        Poor Relationships 21
        Alcohol Abuse, Drugs, and Addictions 23
        Growing Crime Rate 24

CHAPTER TWO: Self-Love Lost 26
        Early Childhood 27
        School and Growing Up in America 32
        Modern Advertising 34
        "God Hates Me" 35
        Life-Long Coping Habits 37
        Need to Evolve Higher 38
        Diminished But Not Destroyed 39

iv/*Contents*

CHAPTER THREE: Necessary Dispositions 41
    Enough Is Enough 42
    Resigned to Work with What You Have 43
    Accepting the Inner Journey 44
    Making a Commitment 47
    Resistance 48
    The Miracle of Consciousness 49
    "Original Sin" 50
    King Baby 51
    Further Handicaps 56
    Out of Our Control 57
    A Higher Power Can Help 60
    Surrender 64

CHAPTER FOUR: All That Self-Love Isn't 70
    Arrogance 72
    Selfishness 73
    Selflessness 74
    Feeling Successful 75
    Having Possessions 76
    Self-Pre-Occupation 77
    Feeling Good 78
    Willfulness and Power 78

PART TWO: Self-Love Recovery

CHAPTER FIVE: Getting to Know You 83
    Impossible To Know Ourselves Directly 85
    Ultimately, Who Am "I"? 86
    What We Think *About* Ourselves Matters 89
    Fundamentally, What Do You Think
        About Yourself? 90
    Meant To Be 92
    You Are My Beloved 94
    What Makes Us Run Away? 96
    Rediscovering Our Spiritual Roots 97

CHAPTER SIX: Inner Work: Re-Programming 99
    Inner Work Needed 100
    Get a Life 103
    Self-Love Is Not a Feeling 104
    Love Is as Love Does 106
    Becoming Aware/Observing 107
    Changing the "Tapes" 109

CHAPTER SEVEN: Inner Work: Affirmative Action (Part I)
                  Primary Principles 116
    Assert Your Self: *A Right To Be* 118
    Be Who You Are: *Uniqueness* 120
    Own Your Self: *Independence* 122
    Take Responsibility for Your Self:
        Moral Accountability 125
    Believe in Your Self: *Empowerment* 128

CHAPTER EIGHT: Inner Work: Affirmative Action (Part II)
                  Self-Loving Actions 131
    Live Now 132
    Grow Up 133
    Discipline Your Self 135
    Do Your Own Driving 136
    Make Your Self "Adequate" 137
    Face and Solve Problems 138
    Be Direct 141
    Ask for What You Need 142
    Affirm Your Self 144
    Stand Up for Your Self 146
    Be All You Can Be 147
    Discover Your Self 149
    Define Your Self 150
    Determine Your Perceptions 151
    Live Off Your Assets 153
    Invest in Your Life 154
    Involve Your Self 155
    Risk Your Self 156

Be Gentle with Your Self 160
Accept Your Feelings 162
Treat Your Self Special 164
Enjoy Your Successes 165
Present Your Self Appropriately 167
Take Care of Your Health 167
Allow Your Self Freedom 168
Give Your Self Work You Love 169
Spend Time Alone with Your Self 171
Allow Your Self To Love Everybody 173
Allow Your Self To be Loved 175
Be Grateful 176

CHAPTER NINE: *De-Programming 180*
Refuse To Be Victimized by Opinions, Expectations, and Criticism 180
Refuse to Be Victimized by the "Shoulds" 182
Don't Stay Stuck in Self-Diminishing or Non-Nourishing Religious Systems 184
Refuse to Sit in Judgment 187
Never Harbor Ill-Will, Hatred, or Unforgiveness 189
Don't Isolate 192
Don't Amplify 193
"Fear Not" 195
Don't Worry 196
Don't Rely on "Logic" 198
Stop "Personalizing" Every Mistake 199
Avoid Envy and "Wishful Thinking" 200
Don't "Take" Care of Others 202
Avoid Toxic People 203
Don't Wait for Someone Else To Do It for You 204
Don't Give Up on Your Self 205

PART THREE: *Continuing Care in Self-Love Recovery*

CHAPTER TEN: *Twelve-Step Spirituality 211*
The First Step 213

Step Two   214
Step Three   215
Step Four   217
Step Five   217
Step Six   218
Step Seven   219
Step Eight   220
Step Nine   220
Step Ten   221
Step Eleven   222
Step Twelve   223
A Personal Spiritual Inventory   225

CHAPTER ELEVEN: *Self-Loving Affirmations*   227
   Affirmations for Co-Dependents   227
   One Hundred Helpful Self-Affirmations   241

CHAPTER TWELVE: *Developing Detachment of
                     the Observing "I"*   248
   Out of Your Mind   249
   See for Your Self   251
   Open Doors   253
   Talk to Your Self   254
   Higher Consciousness   255

CHAPTER THIRTEEN: *Use Your Imagination*   256
   A Powerful Tool 257
   How Do You Picture Yourself?   258
   Think and Act "As If"   260
   Imaginative Dialogue with Your Self   262
   Refuting Our Inner Critic   264
   Using Models   266
   The Good Old Days   266
   Vanity of Vanities   268
   Your Inner Voices   268
   Seeing Your Self In Action   269

CHAPTER FOURTEEN: Loving Your Self Through Times of Crisis 273

Optimists vs. Pessimists 275
Why Me? 276
Powerlessness and Surrender 277
Powerless But Not Helpless 279
Don't Deny Feelings 280
Talk About It 281
Discipline Catastrophic Thinking 283
Stick to a Routine 286
Be Vigilant About Diet 287
One Day at a Time 288
Use Techniques for Handling Stress 289

CHAPTER FIFTEEN: Managing Stress 290

Are You Stress Prone? 291
What Is Stress Telling You About Your Self? 292
Surrender 293
Deal with the Problem 294
Discipline Distorted Thinking 295
Change a Stress-prone Life Style to Its Opposite 297
Practice Direct Stress-Relieving Techniques 299

Bibliography 300

This book is dedicated to Laura, who models its principles and lives by its practices as few I have ever known.

Introduction

THE UGLY DUCKLING

I trust most of us grew up as children having heard the fable of "The Ugly Duckling." I've seen some different versions of it, but, simply told, a swan's egg ends up in a clutch of duck eggs. The mother duck incubates all the eggs until they hatch. Needless to say, the newly hatched swan looks significantly different from the other ducklings in the nest. The difference becomes even more appreciable as they grow up together. The ducks all end up looking very much as growing-up ducks should, but the fledgling swan is too large, too overweight, too ungainly, and worst of all...it honks rather than quacks.

The swan, quite predictably, develops a terrible inferiority complex. It is humiliated for being different. It is picked on, ridiculed, avoided and scorned for not looking and behaving as a real duck should. The swan just never fits into polite duck society. And that's an awfully lonely way to be.

Good fables however usually end on an upswing. So finally one day the swan goes through its final molting and shows itself to be the beautiful swan that it is. With the envy of its now lesser looking duckling companions, the swan floats onto the pond to join other swans in swanland, and lives happily ever after.

The swan of the fable was lucky. After many growing up crises, the swan finally comes to realize it is a beautiful swan. After a period of feeling bad about looking different, the swan finds happiness in discovering what a beautiful work of creation it is. The swan has learned to love itself.

But what if the story didn't end up that way? What if the swan forever kept on thinking it was a duck? Not a swan at all,

1

but an ugly duck? What if the swan never knew what being a swan was all about? What if the swan never had healthy swan models to compare itself with? What if the swan always figured that being a duck and looking like a duck was the only right way to be? No question, it would go through life with a defective sense of self-worth, self-appreciation, and self-love. Whenever it saw its reflection in the smooth surface of the pond, it would never see and love graceful beauty; it would always see and despise an ugly duck.

A swan has to know it is a swan to feel good about itself. A swan that thinks it is a duck, and that it should be a duck, will never feel good about itself. A swan that thinks it should be an eagle, or a peacock, will never love itself. A swan must know and accept itself as a swan to ever love itself at all.

"UGLY" AMERICANS

For almost three decades of ministry I have counseled thousands of people burdened with marital and family problems, people afflicted with loneliness, depression, grief, and inner "emptiness." Listening to their stories, I have long come to the conclusion that one thing all these troubled people had in common was that they didn't like themselves. Inevitably, after closer analysis of the problems presented, it became clear that their problems were not outside, but inside, themselves. Their issues were self-love issues.

In reading mental health journals and from speaking with a large number of friends who are in counseling professions, it has long become clear to me that lack of self-esteem and self-love is a problem of major proportions in the lives of modern day Americans, myself included. I conclude that most of us can relate to this fable of the ugly duckling because we have never come to know or love ourselves as we need.

We live with ourselves twenty-four hours a day, and yet we are a mystery to ourselves. For the most part we are intelligent and well-informed on a variety of topics, but we don't know very much about what makes us tick, or why we tick the way we do.

We feel good or we feel bad, and often can't explain why. We are easily hurt and offended. We are sensitive to the slightest criticism. Our self-esteem may hang by a thread. We don't understand why we so often engage in self-destructive behaviors. We don't know why some things bother us when they don't seem to bother anyone else. We don't know why we're not "making it" better than we do. We find it increasingly difficult to cope with the world that surrounds us. We don't feel adequate to life. We don't feel properly equipped. We don't feel we "fit."

We lack a sense of self. We lack a sense of purpose and destiny. We are not engaged in living as much as we are resigned to living. We are not invested in our lives; we mechanically go through its motions. We don't have clear answers to some of the most important questions in life. As a matter of fact, we find it difficult to frame important questions. We are aware of an empty feeling inside, a hollowness, a "hole in the soul." Something fundamental seems to be missing. No matter how we address it, no matter how many self-help books we read, no matter how many compliments we take in, a "black hole" sits at our center, swallowing everything into its vortex, and giving back little light.

There has been much media discussion recently of how glum Americans have become. A pall hangs over the nation that is more than an economic slump. We seem to be losing confidence in our way of life. We seem to have lost confidence in ourselves. We are trying to live out the American Dream, but for many the dream is becoming an illusion, if not a nightmare. We are not a noticeably happy people. We are full of envy and often wish we were someone else. We don't like ourselves very much.

SHAME AND SELF-ESTEEM

You cannot love what you are ashamed of. In an article featured in the February 1992 issue of the *Atlantic Monthly*, Robert Karen examined "Shame," which in the eyes of many contemporary psychologists is being called "the master emotion, the unseen regulator of our entire affective life." Shame is believed by many analysts to be "the pre-eminent cause of emotional distress in our time, a by-product, some contend, of social changes and child-rearing practices that have made us unusually insecure about who we are."

Shame is a feeling of fundamental unworthiness. Shame is not guilt. Shame is not the same as feeling guilty over something we have done wrong. Shame is feeling bad about who and what we are. Guilt affects our deeds; shame affects our essence, the legitimacy of our existence, our very being. The swan has done nothing wrong, but when it looks upon its reflection, it sees an ugly duck.

While much of our shame is repressed, it can be triggered by almost anything: losing a job, a confrontation, a slight criticism, being asked to give an accounting for one thing or another, being asked to give an opinion, fear of coming up short on the rent, being refused a request for a date, breaking off a toxic relationship, leaving home, becoming ill, and so on. Losing a job in times of recession is a hard fact of life. However, many who lose their jobs because of financial cut-backs feel personally shamed. They interpret a job loss as a personal indictment of their fundamental unworthiness. "I feel like a total failure."

In the same month of February 1992, Newsweek featured an article on "The Curse of Self-Esteem." The article questioned the validity of the "feel good movement" as a program for restoring a genuine sense of self-worth. "Self-esteem" has been called "the biggest personal issue of the 1990s." Millions of words have been written on the subject in best-selling publications. It is a hot-selling issue and a hot topic of conversation. People are not happy about who they are. We are a nation of people who want to feel good about ourselves, but apparently not too many are succeeding.

THE CULT OF NARCISSISM

"Narcissism" became the psychological "in" word of the 1980s. Therapists had a field day labeling their clients as "narcissistic." Our whole culture has already been defined by social historians as "narcissistic." A "narcissist" is someone who is so tuned in to himself or herself that little else in this world counts, except one's self. One's ego and ego satisfaction are all that really matter. Attending to one's pleasures is of primary and exclusive concern. The world, and most people in it, are seen, judged, accepted or rejected, in terms of how they feed one's ego needs.

It is good to have self-esteem. It is good to like oneself, to take care of oneself, to nurture oneself. It might appear that as narcissists, most of us love ourselves too much. It might appear that adequate self-love is not an issue, that most of us love ourselves more than we need. But is such the case?

Someone classified as "narcissistic" is someone who is self-inflating. Someone who has a need to "inflate" himself or herself is someone who feels deflated. We only need to inflate ourselves when we feel that the self we have is inadequate. That is why narcissism is classified as a personality disorder. Self-inflation is a cover-up for a self-image that is perceived as defective. Narcissists really don't love themselves at all.

Thomas Wolfe once labeled us latter-part-of-the-century Americans as the "me"-generation. He put a label on something which probably does not surprise us: that we are really into ourselves, into our own agendas, into our ego satisfactions. "Looking out for #1" is not only the great American pastime, it has become the great American pre-occupation. Everything matters in terms of what is significant for, or satisfies, me. The vast population of these American states could be said to have narcissistic fixations. We are the most vocally dissatisfied, hyperly-critical, extremely demanding, and litigious people on the face of the earth.

But this is only indicative of how un-self-loving we are. Counseling offices are crowded with patients who don't like themselves. Millions of people are walking the streets who feel deep shame about who and what they are. For all their self-serving, narcissists are basically insecure about themselves. They spend most their waking hours in a self-defensive posture. They live in a self-aggrandizing mode because they are fundamentally unsure and uncomfortable with their self-image. Self-inflation camouflages a fearful and emotionally damaged ego—an ego which is ashamed of its self and needs consistent pumping up to appear somewhat presentable.

The cosmetic industry in this country feeds on narcissism and currently shows profits running into the billions of dollars each year. Men and woman, teenagers and children, spend lavishly on making themselves appear better than they feel. Styles and fashions change rapidly. Advertisers prey on the inner insecurities that most of us have about ourselves and successfully persuade us to keep pace with the changes. And, compared to the glamorous stars and fashion models that are paraded before us, few of us stand a chance of liking what we see in the mirror in the morning. Even if we are attractive, it is difficult to *feel* attractive, for any length of time. The fashion industry, or the advertisers, can change a trend in a wink of an eye, and "in" is "out."

Evidence of damaged self-images abounds in our society. Addictions are epidemic in all large American cities. Addicts are readily diagnosed as having poor self-esteem. Social psychologists claim the rapid rise in crime today has much to do with self-worth issues. Education experts claim that the poor record of our school systems, and the lack of motivation on part of students, are intimately tied up with crumbling self-valuing, as is the accelerating suicide rate among the young. Studies reveal that the bulk of emotional problems and disorders in our adult population are rooted in problems with shame and deficient self-esteem.

SELF-LOVE IS LEARNED

The analysis we have gone through so far would be pretty dismal if there wasn't much hope for coming to appreciate and love ourselves as we need. The fact is, however, that we can come to know and love ourselves adequately and appropriately.

Many people do. We can face our shame and reject it for healthy self-esteem. We can learn to let go of our guilt and our self-defeating attitudes and behaviors. We can face our limitations and nonetheless live with dignity and self-respect.

We all go through life saddled with a variety of character defects and disorders, physical and intellectual limitations, emotional problems and hangups. We are all imperfect, and our many imperfections bring us pain and frustration. The world and other people are imperfect and this puts great strain on our coping skills. Life is painful. It is impossible to escape pain and limitation. We have to learn to cope. Unfortunately, many of our coping strategies have led us into a variety of blind alleys.

The best means of coping, we will see, is learning to love ourselves as we need. But this is not easy. With few exceptions, adequate love for ourselves does not come about automatically with our upbringing. Nature provides us with the drive and tools for survival, but mature self-love, or love of any sort, is something which is learned. Self-love does not come to us without effort. Defensiveness does. Self-protection does. The tendency to inflate ourselves like a puffer fish does. Love, self-love, is an art and a craft. We achieve it, and get better at it, only with insight and practice.

WHY THIS BOOK?

Many fine books have been written about self-esteem. Why is there need for another? In the first place, it is often assumed that self-esteem and self-love are interchangeable terms. They are not. "Love" and "esteem" are not synonyms. I can admire others and have great esteem and respect for them, without loving them at all. Briefly, as we shall see later, self-esteem is something we possess; self-love is something we do, for ourselves. There is a difference—a big difference. Self-esteem can be enhanced by upgrading "thinking" about ourselves; self-love is built primarily by loving actions we take on our behalf. While there is a strong and obvious connection between self-esteem and self-love, self-love involves dynamics that merit their own consideration. This book will treat those dynamics directly and explicitly.

Most treatments of a subject like "self-love" are very often incomplete. Some authors affirm how important self-love is to a wholesome and satisfying life, and offer excellent analyses of how self-love is lost or diminished, but fail to offer programs or methods by which self-love can be recovered and actually experienced. Others offer imaginative and "clinically-tested exercises" for regaining self-assurance and feelings of self-worth, but refrain from exploring the spiritual insights which could provide a more solid and permanent foundation for self-love. Many of us who tried these self-help remedies often found ourselves right back at the booksellers, searching out the latest offering to help us gain the meaning and happiness we wanted. We did not eat and become satisfied; we continued to look for more and more menus.

Although "exercises" will be offered to boost self-appreciation, this is not a quick-fix manual to puff up a deflated ego. We will not be introduced to a series of emotional calisthenics geared to tricking your imagination into grandiose ideas about yourself. This is not an attempt to start you on an ego trip with an exaggerated estimation of yourself nor an invitation to find or refine your own personal style of narcissism. It is my contention that mere techniques and exercises lack depth and of themselves cannot assure a recovery of self-love that is both permanent and genuine. A spiritual foundation for self-love recovery is essential. This book brings both spiritual insight and methods of self-love recovery together.

Furthermore, the topic of love is inexhaustible. The "last word" on the subject will never be spoken. Self-love is the basis of all personal happiness and satisfaction in life. On the other side of the coin, an absence of self-love is the basis of most of our unhappiness and dissatisfaction. As we will see in the first chapter, an absence of self-love is at the root of many, if not most, of the debilitating problems we face as individuals and as a society. We will never cope adequately with these problems until we learn to love ourselves as we need.

There are millions who still haven't picked up the motivation or the skills necessary to love themselves as they need. There are millions who are numb with fear before life and either withdraw in isolation or overcompensate with destructive behaviors. There are millions who dislike themselves so much that they are forever wishing they were someone else. They live life vicariously as "fans," or immerse themselves in the fantasies of sitcoms, soap operas, and supermarket tabloids. There are millions who consider themselves loving and caring people and can't understand why they feel so "empty." There are millions of people who are swans, yet continue to perceive themselves as ducks. Ugly ducks at that.

For a swan to see itself as a swan, and not as a duck, requires an awakening, an enlightenment, a spiritual transformation. From the very beginning of our self-love recovery program we will explore the spiritual insights that are essential to this kind of "conversion." For this we will be indebted to the great spiritual traditions of humanity that are so sadly, and unnecessarily, eclipsed in our materialistic culture. We will also be indebted to the insights and practices of the Twelve-Step program, which has had phenomenal success in bringing addicts, especially alcoholics, to sobriety, dignity, and genuine self-love, where nothing else has worked.

The principles and practices of self-love recovery contained in this book have been culled from extensive research and above all from personal experience. I present these principles and practices here because I know they work. They have worked for me in my own self-love recovery. They have pulled me through some incredibly trying times that have tested my self-love and self-esteem to their limits. In my indebtedness to so many others who have shared their insights with me, I offer to share them with you.

In Part One we will examine the dispositions we need to begin self-love recovery and enhancement. We will see what a lack of adequate self-love costs us, what factors are involved in loss of self-love, and what will help us begin self-love recovery. We will investigate how much control we have over our self-love recovery, what could prove a major block in our recovery program, and what self-love recovery isn't.

Part Two will explore insights and spiritual dispositions which, I propose, are essential to self-love recovery. We will outline action programs that make self-love operative. We will examine who we really are, and if there is a "Higher Power" operating in our behalf. We will determine what inner work of re-programming needs to be done to open ourselves to self-love recovery. What self-affirmative actions can we take on our behalf? What actions can we take to de-program ourselves of whatever damages our self-love?

Part Three will examine disciplines, exercises and techniques that we can use to continue our self-love recovery, especially in difficult times and threatening situations. We will outline the Twelve-Step spirituality program which is the backbone of many addiction recovery programs today. We will learn effective self-affirmation exercises. We will learn how to become more detached observers of the drama of our lives, how to use the power of our imaginations in self-love recovery, how to take care of ourselves in times of crisis, and how to handle stress.

Self-love is the foundation of all loving relationships. The most important relationship you will ever have (outside of God as you understand him) is with your own self. What follows in this book is an invitation to a spiritual quest, to an honest reflection of who and what you really are. Throughout this book "self" is used as a separate word instead of "myself" or "yourself," for example. This is not a typographical error. It is an encouragement to look upon your self as a friend and life-long companion who needs your attention, love, care, and nurturing.

Finally, I deliberately entitled this book *Falling in Love with Your Self.* I am well aware that "falling in love" is a transitory phenomenon. Many of us have fallen in, and out, of love many times over. "Falling in love" in our culture also connotes infatuation, most often tinged with highly erotic impulses of short duration. Be that as it may, I believe that coming to genuinely love ourselves may be a "first-love" experience for many readers. Loving ourselves adequately and appropriately on a more permanent basis just may need to be triggered by a falling-in-love enticement. This book, therefore, is an invitation for the swan to see how beautiful it is. This book is an invitation for you to appreciate that you are already a work of art.

Your life is a work of art. We are called to life to make a masterpiece of ourselves. Tragically, many of us are afraid to pick up our paint brushes. Many let others paint on their personal canvasses. This book is an encouragement to pick up our own brushes and do our own painting. The brushwork is the loving actions we take on our behalf.

As you continue to create your masterpiece, you will come to love it more and more. You fall in love with your self as you fall in love with anyone. You are attracted to what you see. You admire what you observe. You want to make a connection with what you are coming to see is lovely. You are lovely because you are, and you need to learn how to paint your self that way.

It is the YOU that is lovely and lovable that we want to look at.

PART ONE
BEFORE YOU CAN FALL
IN LOVE

1

In the Absence of Love

> *The remarkable thing is that we really love our neigh-*
> *bor as ourselves; we do unto others as we do unto our-*
> *selves. We hate others when we hate ourselves. We are*
> *tolerant of others when we tolerate ourselves. We for-*
> *give others when we forgive ourselves. It is not love of*
> *self but hatred of self which is at the root of the trou-*
> *bles that afflict our world.*
>
> —Eric Hoffer

We might best begin by acknowledging what lack of adequate self-love costs us. There is a direct connection between an absence of self-love and a great variety of emotional disorders and painful conditions that occupy so much of our life and feelings. Lack of self-love is at the root of most personal problems we face, and, ultimately, at the root of most of our social ills as well.

SHYNESS

Cindy at twenty-nine is still as attractive as she was as a teenager. She is employed as a legal secretary to a locally prominent attorney. The attorney calls her a "real find" because she is bright and skillful in her job and never misses a day of work. Her family wonders why she never went on to become an attorney herself. It certainly wasn't for lack of brains or opportunity.

15

The problem is that Cindy is extremely shy. It hurts her to talk to strangers or to be anywhere in the public eye. She loves her job because she works in a safe, well-defined little cubicle. Her salary is decent enough for her to afford a small and well-furnished condominium. She rarely goes out and has had only two dates in her life, both of which were "disasters." She chose not to become an attorney because she felt she could never handle the amount of contact with people that attorneys engage in. Fellow workers urge her to "loosen up" and to get out more. They suggest she would have no trouble getting dates if she appeared half-way available. But the suggestions fall on deaf ears as she literally freezes up at the prospect of talking to someone new. She feels empty and miserable, but figures that's just her fate in life.

Shy people don't love themselves. Cindy cannot imagine that anyone would find her attractive. She doesn't find herself attractive. Deep down, shy people don't like what they see in themselves. Not loving themselves is precisely what makes them shy. If you don't love yourself, or you feel shame about yourself, you don't want anyone else to notice your self. You look at your self and feel bad about what you see, and that's bad enough, without letting anyone else see it too. You literally "shy away" from giving anybody else a good look.

LONELINESS

Everybody feels lonely now and then. It's part of being human. But there are many people for whom loneliness is a chronic affliction. "Nobody loves me." "Nobody cares for me." "Nobody gives a damn if I'm alive or dead!" Being the social creatures we are, loneliness is one of the most painful feelings we can experience. People who don't love themselves feel lonely most of the time—even in crowds of people.

For people who do not love themselves enough, loneliness operates in two notable ways. Finding little or nothing to love in themselves, they feel empty and hollow. And because "nature abhors a vacuum," there is a desperate need for someone else to "fill" them up. Loneliness is an experience of not being "enough" for oneself and the need for someone else to fill up the vacuum. Outside of co-dependents, no one wants to be used for this purpose, and that is why lonely people tend to be avoided.

On the other hand, finding little or nothing to love in themselves, they feel they have nothing good to offer anyone else. They may actually put out bad impressions about themselves which tend to keep potential friends at bay. And then they are stuck with the only company they have: themselves. The pain of loneliness is not simply being alone. Loneliness is being stuck alone with someone you just don't like: your self! Loneliness is being stuck with a companion you would never choose: your self!

Craig is an average college student, who walks around with a proverbial chip on his shoulder. He has an attitude problem that readily turns people off. Whenever someone gets too close to Craig, he pushes them off with some insulting remark or putdown. He claims he doesn't mean to do it. He tells his counselor that he doesn't know why he does it. He hates being lonely and wishes he could have some good friends. But he is convinced that he really doesn't have anything to offer anyone else—nothing for which he could be appreciated and respected. "Why would anyone like me anyway?" he laments. "I'm just bad."

No one gets a chance to like Craig, because Craig doesn't like himself. If you're convinced that there is little or nothing likeable about you, you will never be convinced that anyone else could see something likeable about you either. Anyone who would see something attractive in you would have to be "misguided." Or else you would assume there was a hidden agenda to get something from you. If you don't love yourself, it can't make much sense that anyone else could love you, for yourself, either.

People who love themselves rarely feel lonely, because even if they are alone, they are always with someone they like, namely, themselves. People who don't like themselves are predictably lonely, because they are burdened with the companionship of someone who turns them off completely, namely, themselves.

CHRONIC DISSATISFACTION

I am surprised at the number of successful people I meet who don't show much satisfaction about their achievements. They work hard and have all the material rewards to prove their success, but they don't *feel* good about themselves. Joe is an investor and has worked his way to a top tax bracket with salary and commissions. He's a workaholic, but claims that he loves his work, and that for him "work is recreation." Be that as it may, he lives with chronic dissatisfaction. It is only when he is working in his high pressure job that he is able to forget how dissatisfied he is.

In a counseling interview, Joe reluctantly admits he doesn't like himself. He never has. He has never been satisfied with anything he has done in his life, because nothing was ever "enough." Not loving himself, he cannot enjoy himself. He cannot be "in joy" with himself. He cannot enjoy himself because he is always trying to make himself feel better through what he does. He wants to "fix" himself. It's not a matter of what he does or doesn't do. He doesn't like who he *is*. And so he spends most of his time working, in hope that work will make him better, and therefore more likeable, if only to himself.

But it's a never-ending endeavor. The ritual is never over. The train never comes into the station. If you don't love yourself, you can never do enough for yourself. You can never feel satisfied. Whom are you trying to satisfy anyway? Your self. How can you ever please a self you don't really like in the first place? There will never be enough makeup in the whole world to cover up a self that you are basically unsatisfied with or ashamed of.

The majority of people living in the United States are endowed with the highest standard of living in the history of

mankind. Our economic anxieties, fears about the environment, worries about the future of our society, are substantial
and substantiated. However they cannot take away from the fact
that most of us live well, with more than a modicum of security.
And yet so few seem to be satisfied with anything. Few workers
love their jobs. The majority of those who get married end up
unhappy with their spouses. Millions of citizens are dissatisfied
with government and political leadership. Millions have become
disillusioned with institutional churches and religion in general. The vast majority of Americans still claim they believe in
God, but he is often a disappointment too.

Normally we handle our dissatisfactions by blaming someone or something "out there." The point about "out there,"
however, is that it is basically neutral. It is just there! We
become affected by the outside world only insofar as we react
and interpret that outside world as affecting us. The farmer wel-
comes the spring rain because it waters his crops. The business
man on vacation hates the same rain because it is spoiling his
plans to get an early suntan. Spring rain is just spring rain. Our
welcoming it, or being bothered by it, depends on where we are
coming from, not on where the rain is coming from.

Satisfaction and dissatisfaction are basically internal attitudes that we project onto reality. The emotions of satisfaction
or dissatisfaction come from within, not from without. If you
are in a good mood, your wife's forgetting to turn on the morning coffee-maker might not bother you in the slightest. If you
are in a bad mood, watch out! Whether the coffee-maker is on
or off is basically a neutral fact. How you feel inside will make it
an issue.

If you are unhappy with yourself, it cannot but significantly
affect your acceptance and interpretation of all reality around
you. The problem is not out there; it is inside of us. If we are
dissatisfied with ourselves, we will be dissatisfied with everyone
and everything. If we feel sour about ourselves, humor is going
to turn us off, even if it is turning everyone else on. We create
our satisfactions or dissatisfactions by the way we feel about
ourselves.

Control
Competition are
internal

We might speculate further on this issue with insights from the New Age movement, the human potential movements, and the observations of counselors working with addicts. These insights would lead us to believe that even if we do love ourselves in general, we may not love ourselves at our current state of personal development. Often in therapy, some chronologically mature adults discover themselves to be fixated at the psychological age of an eighth grade child or mid-adolescent. We might attend a twenty-fifth class reunion, where Charley "the clown" is still acting as immaturely as the day we graduated from high school. Any of us can achieve maturity in one of the many stages of human development, but remain stuck there. We can be fixated at a certain level of consciousness. We may be stable, but, at the same time, be stale, bored, and "stuck." We don't like ourselves the way we are at a particular stage of development in which we perceive ourselves. We vaguely sense a restlessness deep in our hearts that we should be moving on, and up, to deeper wisdom and openness to the world. It may be subtle or it may be obvious, but we are dissatisfied with ourselves because we have not moved on to a higher state of consciousness that is part of our natural evolution. Chronologically we should have our heads in the stars, while psychologically we are still playing in a sand box.

DEPRESSION/FEAR/ANXIETY

Depression is the most commonly treated ailment in psychotherapy. Fear and anxiety are often depression's closest playmates. There is a clear connection between not loving oneself enough and being a victim of these disorders.

After the untimely, accidental death of her parents, Brenda was raised from early childhood by an invalid aunt and her three elder brothers. Under normal circumstances, older brothers are well-known to fawn on "baby sister," but in Brenda's case it didn't work out that way. Her brothers all possessed a mean streak and had no inhibitions about relentlessly teasing her with jibes and taunts. She was often the butt of their jokes. She was told she was a "born loser," "a birth defect," and that she would "never make it" in the world. Her aunt never came to her rescue or support.

Brenda believed all the put-downs about herself and ended up not only shy, but overwhelmed with fear of even walking out of the house. Teachers found her either morosely depressed or a bundle of nerves. She was afraid of everyone and everything. She never laughed or was ever at ease with classmates. By the time she entered high school, she was on medication for colitis.

Depressed, fearful and anxiety-ridden people lack adequate self-love. They live with an emotionally abused and put-down image of themselves. They feel like an "ugly duckling," and no one is likely to convince them otherwise. Depression stems not so much from the bitter problems life can throw our way, but from a deep inner belief that we are not able to cope with them. Depressed and fearful people feel they "haven't got what it takes." They interpret themselves as unequipped or inadequate. Brenda believed she was defective. She would look at herself and see someone who just didn't have what it takes. Her brothers convinced her of that, day after day. Her inferiority complex almost completely debilitates her. At nineteen she assumes that her fear and trembling, that persistent knot in her stomach, is simply the natural way for her to be.

POOR RELATIONSHIPS

Many of us have difficulties with relationships: getting them started and making them last. One of two marriages today ends up in divorce. Long-term and satisfying relationships are few and far between. Many of us have trouble having our intimacy needs met, adequately and appropriately. Much of it has to do with a poor self-image and lack of self-love.

Rose and David had a "marriage made in heaven." So said the preacher on their wedding day. Guests agreed that they were "meant for each other," so compatible did they appear.

Rose and David believed they were a "perfect match" because they supplied so well for each other's needs. It never occurred to them that they might be in a co-dependent relationship, that each felt a fundamental insecurity the other made up for. David had a successful career going for himself but believed it was all a matter of pure luck. He needed an attractive wife to uplift his self-image and make him socially presentable. Rose knew she was attractive, but she needed a husband who was "going somewhere" and would take care of her voluminous emotional and material needs. Insecure in themselves, they fed on each other. It wasn't long, however, before each felt "used." Resentment followed, and only one year after the marriage, the "ideal couple" found themselves in the throes of bitter divorce proceedings.

The lyrics of much popular music cater to, and reinforce, a deficient self-image that so many of us, especially young people, possess. "I need you, baby!" "I can't live'without you." It sounds flattering; it sounds like love. But is it? If I need you to make up for an emptiness I feel about myself, am I demonstrating love for you, or am I really hoping to use you as a coping device? No matter how much Barbra Streisand sings that people who need people are the luckiest people in the world, using others to bolster our self-image is a losing game. We pick up on people who are using us, and we resent that. Others pick up when we are using them, and they resent it. No matter how much love-talk I put into it, if much of what I'm doing is using you to make me feel better about myself, it will get to you sooner or later. Lack of self-love, and using others to supply for that deficiency, is the major reason why most relationships crumble.

It is not without deep insight that spiritual masters have always taught that personal happiness and peaceful social order depend on "love your neighbor as *yourself.*" For Christians it is the second most important commandment given by Jesus. Jesus himself was echoing a hallowed Jewish mandate. Loving oneself comes first, before one can love another. If we do not love ourselves as we are, we won't believe that anyone else could love us as we are. If we don't love ourselves, there is no love to be given to another. What kind of love can an unloved soul offer?

ALCOHOL ABUSE, DRUGS, AND ADDICTIONS

Stefanie is a recovering alcoholic who credits much of her recovery to her Alcoholics Anonymous program and to her much improved self-esteem. Stefanie admits she began drinking to cover her pain. As a youth, her only hobby was reading romance novels and glamor magazines. She would spend hours imagining how wonderful it would be if she were someone else. She was very overweight in her teen years and suffered miserably from the taunts of her fellow classmates. Her embarrassment over her weight and unpopularity only made her continue to turn to food as an escape from the emotional turmoil she felt—which only made her heavier, and more abused. The cycle went on and on.

She learned to drink on the senior trip. Some of the boys thought it would be "a real gas" to see her "plastered." Stefanie felt no abuse as she took one proffered drink after another. As a matter of fact, she felt no pain at all. The quick euphoria was a godsend that put away the terrible feelings she had about herself, if only for a little while—until that "little while" eventually became longer and longer, and Stefanie became hooked on her daily quart of vodka.

As a group, addicts of one kind or another are burdened with poor self-images. All of us are addicts. We all have addictions to one thing or another. All of us have any variety of things we are "hooked" on. Some addictions are more self-destructive or socially unacceptable than others, but workaholism, the need to be perfect, the need to be "right," the need of material possessions, smoking, sweets, etc., can be just as addictive and self-destructive as alcoholism or compulsive sexuality. Lack of self-respect and self-love blaze the trail in the torturous journey of addiction. Addiction is a way to ease the pain of feeling inadequate. A skid-row alcoholic looks in a mirror and can't wait for another drink to obliterate what he sees and despises. Addicts are looking for a pain-killer—anything to give even a few moments respite from having to face the consequences of a fractured self-image. Addictions are a punishment to a self which is not liked, loved, or respected.

GROWING CRIME RATE

The rising crime rate in this country has caught world-wide attention. Who would believe, in this most affluent nation in the world, where the standard of living for the majority of citizens is exceptional, and where educational, cultural, and career opportunities abound, that crime statistics would be sky-rocketing and prisons would be overflowing?

There is a close correlation between lack of self-love and criminal behavior. Studies investigating criminal personalities indicate high levels of self-hatred, especially in criminals involved in violent crime. The origins of criminal acting-out can be traced readily to an unhealthy, or abused, self-image. The rule is, if you don't love yourself, you're not going to make much of an effort to keep yourself on the straight and narrow. Whatever for? If you feel there is nothing good about you deep down, why not act out the way you feel about yourself. A crook always feels he is being "honest."

Crimes of violence are expressions of self-loathing. Criminals act in accordance with their perceptions of themselves. A prison guard once related to me that some prisoners often act like "swine," because "that's exactly what they think they are." Sowing the seeds of self-contempt in a small child's mind may blossom into the next generation's hardened criminal. As a matter of fact, it's likely.

War, and all forms of social aggression, are expressions on a grander scale of lack of self-love. One country sees in another country something it is lacking in itself and decides to take it by force. We saw an example of that in the aggressive action taken by Iraq against Kuwait.

Many more examples could be given. We could go into many more personal and social issues but the story would be the same. It should be clear how costly lack of self-love is in terms of personal and social ills. So much of our inability to cope, our depressing feelings, our unreasonable fears and hostilities are tied up with a poor self-image and our inability to love ourselves as we need. Understanding that connection can help motivate us to begin our journey toward self-love recovery.

2

Self-Love Lost

Hidden like this, shame can stalk one's being, inflict-
ing an unconscious self-loathing.
—Robert Karen

People who do not love themselves enough often live in a fog where one's negative self-image is never questioned or challenged. The negative self-image is just there, and lived with. Awareness is a key to self-love recovery. Becoming "aware" is the magic wand opening the door to genuine love of self.

One of the first steps we need take in recovering love for ourselves is to become aware of how victimized we may have been, that not loving ourselves as we need came about as a result of circumstances for which we were not responsible. Most of us who do not appreciate or love ourselves enough have likely been fashioned that way from our most formative years—without our consideration and without our consent.

We accept today, for example, that alcoholism progresses as a disease. Alcoholics do not choose to be alcoholic. Alcoholism is not a result of free choice or evidence of deliberate moral failure. Alcoholism is a disease influenced by genetic disposition, social conditioning, and innocent-enough small steps that eventually led into full-flung addiction. As a disease, it is accepted without lifting moral eyebrows against the alcoholic. This is part of the success story of the Alcoholics Anonymous program. Knowing that alcoholism is a treatable disease, and not an indictment of moral turpitude, is a great encouragement to the alcoholic to begin the arduous journey to sobriety.

This does not mean that the alcoholic has no responsibility for his or her problem. We can take steps in our recovery process. I am not contending that we have no responsibility for our lack of adequate self-love, only that most of our lack of self-love has come about as a result of circumstances beyond our control, and certainly without our consent. We never decided to be unlovable. A child does not inherit a sense of self-loathing. It is not in its genes. As a child grows up, he or she learns about his or her lovableness in a reflection of self that is picked up from the eyes of significant others. A child learns whether it is lovable or not. Loving oneself, or not loving oneself, is not a given, it is *learned*.

I emphasize this "victimization" only that we may become aware and reflective about the way we grew up and were raised. With a little understanding of the influences that affected our sense of being lovable, we can be more gentle, tender and compassionate with our selves—especially with our selves that have been abused, neglected, mistreated, misinformed, terrified, or browbeaten into believing things about our selves that simply were not, and are not, true. Recovering love for our selves is a delicate and gentle process. We are most often dealing with a bruised heart that is exceptionally sensitive. Being aware that we are not at fault for the way we have felt about ourselves can help relieve us of the shame that often stands in the way of self-love recovery.

The good news is that what has been learned can be unlearned. The good news is that we can begin learning to love our selves as we need by becoming aware of where we are and how we got this way. Let us now examine therefore some of the most ordinary but striking influences that handicap our loving our selves as we need.

EARLY CHILDHOOD

I have a friend who is heavily invested in the fashionable hobby of bonsai. Bonsai is the delicate art and craft of growing trees in miniature. By fashioning (literally, contorting) a young seedling and by constant careful pruning, the bonsai tree is kept dwarfed, but recognizable, in a shallow planting tray. Some have been around and cared for this way for hundreds of years.

Two things I have learned from bonsai are that the earliest fashioning of the seedling's limbs will stay with it for life, and that constant pruning keeps it from growing into the kind of tree it was meant to be. It is contorted to prohibit it from its natural growth and destiny. It is beautiful to those who ply and appreciate this craft, but it is not what nature meant it to be.

Our earliest baby and childhood experiences are indelibly cast upon our souls. We were formed and fashioned from our newborn hours by people and circumstances totally beyond our control. From cradle to grave we carry those first impressions, those first castings, that fashioned the exquisitely soft clay of our budding personalities. The love and tender loving care that a child receives will be carried for a lifetime—as will any lack of love and tender loving care.

There is never anything "neutral" about early childhood experiences. Every experience for a growing infant is flushed with meaning. A child is born with a drive to survive, but is not born knowing whether or not it is lovable. It learns it is lovable reflexively through the loving attentions and ministrations it receives from others, especially its parents and other caretakers. A child comes to understand and love itself through the self-reflections it sees in the coos and aaahhs, in the affirmations and cuddlings, in the admirations and approvals it receives through those critical developing years. In like manner, a child who does not receive these coos and aaahhs, these affirmations and cuddlings, these uplifting admirations and approvals, will see itself as diminished and unlovable proportionately.

There are fortunate children who are raised in the warm, nurturing environment created by mothers and fathers who love them unconditionally. Unconditional love is hard to come by, however. All parents have their flaws and human limitations. Despite their best intentions, most parents are going to make mistakes in the way they bestow or withhold the love they have for their children. Therefore, many more children go through life never being quite sure of their lovableness because the love they received "depended"—depended not on how good and lovable they were in themselves, but on how well they could please mommy and daddy. If they "acted right" they were smiled upon with affection. If they didn't act right, love was withdrawn. A child raised under conditions where love was never enough, or where love was bonded to mixed messages, can never be sure if it is lovable for itself alone. Love cannot be counted upon. It is haphazard and seems to depend only on what one can do, or on how one performs. From these beginnings, a child never feels adequately valued and assured of adequacy to meet life on its own terms.

Self-love is more severely damaged when a child is subjected to abuse of any kind (physical, mental, emotional, sexual), to reprobation, put-downs, sarcasm, neglect, and abandonment. Millions of children today are raised in dysfunctional family systems, or with parents who are addicts. Simple emotional survival of the fittest is a daily battle. Divorcing parents cause well-documented havoc in a child's emotions and sense of self-worth. Many parents today are into "their own agendas" and their children feel they are not worth their parents' time and effort. Children can begin to feel "unworthy" in their earliest years.

Children can also begin learning in their earliest years that there is something fundamentally wrong with their very being. They are told that they shouldn't make mistakes, that they "make" mother unhappy, that they "broke daddy's heart," that they are disappointments for the choices they make. They are taught that they not only make mistakes, but are "bad" for making them.

Discipline, for example, is necessary in any child's development. How it is administered, however, is quite another issue. Little Laura at three years old is caught stabbing at another playmate with a handful of crayons. It is without question a dangerous act and has to be stopped. Laura's mother gently removes the crayons from her tight little fist and tells her such actions can hurt someone else and must not be done. She encourages both children to play together and affirms them when they do so amicably.

Jason is also three years old. He has been helping his father wash the family car. His attempts at holding the soapy sponge and doing any kind of washing job brings smiles and encouragement from his father. His father has just finished drying the car to a fine shine when little Jason picks up a handful of mud and smears it on the front fender. Jason means well. The mud looks somewhat like the wax his dad uses. He thinks the mud can polish the car even brighter, and then he will win more admiration from his idolized father. His father turns on him, however, and scolds in an angry and abusive tone: "Now look what you've done. You are a bad boy. You ruined my car." Dad reinforces his put-downs with a sharp slap on Jason's arm. Jason in tears has learned that the car may be more valuable than he is.

Many examples could be offered of how a child's budding self-image is formed and fashioned. We all have memories, deeply buried in our unconscious, of how we were treated or mistreated in our childhood. There is obviously a difference in the way Laura and Jason are being disciplined. It is a discipline that radically influences their self-image and understanding of their lovableness. Laura is admonished for something she *does*; Jason is admonished for what he *is*. Laura is being told that certain behaviors are unacceptable. Jason is being told *he* is unacceptable.

If the messages Laura receives about herself are consistently upgrading, she will continue to feel good about herself, know that she is lovable, and learn to love herself. Jason, on the other hand, may not be so fortunate, especially if his father's method of discipline consistently deflates his fledgling ego and tells him bad things about himself. The constant pruning of his self-image with put-downs will stunt his sense of lovableness, just as the pruning of the bonsai stunts its growth.

Shaming is one of the easiest and most common forms of discipline that parents resort to. It is a powerful tool because it affects a child's self-image directly. It affects the child where he or she feels it most: deep down inside. When little Clayton falls down, he hurts and cries. It's wonderful to be hugged and cuddled, so he jumps into dad's lap, hoping for affection and support. He loves to express affection, and hugs his playmate Tommy. He enjoys playing and picks up his sister's doll. There is nothing inherently wrong with any of these actions. He cannot reason that he is being manipulated to fit into some completely arbitrary prejudices. So, when little Clayton is shamed and called a "sissy" for doing these things, he concludes there is something revolting about *himself.*

When little Suzie is pushed off a swing, she expresses herself in anger rather than tears. She may see great fun in playing with her brother's toy soldiers. She prefers playing in the sandbox rather than playing with dolls. She loves getting hugs and giving hugs. She loves to hug her little girlfriends and little boyfriends. When she hears, "Shame on you—nice girls don't do that," she picks up that there is something repugnant about her for doing things she enjoys. At a tender young age she already begins to question if she is really worthwhile.

We can never put too much emphasis on the importance of early self-imaging in a growing child. Self-love is taught from the earliest years of life. So is self-depreciation. A child cannot intellectually think through or refute insults and put-downs that are tossed at his or her self-image. A child can only absorb and feel reflections of itself coming through the eyes of significant others. A child does not decide to love or not love itself. A child is not responsible for feeling unlovable. The child is at the mercy of those reflecting its lovableness.

If you feel victimized with a poor self-image and defective self-esteem, you might well look back on your childhood formation. Can you remember times you felt affirmed and applauded? Or do you more remember times you were made to feel ashamed of your very self? That it wasn't so much what you *did,* but how you were valued or devalued for what you *were?* Those memories have never left you. They affect the way you feel about yourself to this day.

SCHOOL AND GROWING UP IN AMERICA

For most children going through the American educational system and socialization process, growing up is an ordeal to sorely test anyone's sense of self-love and esteem. Those who enter school with a good sense of self-worth may find that worth suddenly eroded. Those who enter without a good sense of self-esteem will most likely find justification and reinforcement for an already poor self-image.

I am not offering a critique of American education. I am reflecting how school years affect the way we end up loving ourselves. Schooling provides society with three basic evaluations. Who is smart and who is not so smart? Who is competitive and will tend to have leadership qualities, and who is not competitive and will tend to follow the crowd? Who is socially promising and who is socially disadvantaged? What we are talking about here is a grading system that separates the "haves" from the "have-nots."

The day most disliked and feared by students is the day report cards are passed out. And with good reason. Report cards present evaluations. Grades. Grades directly tell you how a teacher has evaluated you on passing a certain course. They also tell you, and anyone else who might be interested (like parents and admissions boards), how smart you are and what part of the grading scale you merit in reference to everyone else in the class. Grades and class standing cannot help but affect one's self-image and self-respect. Over the years I have heard many students lament their grades with a self-judgment, "I just can't do the work; I'm dumb." Can we imagine how self-demeaning that statement is if the student really believes that of himself or herself? "No, my family won't be disappointed with these grades; they always said I was stupid."

On the other hand, students who get decent grades may write them off with a disclaimer, "I just got lucky, I guess." Many students worry themselves sick about their grades precisely because of the image about themselves that grading challenges or reinforces. The grading system provides a measure of personal worth. It is unlikely that the grading system will ever be dropped, but we should be alert to its capacity for harm. At best it can confirm a child's sense of high self-esteem, but more likely it can diminish it.

Sports and games mean competition. The end result of all sporting events is to decide the "winners" and the "losers." Competition can be healthy and helpful. It can motivate growth and accomplishment. But there is a downside to competition. Winners often develop a sense of self-worth only in terms of beating out the competition. I am good or better only because you are bad or worse. Self-esteem is reinforced, artificially and unreliably, in terms of another's defeat. I have met businessmen in their forties and fifties still talking about catching a game-winning touchdown pass in their high school years, as if it was the most important thing that ever happened in their lives.

Losing in competition, on the other hand, reinforces a shaky ego with internal messages that "you're a loser." Suicides have been recorded over a teen's despair for not making the varsity. Murder has been conspired in an effort to get a high school student on the cheerleading team. And imagine the thoughts that go through the minds of those who are never picked for a team, those who were never good enough to be "included."

Young adolescents are painfully concerned with the self-image they project. Along with schooling, peer and cultural pressures have a tremendous influence on their self-love. Having the "right" hair style, or wearing the "right" designer jeans, or belonging to the "right" group, determines one's acceptability. Popularity is a burning issue with teens—who is attractive, who is so-so, and who would "scare the warts off a toad." Adults with serious self-esteem problems can usually spin off a variety of tales of rejection and not "fitting in" all through their school years. Self-love was eroded away with every failure to be picked for the team, to be asked for a date, or to be invited to a party.

MODERN ADVERTISING

The most powerful image maker in our culture is the advertising industry. From billboards on the highway to newspaper ads and television commercials, we are saturated with advertising. Contemporary advertising has become the most successful propaganda force known in human history.

Advertising plays up directly to self-image and self-love. It makes no bones that it has something to tell us about ourselves. All of us love to be noticed, admired, and thought well of. Advertising tells us just how well we are doing on that score. Advertising tells us how we should look, how we should dress, how we should smell; what we should drive, what vacations to take, what headache pill we should be using; what we should eat and drink, and what garbage bags are most acceptable for our refuse.

Advertising usually gets us to use a product or service, not by scientifically proving a need, but by playing up to our sense of self-worth. If you're not using a certain brand of mouthwash in the morning, or not dousing your shoes with a particular brand of foot deodorant, people are fainting all around you, without your even noticing it. If you are not drinking a certain beverage, you are not only "out of it," you are one of life's losers. If you are using a competitor's brand of detergent in your dishwasher, you are likely ending up with disgusting spots on your wine glasses. Dinner guests who will use those glasses can only conclude that you yourself are disgusting.

Advertising does not simply tell us what is available on the market. At the bottom line, advertising tries to tell us something about ourselves. At the bottom line, modern advertising inevitably victimizes anyone who believes in it. Advertising appeals to self-esteem and self-love. The purchase, or non-purchase, of one product or another reflects something about you. Your self-image is constantly being put on the line and bombarded. A product sells by convincing you that you are not O.K. without it. And you simply can't buy all the products being touted on the tube. You are going to fail to meet all the standards the image-makers have established. One way or another you will be victimized. Without this product or that service, that message is that you are not good enough.

"GOD HATES ME"

All religions, whatever their persuasion or doctrinal positions, lay claim to offering mankind direction and meaning through the hazardous journey we call life. Religion offers salvation in terms of redemption, forgiveness and reconciliation. Many religions, however, employ an ample dosage of "scare techniques." Scare techniques may speak of a loving God, but impose significant doses of guilt on believers. Having accepted a God portrayed as a reigning potentate with a heavy hand of judgment and justice, few adherents ever escape shame, guilt, and scruples over the countless failings we have as finite human beings.

Often unwittingly, religions that preach love possess a tremendous power for reinforcing depreciated self-images. They actually impede genuine love of self and others. A casual observance of most Christian communities will reveal a goodly number of members who reasonably reflect the teachings of Jesus. But a casual observance will also reveal some of the most uncharitable, mutually-abusive, manipulative and dysfunctional people that one could find in any non-religious group.

John is a plumber, and a good one. Married with three children, he makes a good living because his customers like him and spread the news about his honesty and workmanship. Faithful, quiet and reserved, generous, and with a good word for everyone, he is a well-liked neighbor. He attends mass daily at his local Catholic church, where the priests and members of the congregation consider John to be a "saint." "You can call on him for anything." And people do.

John, however, does not feel like a saint. From his late adolescent years he has been plagued with irremovable feelings of guilt and shame. He had heard sermons at mass and on retreats of "what our sins have done to Jesus," and, ever since, John has taken his faults very seriously. He makes a confession to his priest once a week, but sacramental absolution gives him only a brief respite from his nagging conscience. John cannot believe God could love him because of his many sins over a lifetime. John is honest, generous, faithful and reserved, not because he has a healthy image of himself and loves others as he loves himself. John is honest, generous, faithful and reserved because he hates the sinner he feels himself to be, and fears the hell that surely awaits him, should he die in the state of sin.

We all make mistakes. We are all too human with our limitations and failings. Guilt can be growth promoting by providing motivation to be honest about ourselves and our mistakes, and about our need to make amends where possible. But there is also guilt which is more destructive than saving. A guilt that represses and depresses. A guilt that fills us with shame and makes us feel unworthy as human beings. A guilt that makes us feel that God hates us and looks upon us with disgust. A guilt that millions of Americans have been, and are, burdened with because of the pronouncements and preaching of even well-intentioned clergy.

A religion that encourages us to "love our neighbor as *ourselves*" can unwittingly make sure that never happens, by handicapping our self-love with guilt trips. We cannot feel good about ourselves, much less love ourselves, if we esteem ourselves "despicable sinners" and "offal in the eyes of God."

Worse yet is the misguided pronouncement of some preachers that self-love is evil, that self-love is "the pride that brought down Adam and ruined our chances for paradise." Admittedly, a self-love which is synonymous with egocentricity is not a virtue in our context. But few preachers I have ever heard on the subject were careful about making the distinction between honest self-love and its counterfeits. They simply depreciated all forms of self-love and left their listeners with a feeling of self-remorse. Some preachers actually achieve fame for their talents in making their audience feel like "worms."

Another misguided pronouncement is that we should not

be thinking of ourselves at all, but, "like the saints above, only be concerned about the well-being of others." Charity and self-sacrificing service for the welfare of others can never be discounted. Moreover, altruism is one of the best indications we have that we are reaching our highest potential of self-love. But there is something very psychologically sound about the command of Jesus and other spiritual leaders that we love and serve others *as* we love and serve ourselves. Self-love comes first before we can authentically love others. Genuine self-love is naturally outpouring and giving. Diminished self-love can lead to a "service" of control, manipulation, emotional terror tactics, keeping the faithful in subservience—all highly recognizable qualities of dysfunctional churches and church people. While proclaiming themselves to be "servants" of the people of God, all too many clergy and church leaders actually operate as overlords. And they will remain such as long as there is a congregation with poor enough self-esteem who will continue to empower them.

A healthy self-love brings freedom and joy. A self-love handicapped by religious peroration attracts shame, guilt and a sense of defeat, not redemption.

LIFE-LONG COPING HABITS

Unhealthy and unchallenged habits of coping can be very self-damaging. Certain ways of coping may have been useful at one time, but have become self-destructive in changing situations. Self-love is continuously damaged by the unchallenged coping habits we build up over a lifetime.

Megan has been married to a practicing alcoholic for fifteen long and painful years. She has endured years of chronic tension, deprivation, and abuse to herself and her two children. Megan is in a co-dependent relationship with her husband. Having no will or courage to just leave him, she "suffers in silence." She covers up for him on those days when he misses work. She lies about his drinking problem to family and friends.

She has trained her children to put up with the abuse they receive. She puts up with misery and somehow feels that she actually deserves the ill-treatment she receives. And somehow she guarantees that this misery will continue. In putting up with her husband's drinking, refusing to leave him, and making excuses for him, she is actually encouraging his addiction with her covering-up support.

In therapy, Megan is coming to appreciate that this has been her "style" of life since she was a child. Having grown up in a dysfunctional family herself, where her mother and father were both alcoholics, she continues to use the only coping habits with which she is familiar—coping habits which continue to diminish her self-love.

Habits become habitual. Unless they are challenged and replaced, they continue to devastate our self-love. It is easy to get into habits, for example, where we continue to jeopardize our welfare and happiness because we are too absorbed in the needs of others. We "care-take" others at the expense of having our own needs met. It is easy to get into habits where we allow others to "walk all over us," using us as doormats. Some of us can appear to be almost masochistic in our desire to please, no matter what the cost to our self-respect. We learn to "make fools of ourselves" by waiting for that call that never comes. By accepting criticism for mistakes we never made. By allowing ourselves to believe we are "failures" because we haven't lived up to someone else's arbitrary expectations. By letting ourselves be "used" by someone who has no respect for our boundaries. And we do all this because, "this is what I've always done."

NEED TO EVOLVE HIGHER

Another significant factor that strongly affects our self-image and love of our selves was touched briefly in the previous chapter. We human beings unquestionably evolve through life cycles. There are rather obvious stages of physical, intellectual, and emotional growth. The self evolves in consciousness to higher and higher levels of awareness, comprehension, and wisdom.

We are evolving to the day we die. (Most religions teach that our evolution continues even after death.) The great spiritual traditions of mankind have noted and graphed these stages in a variety of ways. For the most part, these stages are steps in "awareness," from reptilian consciousness of life-threatening situations, to union with the "Ground" of all being.

We cannot discount the fact that if there is a personal evolution that is part of our very makeup and destiny, that if the self itself has a natural course of development, that if there are higher and higher states of consciousness that are part of our natural endowment, that if we have a destiny that outdistances mere survival of the fittest, then we are not going to be satisfied, happy with our selves, or self-loving if those selves are not where they belong in a natural evolutionary process.

If, in the course of development to your greatest potential, you should be at a stage of being in communion with God, and you are still immersed in "dog eat dog" competition to make payments on a second home in the mountains, it's going to take its toll on you, and on how you appreciate your self. You are stuck in a self-image that is no longer appropriate to your potential, and you're going to feel it. You won't love your self, because your self is "out of order." You are not where you need to be. Under those circumstances, you will not love your self as you are.

DIMINISHED BUT NOT DESTROYED

We can end this chapter then by acknowledging that many parental, social, educational, cultural and developmental influences have affected the way we feel about ourselves. None of us choose to not love ourselves. None of us had control of those powerful forces that created the earliest images of ourselves that we carry through life. If we come from a dysfunctional family system, or didn't receive enough love and affirmation, we are handicapped. And it isn't our fault. We are not to blame. It is unjust and illogical, therefore, to blame ourselves, or put ourselves down, for not loving ourselves enough. Somewhere along the path of our development, a gift was taken from us, and we simply learned to survive.

The good news is that while we may be diminished in self-love, we are not destroyed and hopeless. The good news is that we can be responsible for ourselves from here on. We can choose to unlearn some bad lessons. We can choose to learn some good lessons. We can decide to learn the truth about our selves. We can decide to fall in love with our selves and take care of our selves as we would anyone we truly loved. We may have our handicaps and limitations, but we are not condemned forever to live in self-diminishing way. There is a way out. There are steps that can be taken. Others have done it, and so can we.

3

Necessary Dispositions

Trust in the Lord, and lean not on your own understanding.

—Proverbs 3:5

Thy will be done.

—Lord's Prayer

We have seen that many personal and social ills are connected to an absence of self-love. We have examined a variety of factors that conspire to rob us of the love we need for our selves. We have learned that we need not blame ourselves if our self-love is not what we want it to be. Moreover, our awareness is growing that we can take steps in self-love recovery.

It is one thing, however, to know we are stuck in quicksand, and quite another to get ourselves out. Knowledge and insight do not of themselves guarantee recovery. Clients can be in psychoanalysis for years and finally come to understand why they feel as badly as they do, but the insight itself doesn't automatically make them feel better. They simply know why they feel badly.

Self-knowledge is not self-love. We can know with complete clarity that something needs to change in our lives, but never take steps to make a change. We simply endure. And it's incredible what human beings are capable of enduring. Many of us may go to our deathbeds without ever having made the simplest of changes that could have given us a happier, fuller, and more satisfying life.

We have a better chance of making necessary changes in

41

our lives as we become more *disposed* to make them. We need to discuss dispositions for self-love recovery. Without suitable dispositions, we tend to go nowhere. What dispositions, therefore, are needed for us to make a start in achieving the love for our selves that we need?

ENOUGH IS ENOUGH

Nikki states that her road to self-love recovery began when "I just got sick and tired of feeling bad about myself all the time. Enough is enough!" One of the very first dispositions we need for self-love recovery is becoming *fed up* with the way things are. Changing ourselves is very difficult. We may not like ourselves the way we are, but we're all we got. We've gotten used to ourselves. We've gotten used to our thoughts, our "styles," our beliefs, our feelings, our prejudices, our ways of looking at things, our behaviors. They make us who we are. They make us recognizable to ourselves.

We will discuss "resistance" to change further on, but right from the beginning we need to acknowledge our deep reluctance to effect *any* change in our lives. Change means dismantling ourselves in some way. It means taking our selves apart. It implies dispensing a part of ourselves with which we have become accustomed. This is never easy to do, even when there is something about ourselves that is causing us pain or discomfort. As a matter of fact, most of us will endure all kinds of pain and discomfort rather than go through a changing process. "Better the devil I know than the devil I don't."

There is only one factor that can provide enough motivation for us to change: a *sufficient amount of suffering*. We have to reach a point where "I'm not going to take it anymore!," where "Enough is enough!" It is only when the suffering is sufficient that we reach a point of no return and resign ourselves to make some long overdue changes on our behalf.

We will be most disposed to begin a self-love recovery program when it starts costing us too much not to begin. What that "sufficient amount" of suffering is will vary with each individual. For some, like the alcoholic, he or she may need to hit the "bottom of the barrel." For others, it may be enough sleepless nights, enough sad mornings, enough rejections, enough knots in the stomach, enough tears, enough phoniness, enough hollow promises, enough half-hearted resolutions, and enough failed relationships. When "enough is enough," it can be amazing how quickly recovery can begin.

Getting to the point where "enough is enough" can be aided by an honest reflection of what our current attitudes and behaviors are costing us. We are perfectly free to live in misery, depression, chronic fright, emotional instability, sadness, and self-doubt. But what price are we willing to pay? And are we willing to continue paying the price to maintain a self-enervating status quo? Life is so short; we deserve more than this. When will enough be enough?

RESIGNED TO WORK WITH WHAT YOU HAVE

"I've never liked myself. I've always fantasized about being someone else. But I've come to face the fact that, for the life of me, I'm stuck with my self. My self is the only self I have in this life and I will never be able to change that. Denying it, moaning about it, is just a waste of time. I'm learning to accept my self and work with what I have."

All of us at times wish we were someone else, that we had someone else's looks, intelligence, personality traits, coping skills, successes, material advantages, social opportunities, and the like. At times such envy can be motivating. It can energize us to work on improving ourselves and becoming the best that we can be. But, most often, wanting to be someone else is just another way of saying we don't love our selves. And, rather than become energized, we sink into depression.

Linda, in her statement just quoted, has come a long way in recovery from severe depression. She has had "so many hard knocks, on top of bad luck" all her life that she was led to believe that "fate designed me for a life of misery, and there was absolutely nothing I could do about it." In her recovery program, however, she has come to learn that something more than "fate" is affecting her destiny. She has come to recognize that by refusing to accept her self, she continually sets herself up for most of the problems she encounters. Being sour about who she was, she soured everything she touched. Not wanting to be herself, she acted in "strange ways," and gave others the impression that she was mentally disturbed, if not schizophrenic. A big step in her recovery was coming to accept the self that she had.

She still has a way to go on her road to recovery, because she still hasn't found the happiness she wants, and deserves. At this point, she is only "resigned to my self." But that's an important beginning. Changing your self requires that you accept the self you have. You can only work with what you've got.

Acceptance of your self, not someone else's self, or someone else's idea about your self, is a good first step in realism. Your self is all you really have to work with. It will be your constant companion for the rest of your life. It stands to reason that you put aside illusions and distractions about "how lucky everybody else is," and get working on the self you have.

ACCEPTING THE INNER JOURNEY

Being "resigned" to the self we have is still a long way from actually loving our selves as we need. Being resigned to our selves could mean we are simply willing to put up with them. Loving our selves implies a willingness to explore our selves to discover how lovable they are.

Self-exploration does not come easily. Self-exploration is an inner journey, and we human beings have an almost irresistible penchant for *externalizing* our issues. We do this primarily by "blaming," and by expecting the solution to our problems to come from someone or something outside of ourselves.

We have two major externalizing tendencies that easily

become roadblocks to self-love recovery. The first tendency is "blaming." Blaming is a device for externalizing responsibility for personal problems. We hate taking responsibility for our messes. The first thing Adam did when he got caught with his hand in the apple tree was to blame Eve. The first thing Eve did when blamed by Adam was to blame the serpent. And so the story goes since the beginning of human history. It's part of our survival strategy. We shift attention off of ourselves by blaming someone or something else. It gets us out of the spotlight. It gets us off the hook. The problem is that, while blaming gets us temporarily off the hook, we can get hooked on blaming. We can spend so much time and energy on blaming that we neglect to take care of our selves and take the steps we need to ensure adequate self-love recovery.

There is never a point in blaming. Blaming never solves anything. Blaming only gets us involved in heated arguments, semantics, recriminations, and resentments. In the previous chapter, for example, we examined how "victimized" we were in having our self-love diminished, discredited, or abused. But even there, I am not assigning "blame" for our diminished self-love. Much damage to our self-appreciation came about through the best intentions of others. Our significant others thought they were acting out of our best interests. I remember often being told by my parents, "This hurts me more than it hurts you." Perhaps our parents themselves were not loved enough by their parents and therefore simply did not have the wherewithal to give us the love we needed. So we are not sitting in judgment and casting stones at others. As far as building love for our selves is concerned, blaming is a total waste of time. Blaming is a diversionary tactic to externalize issues that need to be addressed internally.

The second major tendency we have in externalizing our issues is to believe that what we need most must come from something outside of ourselves, that the solution to our personal problems will come from someone or something "out there." If people were more understanding, if we had a better job, if we made more money, if we lived in a better neighborhood, if we were able to retire, if we didn't have family responsibilities, if our children were more appreciative, if we had been given a better education, etc., we would be a lot happier. Basically, we want to be taken care of, just as we were when we were infants. We want someone else to stop our pain and create our joy. We blame others for our pain and then expect others to make our pain go away.

But it doesn't work that way. As we will see more fully in a later chapter, self-love recovery is *inner* work. The resources we need to help us love our selves as we need and to be happy will be found within us. If we think that happiness, feeling good about ourselves, confidence, and self-esteem are gifts being held in someone else's hands, we are living with an illusion. If anything, we should have learned by now that outside sources have failed us time and time again.

Today, former major sources of self-love support are themselves in crisis. Support systems that once protected, enhanced, directed, and nurtured the self have fallen on hard times. Tight family connections, permanent relationships, "the old neighborhood," the government, the churches, "experts," strong beliefs and values, once gave structure and meaning to the self's experience. The self always knew its value, its supports, and where it stood in the scheme of things. Today, however, things have changed dramatically. Never before in the history of mankind have so many millions of people felt so unconnected, isolated, rootless, and insecure. Never before has there been so much self-doubt, combined with a lack of confidence that anybody else has "answers."

Family life for many has collapsed, or has become dysfunctional. "Community" has become a lost experience. Confidence in government and "experts" has all but eroded. Few believe that any political party or think tank of intellectuals has solutions to pull us through the countless crises that comprise the American scene today. The established churches are going through their own identity crises and are facing continually dwindling membership. Value systems have become sketchy and self-serving in a way that "everybody is out for themselves."

There is a sense that "the whole world is falling apart," and that our survival depends only on what we can selfishly salvage for our selves.

It is escapism, therefore, to externalize our issues. Blaming and expecting others to provide for what we need most are inevitably self-defeating and a waste of time. Self-love recovery will not come from without. Even this book can only provide some insights, suggestions, invitations, and programs to help you with the inner work that needs to be done. Recovering the love for our selves that we need means disposing ourselves for an inner journey. The great spiritual masters have always taught that we must look "within," that all the tools we need to come to know and love ourselves as we ought already lie within us.

MAKING A COMMITMENT

Commitment is a necessary disposition in self-love recovery. Commitment not only disposes us to an inner journey, but to an acceptance that inner work is really going to mean *work*. I believe it was Mark Twain who once said that the world can be divided up between the do-ers and those who talk about doing, between those who do and those who just complain and endure. Complaining, feeling bad about ourselves, wallowing in self-pity, analyzing how bad life is, moaning about bad luck, can easily become habitual ways of coping. Self-love recovery requires feeling not only that "enough is enough" but that a commitment be made to do something about it.

It is up to us to decide that we are worth every effort we put into our selves. It is up to us to undertake the inner work we need for self-love recovery. We are talking about adopting a fundamentally new attitude toward our selves. We are talking about falling in love with what is the most intimate of our relationships: our selves. We need to know, appreciate, nurture, and love our selves. This will require time and effort—time and effort that will require a commitment, a commitment to do "whatever it takes" to put ourselves into a new and healthy relationship with our selves.

RESISTANCE

Easier said than done. Change and growth are very difficult. The difficulty is caused not only by our tendency to externalize our issues, but by another road block called "resistance." "Resistance" is the most commonly observed and analyzed phenomenon in psychotherapy. Resistance is a tenacious will to hang on to the status quo.

Resistance is recognized in the ancient maxim that "knowledge maketh a *bloody* entrance." Resistance is recognized in denials that we have any problem, in irritation at any criticism, in shame at being "found out." Resistance is recognized in reluctance to take a self-inventory, in refusals to forgive, in aversion to seek the help we need, and in procrastination about making a decision to change what we know needs to be changed. Resistance makes us "talkers" rather than "do-ers."

Something within us wars against us taking the steps most necessary for our self-love recovery. We need to examine why this is so. We need to know what we are up against. We need to confront the roots of resistance.

M. Scott Peck, in the concluding section of his best-selling book *The Road Less Traveled*, finds the root of resistance in the second law of thermodynamics. This law states that energy flows from higher states of organization to lower. This law relates to the phenomenon of "entropy," that since the beginning of creation, energy tends to wind down rather than build up. Entropy accounts for the acute laziness that is part of all of us.

For Peck, laziness is the "original sin" which we all inherit, and of which we are all guilty. As a psychotherapist, Peck notes that the great majority of clients will leave therapy because they don't want to undertake the work necessary to recover from their mental or emotional afflictions. They fear what changing themselves will cost them in terms of recovery work. They fear the responsibilities that might fall upon them as a changed person. They don't want to grow up and take responsibilities of being a mature, and maturing, adult. They don't want the responsibilities of mental health and spiritual growth. What they want is just to *feel* better. What they want is to be able to relax and enjoy themselves more, as they are.

Honestly looking at myself and thousands of people to whom I have ministered, I readily agree with Peck. We are lazy. We don't want to make efforts to heal ourselves, even when we are suffering for it. We don't want to make efforts to grow mentally and spiritually, even when a better and more fulfilling life is promised. I believe there is another root in "resistance" to change, growth, and self-love recovery, however. "Laziness" connotes a negative and passive quality in human endeavor, an apathy about making a beginning. My observations, on the other hand, lead me to believe that, over and above laziness, resistance manifests itself in a positive and determined *refusal* to change ourselves as we need.

This refusal is found in the tenacious human trait to be in "control." In my view, "control" is the "original sin" issue. And to understand how "control" operates in "resistance," we need to explore the miracle of consciousness and to be introduced to "King Baby."

THE MIRACLE OF CONSCIOUSNESS

One of the most beautiful programs I have ever seen on Public Television presented, with great artistry and incomparable photography, the conception and birth of a baby. Watching it was almost a religious experience. Viewing the formation of a living human being from microscopic beginnings was utterly enrapturing. I was moved with a profound welling up of awe and wonder at the great mystery of life and the power of creation. A cosmic design unravels in the clustering of chromosomes and the splitting of cells. It energizes the epic achievement of fertilization, the formation and placement of tiny organs, and the chemical activation of their functions, until, ready to face the world, the baby is born.

Wonder that they are, conception and birth are only the beginning of our understanding the miracle of life. Another awesome miracle is revealed in the development of a child's consciousness.

When a baby is born, it is as close to pure consciousness as we can imagine. The baby is one with its environment. It is one with the universe. It knows no distinctions. It has no sense of limits. It feels the entire world around it as nothing but an extension of itself. It identifies with everything. A mother's warm smile is nothing more than a part of itself. The baby is at peace, in an Eden state of joy.

It is a state of being embedded in a child's memory. It is a state of being that the child will remember with longing for the rest of his or her life. It is a state of being that all of us spend a lifetime trying to get back to, with varying degrees of success.

"ORIGINAL SIN"

The child begins life feeling itself to be the center of the universe. Everything is but an extension of itself. Its natural condition is to be one with everything that is. It is a "graced" state of being. It is living in paradise, unaware of separateness, unaware of boundaries, unaware of good and evil.

Some religious dogmas assert that we are born in "original sin." But we are not born in "original sin." We are born in "paradise." We are born united with the eternal Self that forms and energizes all that is. In those initial moments of consciousness, we assume we are the center of all that is. "All that is" is but an extension of ourselves. We assume that we are God.

From the earliest days of birth and infancy, our consciousness growth takes place through a process of learning. And the learning begins with a profound and painful lesson. A lesson we learn step by step, day by day. A lesson that teaches us that reality is *not* simply an extension of ourselves. That mother is different from us. That mother has an existence all her own. That mother can walk away. That the toys jingling above our crib are separate entities from us. That everything is separate from us. That there are boundaries everywhere separating us. That we are not identified with everything that is, not even our own bodies with their many separate parts.

That sense of separateness, that growing awareness of not being identified with all that is, of not being the absolute center and pivot point of the universe, of not being identified with the eternal Self, is the "original sin" inherited by all. And, as life continues to teach us divisions, boundaries, and separateness, the reality and consequences of that "original sin" become ever more apparent.

(We might note here that all major religions are basically systems through which believers can be led back ultimately to the original unity with the eternal Self and all that exists, which was experienced in the first moments of consciousness. Some travel the arduous journey back and achieve the goal in ecstasy. We call them "mystics." Some get side-tracked by some diversion in that journey toward mystical union, "hooked" by the very power of their own seeking. We call them "addicts," and their diversions "addictions." Some never begin the journey, or flounder on the way. We call them "lost.")

KING BABY

The book of Genesis is a remarkable analysis of the development of human consciousness. The book of Genesis concludes the story of the "original sin" of Adam and Eve with God driving them out of the garden of paradise.

Basically, in their original bliss, Adam and Eve felt "connected" with all that surrounded them. That's what made it "paradise." But it came about that they were not content to acknowledge their life, and their life in the garden, as a gift. They wanted to assert their life, and their life in the garden, as theirs by right. In eating the "forbidden fruit," they wanted to make an assertion about their very being. Not content to enjoy their giftedness as blessed "creatures," they wanted to be "like God" and assert their life in the garden of paradise to be theirs by *entitlement*.

Setting themselves up against the real Owner, they lost. In losing, they discovered how different and "separate" they were. With "separateness" was introduced a new experience of "boundaries." A "gate" is placed at the entrance of the garden. It is well guarded—well guarded because of the obvious: Adam and Eve learned quickly just what they were missing. They would certainly want to get back.

This story continues, and is actually retold, and relived, with each of us at our birth and in the development of our consciousness. We do experience an "original sin." We experience it in the very learning of division, boundaries, and separateness. Mommy and daddy are different and separate from us. They go in and out of our sensations. They can leave us in our crib and be away even when we want them around for the good feelings we get from them. That separation is stressful and painful. A child is terrified by any prospect of separation and abandonment. The easy flow of a baby's tears confirms this.

The experience continues as we are persistently pressured to recognize that we are not at the center of all that is. We are not firmly and forever seated on a throne with jurisdiction over everything that surrounds us. As a matter of fact, mommy and daddy begin to say "no!" "No!" to ME! Of course, in the beginning, we refuse to acknowledge "no," and, wretchedly, we even get punished for not complying. What an affront! What a "fall" from original bliss.

The "gate of Eden" appears well-guarded, but that does not prevent us from wanting to get back in. To be back at the center of everything. To feel everything to be an extension of ourselves. To be one with God. To be God. To be "king." To be "queen." There is an impulse in all of us that draws and pulls us back to that unitive sensation in which we were all born. There is a deep-down resentment that we have been torn from the bliss of that state. We want to return to that graced state of being. We don't want to acknowledge boundaries and separation.

There is nothing reprehensible about that desire. We are born in bliss; why can't we keep it? To repossess paradise is a hunger that every human being feels. Religious systems have been founded with just that goal in mind. The religious quest begins with an awareness of "separation," with an awareness of our never-ending longing for "something more." The quest becomes a pilgrimage of humility, struggle, patience, discipline, endurance, and fortitude.

However, few enter a spiritual quest on this "road less traveled." It is too much work and effort. Most of us prefer another strategy: we resist! We simply refuse to admit separation from that paradise into which we were born. We refuse to acknowledge the boundary of the "gate." We refuse to admit finiteness and limitation. We refuse to acknowledge that we are not the center of everything that is. And thus evolves what Freud would call "his majesty, the baby." Thus evolves a demanding, egocentric, imperious, controlling "little ruler," which is popularized by some writers as "King Baby" (which also translates into "Queen Baby").

"King Baby" feels born to rule, as is only fitting for someone born in paradise, at the center of all that is. King Baby knows one role and one role only: to rule and demand. Like Adam and Eve, King Baby assumes everything is his by entitlement.

We never grow up, and out, of "his majesty the baby." King Baby may be obnoxiously apparent in the "terrible two's," and become somewhat tempered and discreet with discipline and painful learning experiences, but King Baby is with us for our lifetime. King Baby wants its rightful place in the garden of Eden. King Baby has no intention of going on a quest or a pilgrimage. King Baby asserts that its existence outside of paradise is simply: unacceptable.

King Baby only knows that he "deserves." King Baby

makes himself heard with the imperious demand: "I want what I want, and I want it now!"

King Baby is the source of all our fears, frustrations, and disappointments. King Baby is working in us with every threat we feel, with every anxiety of losing in competition, with every fear of punishment or accepting consequences for our behavior. King Baby is working in us with every impatience at waiting in line, with every resentment at being refused a raise, with every bewilderment of not being "understood," with every act of punishing others for affronting us with criticism, with every refusal of granting forgiveness.

King Baby is all around us in other people we know and meet. King Baby manifests itself in the rages of an angry boss, in the manipulations of a seductress, in the postures of a pouting adolescent or a passive-aggressive spouse. King Baby is the ludicrous exhibitionist making a fool of himself at the office party. Queen Baby is the simpering mother who uses her tears to break down her children's attempts at independence. King Baby is the failing salesman whose sheepishness is blamed on an inferiority complex, which itself is just a disguise for a manipulative omnipotence seeking control by looking "needy." Queen Baby is the twice divorced wife, taking all the blame on herself for her failed marriages. She even has the brazen audacity of claiming "God could never forgive me." What splendid omnipotence: to be able to read the mind of God!

As entropy is the passive "laziness" in resistance, King Baby is the positive energy in resistance. We will never come to love our selves as we need as long as King and Queen Baby are "on the throne," occupying our consciousness. King Baby does not love; King Baby only demands. King Baby assumes he is perfect, just as he is, and will not hear otherwise. King Baby is not interested in reform and "development."

King Baby assumes that his own imperious self-love (which selfishly does not take into account that there may be more to "us" than himself) is enough. King Baby has only his own interests. Love for our selves will necessitate acceptance of our human limitations. King Baby cannot do that and survive. Love for our selves will mean accepting ourselves as we really are. That we are not omnipotent. That we are not the center of the universe. That we are not God! King Baby will not listen to this. And that is why falling in love with ourselves is so very difficult. That is why falling genuinely in love with anybody is so difficult. King Baby will always stand in the way. King Baby is subtle and resourceful in his attempts to maintain the throne, and is always refining his techniques. King Baby will constantly try to keep us maintaining false assumptions about ourselves and our place in the scheme of things. King and Queen Baby will always have agendas irrespective of our best interests.

It is here that I have a problem with some self-help books and programs that have been popular in recent years. I have a problem with some of the self-help courses that try to restore one's sense of self-esteem and assertiveness in a way that affirms and plays up to one's sense of personal "omnipotence." It may be an exercise in getting someone who is shy and reserved to become an aggressive self-seeker. Or the exercises may be more subtle, and teach the client refined and well-honed skills of assertive manipulation. One way or another, they are techniques of allowing King Baby to rule more successfully.

Audrey simply got tired of being shy and the "butt end of everyone's jokes." Audrey never liked her looks, her personality, her intelligence, her regressive social skills. She was tired of being "everybody's door mat." She took a popular course in "self-assertiveness," which plainly coached its students that the only way to avoid getting trampled on is to "do some trampling of your own." She was bombarded with aggressive jargon and slogans until her shyness faded and she became the "new Audrey" who vowed "never to take 'shit' from anybody."

Audrey did change, remarkably. From a shy, melancholy, reserved young secretary, she became an ambitious, aggressive, driven, CEO of her own small company. She is considered one of her recovery program's greatest successes.

She is also considered "unscrupulous and obsessive" by her competitors, a "perfect witch" by her old friends, a "monster" by her ex-husband, and "seriously dysfunctional and on the verge of breakdown" by her new therapist. Audrey never found the love of herself that she deserves. She found a way to let "Queen Baby" rule without restraints.

FURTHER HANDICAPS

As if entropy and King Baby weren't enough, our resistance to change, to improvement, and to development of self-love is enhanced by an assortment of handicaps. We will deal at length with the handicap of "old tapes" in a further chapter, but immediately it comes to mind that we are creatures of habit. Over a lifetime, habits can be our best friends, but they can also be our worst enemies. Self-defeating behavior can become just as entrenched as self-enhancing behavior. We tend not to think about our habits. They become so much part of us that we wouldn't think of calling them into question.

Memories can encourage resistance. Awareness of our past bad track record of making and keeping resolutions can make us throw up our hands in despair. It is most difficult to make a commitment and develop courage when our memories coach us that we simply don't have what it takes.

Perhaps the greatest handicap, however, is the very self we bring to our self-love recovery program. If our journey is an inner journey, and if we are to find resources for self-love recovery within ourselves, it seems that we approach recovery with the only equipment we have: our selves. We will be using the very selves we feel are deficient.

The problem is that we cannot escape our old selves. Our old selves accompany us like permanent baggage. We seek to escape our problems and all we have to work with are our old selves which got us into our problems in the first place. It seems like hiring a burglar to guard our house.

That is why personal resolutions don't work very well. That is why our willpower seems so flabby. That is why our resolve is so half-hearted. That is why we correct one fault, only to discover that another one has quickly taken its place. (A good friend finally gave up smoking after thirty-two years, and in six months has put on thirty-two pounds.) When we work from our own resources, we seem doomed to use the very instruments which put, and keep, us in our mess in the first place.

Again, that is why we are most often blind to our real needs, and why we tend to concentrate on changing what really doesn't matter. We think that deciding to hold back our temper will make our failing marriage better, when the problem lies much deeper than a few angry outbreaks. We are blatantly prejudiced in our own favor. Only with great reluctance do we admit our faults. Little wonder that age-old wisdom warns us that we are our own worst doctors, our own worst lawyers, and our own worst enemies. Our track record for having adequately taken care of ourselves is most often remiss. In our effort to control our lives and make things better, we often find that we make things worse.

What can save us from "resistance"? What can protect our recovery work from laziness, entropy, and King Baby? What can modify our handicaps in self-love recovery? The answer we will now see is found in the paradox of "surrender." "Surrender" might just well prove to be the most important disposition we need in self-love recovery.

OUT OF OUR CONTROL

I have emphasized from the beginning that self-love recovery will depend on more than a quick "fix" and on more than "techniques" and exercises. A more permanent self-love recovery will need to be based on a spiritual program, a program designed with spiritual growth in mind. One of the most powerful recovery programs for addiction is found in Alcoholics Anonymous. Alcoholics Anonymous is not a religion, nor is it affiliated with any particular religious denomination. Alcoholics Anonymous, however, is a "spiritual" program. It is geared to growth, spiritual growth, growth in self-love, self-esteem, and self-nurturing. Alcoholics Anonymous is affiliated with other addiction-recovery programs in the use of "Twelve-Step" spirituality.

Twelve-Step spirituality, from which we will borrow, is capturing the attention of many recovery programs and many church reformation programs for one substantial reason: it works! I have embraced Twelve-Step spirituality because it works for me, and I have seen it work for thousands of others. Twelve-Step spirituality is based on a recognition of "powerlessness" over one's recovery, and on "surrender" to the help of a "Higher Power."

The "power" for recovery is found in the very *admission and acceptance of personal powerlessness*. The First Step begins: "*We admitted we were powerless (over alcohol, relationships, sex, emotions, eating, etc.) and our lives had become unmanageable.*" This first step is an echo of the self-empowering belief of the early Christians in the teaching of the apostle Paul, who proclaimed a famous paradox: "It is in my weakness that I am strong."

All of us who have felt a personal insufficiency and inadequacy because of poor self-esteem and poor self-love know what "weakness" is. We have suffered with it, and because of it we may be reasonably dubious that adequate self-love is within our reach. We may be hesitant to launch into a self-love recovery program saying: "What's the use? Nothing's ever worked for me before." Furthermore, we can probably relate to the resistance issues as we have been describing them so far in this chapter. We realize that our resistance is tenacious, that our commitment will be handicapped, that we are encumbered with bad coping habits, that King Baby is alive and well on the throne, that we are lazy and full of self-doubt, that as far as self-love recovery matters, we are *out of control*.

It should perk our interest, therefore, that there is a spiritual program that actually takes all this into account. A program that tells us that our very helplessness and hopelessness is the strength and assurance we need to recover love for our selves. A program that says, yes, you cannot recover the love you need for yourself all on your own, from your own resources. That you cannot "control" your own self-love recovery. That you cannot guarantee any results of a self-love recovery program...but that a Higher Power can.

Thanks to King Baby, "control" and our control impulses will always remain a major issue (to our disadvantage) in our self-love recovery program. From babyhood we grew up craving security in an often insecure environment. And we have never lost that impulse. Survival is our strongest instinct. Fear is one of our worst feelings. Fear is what insecurity is all about. We hate to feel insecure. We hate to feel powerless. We desperately want to be in control.

Most of our education and training was geared to help us get control of our lives and our future. We were disciplined in an effort to teach us control. We studied and competed to gain assurance about the reliability of our own resources for control. We were taught to take care of ourselves, to prepare for the future, to equip ourselves for times ahead. We learned the importance of guarantees, and to make sure that we got it "in writing." We were cautioned not to take chances, or to throw caution to the wind. It was important that we remain in control.

As we get older and become more observant, however, we come to realize what little control we actually have. We can't control the weather or the price of tomorrow's tankful of gas. We have no control over the economy, rising taxes, the political tone of the nation, or the rise and fall of the stock market. There is little we can do about the aging process, getting the flu, or making sure there will be social security for us on the day we retire.

All that might be acceptable, if only we could control what happens to us, our jobs, our families, and our immediate circle of friends. If only we had control of our health, our physical, mental, and emotional well-being. But such is not the case. We do our best, but "control" is terribly limited. Illness happens. Accidents happen. Times change. Jobs are easily lost today. Our children become emotionally independent at an earlier and earlier age. Close friends come and go. One of our inherited genes may be deficient and we die at a tender age, or the tiniest of microbes enters our bloodstreams and puts an end to all our dreams.

If the truth be told, there is no real "control" at all, for anybody. At most there are more or less successful attempts at *manageability*. There is no omnipotence for the finite, limited, human beings we are. Life offers no guarantees of anything. We ultimately "possess" nothing. Death will ultimately take everything away. "Health nuts" exercise their way into heart attacks. A fall in the stock market turns a billionaire into a pauper. Howard Hughes, with all his millions, is helpless over the madness that overtook him in his declining years.

Unless we can admit all this, we are living in an illusion. And, admittedly, millions of us do live in illusion. We are still "shocked" and depressed when things don't turn out the way we anticipated. We are outraged when something doesn't go our way. We become bitter when we are criticized. We are affronted when a freight train stops traffic. We feel put upon when someone doesn't see things our way. An accident appears to us as a personal attack. And, as the saying goes, "Life is what happens when you've made other plans."

May I quickly add the reflection here that the first step of Twelve-Step spirituality tells us that it is perfectly OK to be this way. It is perfectly OK not to be "in control." It is perfectly all right to be a limited and finite human being. It is perfectly OK not to be omnipotent. It is perfectly OK to be handicapped in our self-love recovery program. It is perfectly OK not to be God.

A HIGHER POWER CAN HELP

It is only in our weakness that we are able to receive the help we need. It is only in our vulnerability that we are disposed to receive the help we need from something greater than ourselves. To put on a show of invulnerability is always self-defeating because it cuts us off from the help we need, and cannot control. It is only in admitting what little control we have that we can gain some control over the actions we need to take on our behalf. If we have "all the answers," and the answers have not been working very well, we can be assured that they will continue working poorly for us in the future. It is only in humble admission that we haven't got all the answers that we can find answers.

An alcoholic can never recover until he or she hits the "bottom of the barrel" and admits to "no control" over alcohol. Fighting to gain control only aggravates the problem. All of us have a wide range of control behaviors. We become hyperly defensive in the face of any criticism. We may lash out at any attack of our work. We may rage in blame of others for the mess we feel our life has become. We rage that nobody understands us. Perhaps we fight for control by the strategy of isolating ourselves as much as possible from the world around us, becoming recluses in our immediate home surroundings. Many of us try to control our bad feelings with "reasoning" ("I shouldn't feel this way") or repression ("It doesn't bother me"). We seek revenge on those who we've supposed have harmed us. We may even attack and abuse ourselves for being a "misfit" or for making mistakes. We look to a bottle or a drug or a medication to help us avoid the pain, or else we beat ourselves with guilt and shame in an attempt to make ourselves "perfect." We feel that if we can "beat ourselves into shape," everything that is wrong about us can be "fixed" and we will become more lovable.

In truth, all these attempts at "control" only result in making us ultimately feel worse about ourselves. We cannot build self-esteem by attacking others or ourselves as less than worthwhile. We cannot build self-love by beating others or ourselves into submission. All recovery programs require some form of "surrender," a surrender of control. Self-love recovery will not prove an exception.

Control must give way to *acceptance*. Our primary task in life is not to be "in control," but, as Mother Teresa often asserts, *to be faithful*, faithful especially to our selves. For most of us, "faithfulness" will mean taking care of our selves as we need.

For most of us that will mean giving up our control illusions and calling upon "a power greater than ourselves" to assume control for us. The second step of the Twelve-Step program says: *"We came to believe that a power greater than ourselves could save us."*

After humbly, and realistically, forsaking the ineffectiveness of our control strategies, and admitting our fundamental need for help, we come to believe that there is a power somewhere in this universe that is greater than our selves, and into whose hands we can surrender control. In this step we are being asked to discover and admit what should be fairly obvious: life is bigger than any of us alone. There are forces and dynamics in this universe that operate above and beyond us. There are "powers that be." A Higher Power is in control, and it is up to us to be connected with this Power. We don't have to go it alone.

We will be elaborating upon this in greater detail in a later chapter, but for now we need but speculate that there is a power greater than ourselves operating in the living organism we call the universe. The entire cosmos is an unfolding, a birthing, an evolution of Being. And the greatest revelation of all is that the Being which unfolds in the cosmos, and in us, does so in a benign, nurturing, and loving manner. Love not only makes the world go round, it is the life force of the universe—a life force which energizes us as it does all the parts of galaxies too far beyond our comprehension.

It is not my intention to continue a metaphysical treatment of this matter. Sufficient for our purposes here, it is important that we grasp that there is a power greater than ourselves, operating in and around us. A Higher Power that operates for good. A Higher Power that operates for our good. A Higher Power that loves us and can help us love ourselves as we need.

Knowing that we are not abandoned, or left to our own limited resources, is power enough to begin our quest to learn to love ourselves as we need. We may call this Higher Power anything we wish, as long as we recognize that it is a Power greater than ourselves. For many, this Higher Power will be

God, in whatever form they comprehend God to be. For others it might be a universal force for good.

Where does this Power reside? Again, we have not the space to go into a metaphysical treatment of the "location" of our Higher Power. Many are comfortable with "God in his heavens," God as transcendent over his creation, which he cares for and guides. For others, myself included, God is transcendent and immanent within us. In my view, I believe God, the eternal Self, is conjoined with our observing "I," with the "I" that we use when we speak in the first person singular. The eternal Self manifests itself within us. I might go further and state I believe that God can be identified in our unconscious (if not *with* our unconscious, according to some) and dwells within us as our Higher Wisdom, Guide, and Lover. (For excellent elaborations of these concepts, I would urge the reader to refer to *The Road Less Traveled* by M. Scott Peck and to a superb treatment by Ken Wilber in his book *No Boundary*).

In terms of our treatment of this second step, however, I repeat that *where* we understand our Higher Power to be located is not essential to self-love recovery. While I am persuaded of our Higher Power's identification in our unconscious, others who cannot at present comprehend or embrace such an idea of a transcendent and/or immanent God may well find their Higher Power in a loving family, in trusted and supportive friends, in the membership of a Twelve-Step meeting such as Alcoholics Anonymous. For others it might even be this book, with its insights and suggestions. The point is to relinquish our illusions of personal "control." The point is to accept that there is a Power or powers above us that can help us achieve what we cannot do on our own.

Admittedly, this step of acknowledging our need for a Higher Power to help us on our road of self-love recovery may be difficult for many of us. We have become convinced that all plans for life are man-made, that our needs are what count the most in the universe, and that our plans are the only plans that should make a difference (King Baby). We are so "subjectivized" and self-referent that we don't want to admit there is a bigger reality outside of us and that fundamentally we are but parts of a Plan. Belief in a Higher Power, in our need for a Higher Power, and in our Higher Power's willingness to help us can only be enhanced by a consistent review and acknowledgement of our powerlessness and lack of control. As life continues to teach us that much of our "control" is little more than a hope or an illusion, our willingness to "believe" will be encouraged.

SURRENDER

Resistance in its many forms will dog us every inch of the way in self-love recovery. Resistance will always prove to be a handicap to caring for our selves as we need. Resistance will attempt to squelch our commitment to "do whatever it takes" to recover for our selves the love that we need. I propose that the only effective antidote to resistance is "surrender."

"Surrender" is not a coping mechanism, much less a technique to make life easier or make us less put upon. Surrender is a whole new way of life for most of us. Having experienced sufficient pain, and our inability to effectively manipulate life or others in our favor, we turn our selves over. We turn our lives, our wills, and our recovery over to a Power greater than ourselves. The third step of the Twelve-Step program says: *"Made a decision to turn our wills and our lives over to the care of God, as we understood Him."*

It is important that we take note of two significant parts of this step. Resistance may be so powerful in us, or so subtle, that we never come to feel that we can surrender our selves to a Higher Power. The efficacy of this step does not depend on a *feeling* of actual wholesale surrender of our selves, but on a *decision* to do so. The framers of the Twelve Steps knew well that part of our limitations as human beings was our inability to always act in our best interests. Surrendering our selves to a Power greater than ourselves for recovery might be in our best interests, but might also be beyond our capabilities at a given moment. A "decision," however, is well within our means. We can at least make a decision to turn our lives and wills over. We can at least allow our Higher Power the freedom to take over. We can at least be *willing*.

The second point we need take note of in this step is that "God" is never defined. "As we understood Him" allows a wide range for interpretation. "God" is used as a conventional term for a Higher Power, but even an atheist can conceive of a Higher Power that is not identified with the Judaic or Christian God, for example. This step allows us to accept a Higher Power in whatever form is most acceptable and useful to us at any given stage of our development. The important thing again is that we forsake our ineffective and self-defeating control strategies and place ourselves into the hands of a Power greater than ourselves.

Thousands have shown in their recovery programs the importance of humility and surrender. An attitude of "I can take care of myself" might be acceptable, as long as we really are taking care of our selves. But if the "care" we are taking of our selves is proving to be more self-defeating than self-enhancing, such an attitude is little more than arrogant posturing.

It is not without reason that the great spiritual masters have encouraged their followers to adopt an attitude of a "humble pilgrim." Humility and openness of spirit are crucial in self-love development. The ability to ask for what we need is crucial in self-love development, as is the ability to forgive, to be patient, to give up entrenched habits, and to become an open conduit for love. Without an openness to "surrender," these crucial elements in self-love recovery are impossible. We cannot make a "new life" for ourselves by tenaciously hanging onto the ropes that bind us to our old ways. Turning our wills and our lives over gives us the important "release" that we need.

Making a decision to turn our lives and wills over to a power greater than ourselves is opening our hands for help. In self-love recovery, we are offering our selves. It is an offer which a benevolent Power greater than ourselves cannot refuse. Our very understanding of a benevolent Power greater than ourselves is that it is a Power that wishes, and works, for our best interests.

Those who have already surrendered and are well on the way of self-love recovery encourage us never to lose heart. They tell us that surrender is difficult and is never a one-time decision. It is made again and again and again. In the beginning maybe the most we can do is breathe a sigh of release, and "give in." We give up "quick fix" attempts to make ourselves feel better for a while. We give up demanding that things work out the way we have specifically determined. We give up expecting things to work out our way. We give up control and let our Higher Power work with us and through us.

"Surrender" should not be a difficult concept to appreciate. Surrender comes quite naturally to human beings. A little reflection will demonstrate that we are surrendering all the time. We surrender trust to authority figures. We surrender belief to the outpourings of the media and opinion makers. We surrender to our temptations, idiosyncracies, and obsessions. The idea of surrender is hardly new to us. At heart we want to surrender.

The great spiritual masters teach that "surrender" is a natural impulse, that there is a deep and powerful need in all of us to give our selves over in love to someone or something greater than ourselves. It is more than a lazy attempt to become generally passive and apathetic to our responsibilities. It is a natural longing to abandon our selves to something truly worthy.

The great spiritual masters also teach us that there is enormous freedom in surrender. They teach us that the most significant, liberating, and powerful act a human being can perform is to say "Thy will be done." Surrender means "letting go," letting our Higher Power take charge of our lives, our selves, even our self-love recovery. Surrender allows our Higher Power to take over with a wisdom and love that is beyond our comprehension. Surrender allows us to say "Thy will be done" with trust that that "Will" will be the best for us.

In later chapters we will review action plans to recover and enhance our self-love. Loving acts on our behalf do not negate surrender. As a matter of fact, surrender and loving actions on our behalf work hand in hand in self-love recovery. Gerald May in his book *Will and Spirit* asserts: "The paradox of spiritual surrender is that in giving oneself fully, one finds not passivity but intimate involvement, not restrictiveness but endless freedom, not blameless quietude but the deepest possible sense of responsibility."

Surrender, therefore, is not self-insulation. It is not an abandonment to indecisiveness and apathy. Quite the contrary, it represents a willingness to engage life as fully as possible, but (with a willingness to surrender) as it comes and unfolds by the will of our Higher Power. It is not giving up on life, but giving up "control." Surrender is giving up reliance on personal will power to accomplish what we need for our selves. Surrender allows our Higher Power to come alive in us and lead us where we need to go.

As we come to love our selves more, surrender becomes easier and easier. Surrender activates actions on our behalf. The more we surrender, the more empowered we become to perform those actions which will increase our self-love. The more we increase our self-love, the less defensive and resistant we become, and the more able we become to surrender even more. A wonderful cycle begins, spiraling us into higher levels of self-love recovery. Within the cycle, we begin to see the benefits that come our way from surrendering more and more. We begin to appreciate the benefits of letting a Higher Wisdom raise us to a more fulfilling life.

Those who have surrendered assure us that the often painful "dying" to ourselves, which is a hallmark of surrender, is at the same time a rebirth to a new and better life. They assure us that we will experience "salvation." That somewhere down the road we will discover that if we were allowed complete freedom to write our own life story, we would probably have destroyed ourselves, and others. That gratefully our Higher Power has intervened time and time again to save us from our own folly.

Admittedly again, it is difficult to accept and trust that

there *is* a Higher Power that cares about us and can help us. Many of us feel that our prayers, or hopes for help, are rarely responded to. What we may not realize is that what we pray for, or even hope for, may not be in our best interest. Many of the things we thought we "needed" desperately proved later not to have been necessary at all. Perhaps they even proved to be harmful. Nonetheless, it is still difficult to trust, especially when we feel defeated, laid low, oppressed, or rejected. It is at those times that we most feel a need for "strength," not "surrender." It is at those times that we most feel the urge to use our control strategies and take things into our own hands. It is at those times, however, that turning over control is the most urgent and wisest thing to do. Those well into self-love recovery tell us that with time we will come to see and appreciate how well we were led and guarded as a result of our surrendering. That our Higher Power, God, as we understand him, keeps us, and leads us on the track that is best for us.

Paradoxically, surrendering, turning ourselves over to a Power greater than ourselves, is the only way we become empowered to help ourselves. Entrenched in our old habits and self-defeating attitudes, we often behaved with one-track minds. We didn't help ourselves; we hurt ourselves. The "old ways" were not working out for us. That is why this third step takes into account not only to whom or what we turn ourselves over, but what we turn over. We turn over "our lives and our wills." That means we turn over *everything* about us. We turn over what is good about us and what is bad about us. We turn over our attitudes, our beliefs, our prejudices, and our need to feel better. We turn over our ways of handling people, our anger, our temper, and our "sins." We turn over our sufferings, our frustrations, our doubts, our impatience for an immediate solution to our problems, even our inability to surrender as much as we might like. We surrender our selves. We surrender everything.

Surrender, then, not only helps take us out of our guilt and shame (yes, we surrender that too), but also opens us up to new possibilities. Surrender opens us to learn. And that is how we are helped to help ourselves. Learning opens doors, which, in our old mind-sets, we never knew existed. We learn new ways of coping and taking care of our selves. In surrender, our own higher interior powers become activated. "Logic" gives way to intuition and wisdom. We become open and willing. We learn to love our selves as we need.

Surrender is necessary, therefore, because self-love recovery most often necessitates turning our lives around. All our lives we have been persuaded and trained to take and maintain "control." We were expected to "master" ourselves as a means of coping with life and people. In our struggle to gain and maintain control we developed coping habits that many times over proved to be self-destructive to our self-love. Now we need to forsake our habitual means of coping, because they do not work in our best interest.

Our Higher Power must replace King Baby on the throne. This is "revolutionary" behavior for us. We need to be transformed. Our selves need a new configuration. We cannot do this of, and for, ourselves. Our old habits are too ingrained. We are too entrenched in our old lifestyles. We need help. And the only way "help" can be effective to turn our lives around is by our willingness to surrender to that help, by our willingness to surrender all that we are and have.

Make no mistake, we cannot make a new life for our selves without a dying of the old life. We cannot find peace unless we are willing to forsake old coping mechanisms that bring us stress. We cannot find love unless we are willing to "let go" of mind-sets that keep love at a distance. We cannot find joy and happiness until we surrender up our wills for real healing. Without "surrender," all "techniques" for improving self-esteem and self-love fall flat.

4

All That Self-Love Isn't

There is no greater lie than a truth misunderstood.
                                        —William James

We have become aware of the significant influence that
King Baby has on "our lives and our wills." We have seen what
an obstacle King Baby can be to self-love recovery. It should be
obvious that King Baby can fool us into thinking we are more
self-loving than we are. As a matter of fact, King Baby can make
us think that he and self-love are one and the same, that what is
good for him is good for us too. It is important, therefore, that
we be alert to what genuine self-love isn't. We need to appreciate that what might look like self-love may only be King or
Queen Baby in disguise.

Joanne and Susan have made a special point of remembering each other's birthday since they became close friends in college. Both are now married with full lives of their own. While
they see each other only rarely, they still remember each other's
birthday with a card or a call. This year is the first time Susan
did not receive a card or a call from Joanne on her birthday.
There may be a very reasonable explanation why she didn't.
Susan's immediate reaction, however, is sadness and disappointment. She speculates that perhaps, in a world where nothing
lasts, she and Joanne are drifting apart and a wonderful friendship is coming to an end. A day later, Susan's disappointment
turns to anger. She is angry with Joanne for her fickleness in a
relationship that was always important to both of them. After a
week of not hearing from Joanne, Susan feels that her self-
esteem has been affronted. Susan is an intelligent woman and

feels that her self-esteem needs to be protected. She concludes that she doesn't have to "put up" with this "obvious slight" from Joanne. It isn't long before she builds up in her mind all the things about Joanne she never really liked anyway, and wonders how she ever became friends with Joanne in the first place. She is glad the relationship is over. Susan feels that she has protected her self-esteem but it is obvious Queen Baby has made her point. The Queen rules.

Paula is attending a parent-teacher conference for her daughter Rachel. Rachel is in fourth grade and, as far as Paula is concerned, is doing quite well in her school work. Rachel's teacher is elderly and a bit of an old-school taskmaster. For some reason hidden deep in her unconscious, Paula is immediately turned off by this teacher. She feels intimidated and experiences fear and shame simply being in a face-to-face discussion with her. She feels the blood rush to her face. When the teacher implies that Rachel is not quite living up to her potential as a fourth grader, Paula feels a rush of embarrassment. Scores of images flood her brain that recall her own embarrassment as a child who "could never do enough to please anybody." On the verge of tears, Paula excuses herself on the pretext of an emergency and rushes for her car. Out of the teacher's presence, she soon regains her composure. Shortly she becomes upset at her reaction and loss of control. In an attempt to "regain her self-respect," she vows to complain about the teacher, quit her position on the PTA board, and stop making cookies for school parties. Queen Baby has made her point. "Self-respect" has little to do with it. The "baby" pouts.

Luke is a very successful businessman. He looks like a man of utter self-confidence. He gives the impression of being in total control of his life. He has an answer for everything. He "gets what he wants." He eats right, exercises regularly, and takes very good care of himself. He is also abusive. He has been married four times, and the trial evidence in his divorce settlements for "mental cruelty" could make front page titillation in the daily tabloids. His associates complain how much he uses people. Luke justifies all his behavior with: "You have to look out for number one," and "When you like yourself enough, you don't have to worry about what anybody else thinks." King Baby has made his point.

ARROGANCE

At first glance we might assume that arrogant people are extremely self-assured and confident. At first glance it might appear that arrogant people have too much of a good thing. It is good to be self-assured. It is good to be self-confident. These qualities are indications of self-love.

But arrogance falls short of self-love. Arrogance is a demand that others accept us as superior. Arrogance is a demand that others acknowledge our existence as a boon for humanity. More than taking healthy pride in work and accomplishments, arrogant people feel a need to flaunt and parade their accomplishments—which should give us a hint that some kind of compensation is going on.

Arrogance is not just wearing a halo, it is polishing one's halo under the noses of others. Arrogance is putting on airs. It is exaggerating one's opinions and deeds as if they have never been offered or accomplished by anyone else before. Arrogance is a posture of superiority. When we are arrogant, we are not acting out of love for ourselves. As we might suspect, arrogance is King Baby demanding his due whether it is owed to him or not. Arrogance is an obsession with entitlement. Entitlement is what makes us feel affronted when our waiter gives more attention to another table.

If we are arrogant, we are prime candidates for a self-love recovery program because arrogance is fundamentally a ploy to hide a fearsome inferiority complex. Arrogance is a need to hide a self which is felt to be defective. Arrogance is over-compensation for feelings of inferiority. We cannot love ourselves as inferior. By putting on airs, we can at least pretend. What better way to hide the inferiority feelings than by substituting feelings of superiority.

SELFISHNESS

As will become clearer in later chapters, "selfishness" can be considered an asset in self-love recovery. Self-love can be "selfish" in a very admirable way, as when we take care of our selves and do not succumb to the arbitrary expectations of others. Nathaniel Brandon, who has written many fine books on self-esteem, has clarified that rational selfishness is a good indication of self-love. Rational selfishness does not take away from love and concern for others. As a matter of fact, he asserts, rational self-interest is the only way to be genuinely caring of others without the manipulation so often associated with "love." Abraham Maslow also taught that self-interest actually coincides with altruism in highly self-actuated (loving) people.

In our context, however, "selfishness," as it is conventionally understood, does not coincide with self-love. Rather, selfishness is identified with self-seeking and an unwillingness to share. Selfishness is most evident in people who are narcissistically self-centered. Selfishness is King Baby living in the illusion that it is the center of the universe. King Baby demands, "I want what I want and I want it now," and the needs of others are irrelevant. This is not self-love. This is pure egoism.

It is not "selfish" to assert that I live my life to my expectations, but it is "selfish" to assert that you live your life according to my expectations. I am selfish when I do not take your needs into account. I am not selfish in painting my own picture, but I am selfish when I draw you into my picture to suit my desires.

While selfish people often intimate that they are simply taking care of themselves, they blind themselves to the fact that self-care is not "self-seeking." Self-care is not egoism. Self-care is not pandering to the whims of King Baby. Motives give it away. Selfishness is a cover-up for shame. Shame is a reaction to a feeling of personal insignificance. Selfishness is a ploy to disguise or compensate for that feeling of inadequacy. Selfishness is not self-love, but a ruse to hide a lack of self-love—which makes selfish people excellent candidates for a self-love recovery program.

SELFLESSNESS

"Selflessness" sounds virtuous. And in many cases, it is. Saints, heroes, and many ordinary people have demonstrated a healthy self-love and love for others in giving of themselves for the sake of their friends or countrymen. Self-sacrifice is seen written beautifully and deeply on the face of a Mother Teresa. We can admire, applaud and respect this selflessness.

On the other hand there is a "selflessness" that parades around as love, but is actually little more than a manipulative strategy to get others to love us because of what we do for them. While we can selfishly take care of ourselves at the expense of others, we can also "selflessly" take care of others at the expense of ourselves.

"Caretakers" love to be perceived as "selfless" people. Technically "caretakers" are people who take care of others while neglecting their own needs and feelings. "Caretakers" are most often co-dependents whose sense of self-worth and self-love are not "owned" but are dependent on the good will of others. Caretakers are "people-pleasers" who need others to give them a sense of self-worth they don't feel about themselves.

Caretakers are "martyrs" who carry around a fair share of toxic shame. To escape that shame, they go out of their way to cater to, to take care of, and to please others, with the hope that others will think they are wonderful and love them in a way they don't love themselves. They might even put up with an enormous amount of abuse just to receive a little recognition. That's the hidden agenda. Caretakers want to appear selfless. Caretakers are willing to put themselves out and make any sacrifice as long as some admiration and appreciation from others will help fill up the emptiness they feel inside.

If there is a "caretaker" in our lives, what he or she is saying to us is: "I have never felt very good about myself, so I will go overboard to take care of you, to do nice things for you, and to please you. All I secretly ask in return is that you appreciate me, say some nice things to me, and help me feel better about myself than I actually do."

Ultimately, "caretakers" do not help; they victimize the object of the "caring." They use people to make themselves feel better about themselves. They "serve" others in order to receive applause and gratitude to supplement a deep sense of inadequacy. And ironically, for all their caretaking efforts, not loving themselves enough actually prohibits them from taking to heart any applause and gratitude.

FEELING SUCCESSFUL

Feeling successful in a job well-done is nothing we need be ashamed of. It is an indication of self-love that we can take pride in our accomplishments and feel gratified that we have been successful. From our earliest years, we have been coached to "be a winner." We have been indoctrinated in the importance of climbing the "ladder of success." In school, playground, and the job, we have been encouraged to compete. We have been taught that "winning is what it's all about." As we noted earlier, competition can be appropriate. Competition can stimulate us to live up to our potentials. Competition can give us a well-deserved feeling of success.

Competition has a dark side, however. We can use competition to compensate for shame and feelings of inferiority. That is precisely why many "successful" people never *feel* successful. That is why many highly successful people become self-destructive, as was evidenced in the rise and fall of some high-powered bond investors who caused so much financial havoc in the early 1990s. Competition can be used to hide the fact that we do not love ourselves enough. A "drive" for success can be a coping mechanism to escape from bad feelings about ourselves. "Success" and feelings of success are not necessarily synonymous with self-love.

When is "success," and the "drive" for success, not indicative of self-love? Clearly, "success" is suspect if it has to be achieved "at any price." Workaholics, for example, can destroy themselves, their health, and their families with an obsession for their careers. This addiction can be just as devastating and self-destructive as alcoholism. "Success" is also suspicious if it is pursued for its own sake, or if it can only be achieved at the expense of others, rather than on personal merit. If "success is all that matters," or if we can only feel successful by "beating out" the competition, we are obviously compensating. We are using "success" to feel better about ourselves than we do. When we "need" success, or cannot enjoy success, we are candidates for a self-love recovery program.

HAVING POSSESSIONS

In our culture, "success" is normally indicated by the trappings of success: a fine home in the suburbs, a couple of expensive cars, designer clothes, a private pool, roomloads of antiques, a workshop loaded with the latest gadgets, the finest in stereo equipment, original paintings, a condo in the Caribbean, and so on. But it is one thing to have many fine possessions, and quite another to have to *prove* ourselves through our possessions.

We can take care of our selves by providing ourselves with all the necessities and comforts that make us feel suitably rewarded for our achievements. As we will see later, this is an admirable self-loving action. The obsession to possess things, however, or to hang on to things with a pack rat mentality, is an indication that possessions are much more than a reward; they are a compensation for feelings of inferiority and inadequacy.

The number and quality of our possessions are strictly secondary to the good feelings we should have for ourselves. Self-love does not *arise* from possessions. Self-love allows us to *enjoy* possessions. Self-love is not dependent on "owning" anything, but our selves. Again, as we will see, genuine self-love stems from self-appreciation and self-caring actions. When owning possessions becomes a driving force in our lives to "fill in the gap" of empty inner feelings, they are not expressions of self-love, but a cover-up for lack of self-love. In such a case, we do not own our possessions, they own us. Our feeling good about ourselves is at their mercy.

SELF-PRE-OCCUPATION

While it is good to be invested in ourselves, it is easy for us to go overboard, especially with King Baby sitting on the throne. We can take "caring for ourselves" to extremes. We can become self-pre-occupied. This is especially true for those of us who haven't felt very good about ourselves, but are willing to take active measures to change. It is all too easy to become too self-absorbed, too introspective, too self-analyzing, too pre-occupied with our needs and wants.

Self-love is not obsessive. We are not self-loving when all we do is think about ourselves. Self-love is not served by obsessions of any kind, even about our selves. Self-pre-occupation is over-compensation for feelings of inadequacy. Even with the best of intentions, self-pre-occupation is dangerous and self-destructive. We can become pre-occupied about our selves to the exclusion of real life going on around us. Some become so pre-occupied that they lose all contact with reality, and end up mentally ill.

Being occupied with ourselves and our best interests is appropriate. Being *pre*-occupied with ourselves, however, is a sign that we have not yet come to love ourselves as we ought. Genuine self-love is most evident in people of composure, moderation, and balance. Self-loving people are normally outgoing and are naturally absorbed in life and other people. Assured and appreciative about themselves, they live in service of others. Helping others is a reward all its own.

This is not to say that we should forget about ourselves and pursue self-love exclusively in helping others. What we need to strive for is balance. There is great virtue in getting into ourselves, in becoming aware of who and what we are, in discovering our lovableness. But there is also great virtue in getting out of ourselves and into the lives of others. We show true love for ourselves when we feel confident enough in ourselves to pour ourselves out for others.

FEELING GOOD

It is popularly accepted in our culture that if something feels good, it must be good for us. If we feel good, everything must be O.K.

Many self-help programs are directly geared to improving feelings. A program is considered a success when clients feel better about themselves. As we will explore later, however, feelings, while they need to be acknowledged and respected, are terribly temporary, shifting, and unreliable. Feelings are especially deficient as self-love indicators.

Self-love is not synonymous with feeling good. A drug addict can be "in heaven" with his "hit" and be destroying himself with the addiction. On the other hand, a grieving widow can feel like giving up on life after the death of her husband, and yet take self-loving action on her own behalf by becoming involved in local charity work.

While self-loving people most often do feel good about themselves, there are times when self-love will demand taking actions on our behalf, whether they make us feel good or not. If we are going to be dependent on feelings, especially at the beginning of our self-love recovery program, we are not going to go very far. Self-love recovery will mean some changes need to be made in our lives. As we have seen, changes never come easy. King Baby will be up in arms, and our natural resistance to change will make sure that we don't *feel* very good about it at all.

Feelings are important, but are not reliable indicators of self-love.

WILLFULNESS AND POWER

Many self-help books and self-enhancement programs I have examined are ultimately geared to promoting will power in readers or participants. For millions of people burdened with shame and feelings of helplessness, the promise of "power" holds an immediate lure. Many authors are more than willing to show them how to "get it." And they are making fortunes at it.

As we have seen, strategies aimed at "power" and developing personal will-power are music to King Baby's ears. Anything that will offer us power and control will stimulate our interest as few other agents can.

Unfortunately, however, life does not respond to control. As a matter of fact, as daily papers well document, life mocks our attempts at control and power. "Control" and "power" may readily excite our imaginations, but they are illusions. "Control" and "power" may inflate our feelings for a while, but rather than solve our problems, they tend to create more.

It is absurd to believe, for example, that each of us can become "powerful" as the models which are typically offered for our emulation. While we can learn to mimic the best qualities of others, all of us cannot become Alexander the Great, Julius Caesar, Charlemagne, George Washington, Gandhi, Franklin Roosevelt, John F. Kennedy, Martin Luther King, etc. We cannot all be "giants" (nor do we need to) simply by believing in ourselves, organizing our resources, and developing sufficient will power to pursue our strategies.

We have learned that true recovery comes about, paradoxically, from a humble admission of powerlessness. Recovery and the enhancement of self-love are not reflected in personal willfulness, nor will they ever be achieved through willfulness. Self-love is reflected in "willingness" and in a humble acknowledgement of the limitations of our human nature. Self-love is achieved not through a defiant "our will" be done, but in a willingness to surrender to "thy will" be done.

An admission of powerlessness does not weaken us; rather, it helps us face reality. An admission of powerlessness does not make us helpless, but allows us to cooperate with our Higher Power to achieve all that our Higher Power envisions for us. We cannot do it alone, but we can with our Higher Power who works through us and with us.

We can work on control and power until our dying breath and it will continue to be one exercise in frustration after another. Any time King or Queen Baby is energized, we can bet our bottom dollar that it is not ultimately going to be in our best interest. The prospect of more control and power in our lives is enticing, but it offers a hollow reward. We cannot defy the fundamental nature of who and what we are.

Make no mistake, we work at what we need, but our true needs are determined by a Power much greater than ourselves. We work, but we leave the results of our work in the hands of our Higher Power. We work, but leave all "control" and "power" in the will of God, as we understand him.

PART TWO
SELF-LOVE RECOVERY

5

Getting to Know You

You have not chosen me; I have chosen you.

—Jn 15:16

Not that we have loved God, but that He has loved us first.

—1 Jn 4:10

We have outlined the dispositions that are required of us to begin our inner work of self-love recovery. Actual "work" on self-love recovery begins with self-exploration. We cannot love what we don't know. We cannot love ourselves if we don't know ourselves for who and what we are. So coming to love ourselves as we need will involve knowing ourselves as we need. For the ancient Greeks, the highest human wisdom was self-knowledge. "Know Thyself!" was written across the entrance of the cave of the great oracle at Delphi. We must know ourselves to love ourselves. Self-knowledge is not self-love, but it is an inseparable link to self-love.

It is my contention that basically we don't love our selves as we need because we don't know ourselves as we need. Few of us know ourselves enough to give an accurate and adequate description of what makes us tick and what drives us. We are not only mysteries to ourselves—for the most part we don't reflect much on our selves. True, we have a lot of experiences. We feel a lot. Sometimes we hurt a lot. We have a wealth of memories, some good, some bad. We know what makes us happy and what doesn't. We know what gives us pleasure and what gives us pain. We know what we fear and what we hope for. But in truth, we don't reflect much upon *who and what we are.* We simply don't give *ourselves* much thought.

Rarely do we take the opportunity to investigate ourselves in depth. Perhaps those who have been in psychotherapy for some time have deeper insights into themselves, but for most of us, we often know more about our jobs than we know about ourselves. Ask people who they are, and they will likely respond with something they *do*, or tell you something *about* themselves. We simply have never taken the time or industry to give ourselves a more thorough investigation. Self-love recovery will mean taking the time, and making the effort.

Alex Haley's book *Roots* made a dramatic impact in giving black people an awareness of their heritage and dignity. Haley dug deeper than stereotype and superficial impressions about blacks and their issues. He pursued insight into the black soul. Black people, and white people, who took Haley seriously came away from the book, and the television series, not with more revelations of oppression of blacks, not with some nice affirmations about blacks, but with an awareness of what it *means* to be black—what it means to be black, noble, and beautiful.

The more superficial our self-knowledge, the less self-love we will have for our selves. Not knowing ourselves sufficiently, not being aware of ourselves in the "roots" of our being, we will not be able to grasp whether we are truly lovable or not. A fundamental step in falling in love with our selves, therefore, will be made when we become knowledgeable of our selves *in depth.*

It is here again that many otherwise excellent self-help books and programs fall short. While offering excellent psychological insight on the etiology of self-esteem loss and excellent techniques for relieving emotional distress, they do not go to the roots and tackle what is basically a spiritual question: Who am I?

A psychologist friend of mine is a successful behavioral-modification therapist. He is extremely practical in his approach to the common problems besetting his clients. His philosophy is: "What is painful is to be avoided; what is pleasurable is to be pursued—within lawful limits, of course." He is very forceful in leading his clients to accept "reality" and act accordingly. My argument with him is that he doesn't get down deep enough. I argue that he deflects his clients away from their central issues and provides behavioral "distractions" to keep their minds off themselves. While some of his clients have behavioral issues that can be cured with a "quick fix" of behavioral modification, many are laboring under more fundamental issues of "inner emptiness," of "a vacuum in my heart," of "a hole in my soul." There are no simple behavior modifications or "techniques" for these spiritual vacuums. There is an obvious need to go deeper.

We begin the work of self-love recovery, then, by taking a good look at ourselves. We work to become more aware of who and what we are. Are we ultimately lovable? Even over and above our behavior, good or bad? If so, what is it that makes us lovable, fundamentally? What is it about us that can help make self-love recovery a genuine possibility for us?

Is there more to me than meets the eye? Who am I?

IMPOSSIBLE TO KNOW OURSELVES DIRECTLY

In trying to learn "Who am I?" we immediately run into an obstacle—fundamentally a promising obstacle, but an obstacle nonetheless. Walker Percy, in his delightful psycho-philosophical book *Lost in the Cosmos*, agrees that we simply do not know ourselves very much at all. We may be familiar with the movements of galaxies and the laws of subatomic particles, but we are not familiar with ourselves whom we live with, most intimately, every day of our lives. We are not familiar enough with ourselves to be able to write even a convincing one-page description.

I look at myself in a video tape-recording and often do a double-take. "That isn't me!" I listen to my voice on a tape-recorder, and almost always insist that "it doesn't sound like me." I listen to other people's evaluations and critiques of myself and can't believe they are talking about me, especially if their critiques are negative.

I feel I can talk to someone for about an hour and give a pretty good synopsis of a person's personality makeup and character traits. But I would have a very hard time doing that for myself. Why? Maybe it's because I feel I'm too complex for a one-page description. I know for sure that I cannot describe myself by one word adjectives. I'm a bundle of contradictions. I've been good and I've been bad. I'm a hard worker and I'm lazy. I'm full of love and I'm full of hate. I am generous and I'm stingy. I can roll with the punches and I can be as stubborn as a mule. I'm all kinds of things.

Percy notes that "Who am I?" defies a simple answer for one simple reason: we cannot know ourselves directly. I cannot look at "I" directly. I cannot directly look at my who-ness. I cannot turn my eyes within and see who "I," the speaker, am. I can look in a mirror and see a physical *reflection*, but, just as my eyes cannot see themselves directly, I cannot see myself directly either. It is my conscious self, "I," which is doing the looking. The self I am trying to look at is at one and the same time the knower, the perceiver. What I try to become aware of is itself what is being aware in the first place. In trying to perceive myself I am at one and the same time the perceiver.

Who am I? Fundamentally, I am, by nature, a mystery.

ULTIMATELY, WHO AM "I"?

Dealing with a "mystery," however, does not deter exploration of "who" we are. As a matter of fact, the impossibility of knowing ourselves directly may lead us into a profound truth about ourselves, which has already been alluded to in the previous chapter.

The fact that we cannot know ourselves directly has alerted many spiritual masters and psycho-spiritual theorists to assert that there is an "I," an observing "I," which is not to be identified with "me," my self. The "I" is the central self, that which speaks in the first person singular, connected (if not identified, say some) with the Eternal Self manifesting itself in the cosmos—which is an extremely profound thought!

The observing "I" is not identified with feelings, joys, sorrows, or any experience. "I" am not my body; "I" am more than my feelings. Everything outside of the observing "I" are experiences which the "I" observes almost in passing. These experiences belong to me, but "I" am more than my experiences. (The practical usefulness of this insight will be explored more in Chapter Twelve.)

The "I" who I am is unknowable directly. The "I" observes and knows my self. My "self" is what makes me up. My "self" is what "I" have come to know and make of myself. My "self" is a name, a concept, an abstraction, that I give to the composite of all my sensations, feelings, hopes, dreams, memories, "inner voices," instincts, intuitions, the ego, "King Baby," the "inner child," all the experiences of the self on many levels of operation. My "self" is all my experiences objectified into "me," as observed by "I." As God is "embodied" in the universe, so "I" am embodied in my self. "I" live and act through my self. My self is what "I" hope to come to love in self-love recovery.

"I" am embodied, "incarnated," in my self. "I" operate through the "body" of my self. With the passage of time, "I" am "fleshed out" in my self. I am manifest and extended in my self. "I" have created my self with everything "I" have experienced. "I" and my self make me who and what I am. For the purposes of our study therefore, I am all that makes me what I am: "I" and my self. "I" and my self = myself. I, myself, am the composite of all that "I" have experienced and become. Myself is what I have become to the present moment.

The observing "I," that which speaks when I say "I" is not identifiable with any elements of my self, nor with my mind, nor with my memory, nor with my body, nor with anything else that happens in the world outside me. Spiritual masters assert that great bliss can be found in learning to "detach" from, or "unidentify" with, our selves and our experiences, that great happiness can be found in learning simply to "be" (as an observing "I") and not to be "identified" with anything. They assert, further, that ecstasy is found in being one with the Eternal Self, in joining our observing "I" with God who is the ultimate "I" of all that is. This, they say, is the culmination of the great spiritual journey to which all of us are called. This, they say, is the great "awakening" as we progress step by step to higher degrees of awareness and consciousness.

All this may be quite difficult to assimilate in the beginning. Our treatment of this important topic is greatly condensed and only touched on here. But with reflection, meditation, and further exposure to the great spiritual masters (or current writers such as M. Scott Peck, Gerald May, John Hitchcock, and Ken Wilber), we can come to know ourselves, and love ourselves, at our greatest spiritual depth. I would encourage readers to take advantage of the writings of these authors, which today are readily available in libraries and most large bookstores.

Christians need go no further than the gospels. The actual teachings of Jesus (as separated from the interpretations and interpolations of his evangelist commentators) are supremely mystical and self-transcendental. According to Jesus, for example, life is found by "losing" it (surrender). Jesus further proclaims: "Seek first the kingdom of God." And that "kingdom," he said, is "already within you." The "kingdom" is the experience of God's presence within. Union with that presence is "redemption," a return to the experience of the garden of paradise. The Christian vocation therefore, can be summed up in one goal: coming to experience, and unite with, the real presence of God within. Everything else—bible studies, churches, liturgies, theology, rituals, sacraments, hierarchy—is either help, or hindrance, to accomplish that unique invitation.

When the time is right for us to advance to a higher state of consciousness, we will be ready. When the time is right for us to explore our highest spiritual potential, we will be willing. But for the present, we are just beginners on the journey to know and love ourselves better than we do. In self-love recovery, the ultimate truth about who and what we are needs to be explored in ways that are perhaps more accommodating to us as beginners. While the mystery of who "I" am will continue to be explored by philosophers and psychologists, we can learn enough about our selves to continue in our self-love recovery. The fact that we are profound mysteries and cannot know ourselves directly does not prematurely end our attempts at self-exploration. As impenetrable as "who" we are may appear, and as impossible as it is to know "I" directly and objectively, this does not mean that we cannot come to appreciate and love ourselves as we need. We may not be able to know ourselves directly, but we can certainly acquire significant knowledge *about* ourselves. We can certainly come to appreciate what we are.

WHAT WE THINK *ABOUT* OURSELVES MATTERS

When Cynthia came to see me about troubles in her marriage, I could not help but notice immediately how attractive she was. Cynthia was in severe depression and anxiety. Her husband was at his wits' end because she was always putting herself down, never wanted to go out or entertain, was inordinately shy in front of strangers, and felt almost victimized when her husband wished to make love with her.

Cynthia did not like or love herself. That became clear right from the start as she nervously and effusively excused herself for taking up my "valuable time" with her "silly little problems." It was obvious that she was falling apart.

Cynthia could not see herself as attractive to anyone. She recalls how "gross and ugly" she was as a child and how taunted and teased she was in grammar school. With the physical changes of adolescence, however, she blossomed into a beautiful girl. As a matter of fact, she became dramatically attractive. Her physical changes, however, had no effect on her self-appreciation. Early memories had etched themselves so deeply in her subconscious that to this day she cannot see herself as anything but "repulsive." This, despite endless suitors in high school and college. This, despite hundreds of compliments on her beauty that she has received from teachers, co-workers, and friends.

This, despite the regular wolf-whistles she still gets at the beach, which bothers her husband to no end.

The lesson here is that, for all practical purposes in self-love recovery, it's not so much yourself but what you *think* about yourself that matters. Ultimately, who "I" am may be a mystery tied to the mystery of God, but, mystery or no mystery, what we *think* about ourselves is what really matters in self-love recovery.

It is not how attractive or unattractive you are to others, it is how attractive or unattractive you *feel* about yourself that counts. It is not how others tell you how good you are; it is how good you think you are that matters. There is enormous power in your thinking and your feeling to make you happy or sad about yourself. There is enormous power in how you think and feel about yourself that will help you love yourself or not. Self-love is built on self-esteem. What you think about yourself can make you or break you. You must take what you think about yourself, therefore, very seriously.

FUNDAMENTALLY, WHAT DO YOU THINK ABOUT YOURSELF?

One of the greatest concerns an architect has in putting up a building is making sure that the foundation is adequate. The taller the building, the firmer needs be the foundation on which it stands. Most of us who find our lives shaky, overwhelmed with one problem after another, full of fear and insecurity, more than likely have never consciously addressed the problem of our "foundations." We go through life hoping against hope that the building will not collapse all around us. Our goal is survival. We don't so much feel we are living life as we are "making it." "Making it" is not a bad goal, but it is a far cry from finding the joy, love and happiness most of us desire.

Rather than examine the shaky and unaddressed foundations upon which our lives are based, we haphazardly, and often frantically, go from one quick repair job to another whenever parts of our building get shaken loose in a storm. Consequently much of our lives is spent in "damage control" and salvaging. We become "patch-job" artists. Admittedly, this is a way to survive. But is it a way to live?

Adequate self-love will depend on how deeply we explore our foundations, on how deeply we come to appreciate ourselves. Having a philosophical explanation, or even a psychospiritual explanation, as we saw above, of who we are is not enough to bring us into self-love recovery. What we need to know is what we *mean.*

We need to know whether or not, in the depths of our being, we are lovable. We need to know whether our self-love recovery can be established on a substantial foundation of our basic lovableness, or whether our efforts will merely be attempts to bolster our egos.

In order to answer these profound questions, we have to know ourselves in our fundamental meaning. Who we think we are, and what we think we are, needs to take us to the ground floor of how we understand ourselves face-to-face with the whole cosmos in general. Our fundamental spiritual meaning is founded on how we see ourselves in the context of all life in general.

How do we fit into the scheme of all that is? What is our fundamental reality in the face of all creation?

Are we an accident, victims, of a mindless evolution of cosmic dust? Are we orphans sprung from chaotic atomic and electrical energy? Are we of no more ultimate significance in the span of time than a piece of driftwood or a starfish washed up on a sandy shore? Are we pieces of flotsam, galactic debris, haphazardly floating along with all the rest of molecules and atoms in this forever expanding universe?

Or are we in some way here by design? Were we somehow planned for and expected? As tiny and insignificant as we might feel looking up at the countless stars on a clear, cold night, are we children of a benevolent Power—a Power mightier and more magnificent than anything we could possibly imagine? Are we part of a plan? Has a destiny been laid out for us every step of the way along with everything else that is?

How we understand and appreciate ourselves, fundamentally, means everything in the world. What we understand and accept about ourselves at rock bottom will affect all the progress we hope to make in loving ourselves as we need. The rock bottom question we can ask about ourselves is simply: Are we a cosmic quirk or is there poetry in our being.

Enormous repercussions stem from this fundamental appreciation of ourselves. If we are merely "accidents," everything we endure in life is ultimately one terrifying joke. You might as well close this book right now and begin vegetating. If we are not accidents, but are part of plan, we have every reason to take a deep breath of relief that ultimately everything for us is going to be all right.

MEANT TO BE

I would not be writing these words unless I truly believed that all of us do exist *on purpose*, that, fundamentally, we do have meaning, and that, fundamentally, we have a meaning we can appreciate and upon which can build our self-love recovery.

There is poetry in our being. We are not accidents. We have been planned for, and are planned for. We are not chance debris of a cosmic explosion. We are not a collection of molecules just biding time before we lapse into extinction or some other chance form. You and I are children of the universe and are meant to be here.

The very fact that life is so full of mystery, ambiguity, and paradox proves that we and the world around us are more than cosmic dust in a purely mechanical universe. The ambiguities and seeming contradictions in life as we know it would long since have brought a purely mechanical cosmos to a cataclysmic conclusion.

"Mystery" pre-supposes planning. As a matter of fact, the more science reveals the serendipity of sub-atomic elements, the more haphazard things appear, the greater likelihood that life cannot be reduced to a simplistic mechanical explanation.

If you and I have been planned for, it means that we are meant to be here as much as anyone or anything else. We are here by no one's leave but the Power that arranged it all in the first place. We do not need to make excuses to anyone for who we are and why we exist. Our existence is not subject to the benevolence of anyone or anything around us. We are here by eternal design and planning. We have been given a birthright and are heirs of all that is and all that has been. More of our inheritance is yet to come.

Yes, there is evolution and all of us are part of it. Evolution pre-supposes a plan—a plan that has taken all of us into account. What this means is that you are already good, worthwhile and lovable just because you *are*, just because you exist! It doesn't matter what you do or don't do, you are worthwhile *already*, just because a Higher Power has eternally planned for you to be.

There is significant empowerment for self-love in *embracing* that we are part of a divine plan—not just mindlessly assuming it or taking it for granted, not just blandly accepting it as another piece of pious data, but embracing that plan, as a truth, for you.

Appreciation of what we are *fundamentally* cannot be treated lightly. There is power and privilege in accepting that we are children of a Supreme Power that has a plan for us. There is no more important way to come to love ourselves than appreciating ourselves in our fundamental meaning.

For some, just knowing and embracing this fundamental truth about themselves is the apex of their spiritual journey. It is all they need to give their lives meaning. It is all they need to love themselves and others fully. They simply accept their fundamental place in the eye of the Creator and go on to live simple, joyous lives, without need for any more philosophical, theological, or psychological "explanations."

For most of us, however, this appreciation of ourselves remains only a beguiling and pious "notion." We can't sufficiently embrace it to give our selves the love they need. Our exploration must continue.

YOU ARE MY BELOVED

I have never found more beautiful lines in the Christian scriptures than those recorded over the baptism of Jesus in the Jordan River (Mt 3:17, Mk 1:11, Lk 3:22). Whenever I read them or hear them read, a profound emotion always wells up within me that perhaps, until now, I have never been able to adequately explain. In the context of scripture, these words are spoken by God to, or about, Jesus when he presents himself to John the Baptist. The words vary in various translations, but they come down to saying: "You are my beloved. It gives me great pleasure to look upon you."

"You are my beloved. What pleasure I take in looking at you." These words are so stirring for me because with all my heart I long to hear God speaking them directly to me. I want to hear that God is looking at me, that he knows I exist, that I give him great pleasure in my very being, and that he loves me for who and what I am.

We all desperately want to hear words like these—that we are absolutely and unconditionally loved, that we are ultimately valuable, that we mean something of great significance to someone.

Such an affirmation is beyond all affirmations. Such an affirmation heard personally by each of us would change the way we look at ourselves forever. We could not help but love ourselves if we could come to appreciate ourselves this way: as infinitely and eternally beloved to the Supreme Being from whom all creation has come.

But I will tell you an amazing truth. The very fact that I feel such powerful longings and stirrings in my heart is enough to convince me that these words are indeed spoken to me. The fact that I can long for such words tells me that there is indeed more to me than meets the eye.

How on earth can we explain such longings if we are nothing but chemical accidents in a mindless cosmic storm? Can mere bone and blood evoke such an unbelievable prayer?

Think about it. Meditate on it. Let it sink in deeply. "You

are my beloved. I take great pleasure in just looking at you." You are infinitely lovable, because you are infinitely loved by an infinitely wise, powerful, and loving Supreme Being. *This is the fundamental root of all genuine self-esteem and self-love.* It is not so much that we work to love our selves as we need, but that we are infinitely loved already.

An observation was once made to Mother Teresa as she held a dying leper in her arms that she must really love God very much to do the work she does. She replied that she wasn't sure about how much she loved God, but that she did what she did in her ministry *"because I know how much God loves me."*

The truth about our ultimate lovableness is so overwhelmingly enriching that, once comprehended and embraced, you need have no problems with loving yourself enough, again. Nothing else need matter. No other exercises, techniques, self-help programs, need be pursued. Once this fundamental truth begins to sink in, all else is frosting on the cake.

Unfortunately, in our human frailty, with the weakness of our memories, with years of negative thinking about ourselves, with doubts and distractions that capture most of our attention, we cannot hold this truth in our hearts for any length of time. Like children, we often prefer the "frosting" to the cake. It will be up to our Higher Power, to whom we have made a decision to surrender, to whisper these words to us when we need them the most: "You are my beloved, and I take great pleasure looking at you."

Furthermore, is it not reasonable to assume that a loving Supreme Power will pursue us and tug at our hearts with these words? Is this not perhaps the reason that, despite the many good things we possess in life, so many of us feel "empty"? As Francis Thompson's beautiful poem asserts, the "Hound of Heaven" pursues us even when we are running away at top speed. When we allow ourselves to get caught, we get caught. When we surrender to our Higher Power, the gates to our souls are opened. Abraham Heschel outlines the philosophy of Judaism as *God in Search of Man,* which is the title of his book. According to Heschel, God pursues his intelligent creation and eternally wishes to whisper that he is alive and well and wants to be part of our lives—a living God wanting to let us know that we are infinitely lovable.

WHAT MAKES US RUN AWAY?

It is one of the greatest tragedies of our materialistic society that we run liked scared rabbits from the profound truth of a *loving* Supreme Power. Polls continue to show that most Americans believe in a Supreme Being—which means little more than most Americans give intellectual assent, or lip service, to the fact that there must be "something," there must be someone, greater than all of us put together who is responsible for the whole kit and caboodle we call the universe. But surrendering to the embrace of a loving Power is quite another thing. Most of us run from it, or ignore it.

What are we afraid of? Why don't we run into the arms of a benevolent Creator? Why don't we tap into God's absolute and unconditional love? Why are we running away from a God that *loves*?

Why are we afraid to admit our ultimate dependence? Why are we afraid to surrender to power greater than ourselves? We surrender to everything else: worries, demands, passions, addictions, the job, the lure of money, the expectations of others, the latest fads, popular opinion polls, television, "experts," advertising, the promises of politicians, public opinion, et cetera. All the scientific and technological advances that we have banked on have not given us more meaningful lives. They have not made us more content or happier. They have not helped us love our selves more.

You don't have to be a profound thinker to realize, as so many today do, that "something is missing." Something essential is missing in our culture. Our "achievements" so often add up to little more than the greatest carnival of distractions and passing pleasures in the history of humanity—distractions and pleasures that never provide the deep soul satisfaction for

which all of us in our hearts hunger. We run after what we need
the least and we run away from what we need the most.

We are not bad people. We're simply human. We are igno-
rant of what really counts and unaware of what really matters.
We need, therefore, to return to our "roots." We need to understand and love ourselves for what we really are in the eyes of a
Supreme Being.

Some will argue that this takes a great act of faith. But
doesn't it take an even greater act of faith to choose ignorance
and apathy? Doesn't it take an even greater act of faith to
believe that there is no plan? That we are just cosmic dust and
that there is no real rhyme or reason for anything? Are not the
"clues" more in a loving God's favor than not?

A loving Supreme Being is not an illusion we create for
ourselves. It is a reality we can feel when we allow ourselves to
feel it. A Higher Power cannot be glibly written off as a "projec-
tion of a fearful creature, desperate for reassurance," as some
materialist psychologists have suggested. Why are we evading
the obvious? Has Freud given more reasonable explanations to
the riddle of life than Jesus, Mohammed, or Buddha?

(Psychology today needs to come to terms with our basic
spirituality if it is to avoid the charge of benign superficiality.
All the schools of psychology, all the systems and types of therapy that flood the market today, will never effect more permanent healing until they take our fundamental nature and needs
into account. Until the fundamental reality of who and what we
are is treated seriously, until we come to know that we are
beloved by the Creator, we will never achieve the healing or
wholeness we need.)

REDISCOVERING OUR SPIRITUAL ROOTS

Whether we are Hindu, Jew, Moslem, or Christian, all of
our traditions speak of a God who finds his creation very good.
He finds all of us very good. He beholds us and takes pleasure
in our existence. The teachings of the great spiritual masters,

including Jesus, come down to one basic assertion: the Supreme Being loves us and is within us. For all spiritual masters, awareness of the inner presence of God is what spirituality is all about. For us, awareness of God's loving presence within us is what recovering self-love is all about. The "kingdom," Paradise, the garden of Eden, is already within us. Happiness is not "out there," it is within. Joy and serenity cannot be found in someone else or in something else—only within.

The spiritual journey to discover our fundamental lovableness would have us "become like little children" again. Like little children: inquisitive, open, sensitive, and full of awe. To become what years and years of negative varnishing have covered over with layer upon layer of self-doubt, cynicism, anger, shame, and hopelessness.

It is tragic today that "religion" has lost its edge to keep us aware and alive to these fundamental spiritual truths about ourselves. Many churches preach and model everything but. Millions have left church membership because they are not being fed the one spiritual food they need most. We do not need to be convinced that we are sinners. We've known that from the middle years of childhood. What we need is to *experience* the loving presence of God within. We need to be touched by the grace of "awareness." We need to feel the gift of assurance of God's presence within—a presence that tells us we are beloved and pleasing to behold.

The foundations for an adequate and appropriate love of our selves can only come from discovering, appreciating, and embracing what we are: children of a loving Creator. The only permanent realization of love for ourselves comes from embracing ourselves as infinitely and eternally lovable, because we are loved by an infinite and eternal Lover. Only in appreciating how loveable we are will we give ourselves the love we deserve, and perform the necessary loving actions we need on our behalf. And until we can appreciate ourselves in our fundamental lovableness, all "techniques," strategies, exercises, and programs to build self-esteem and self-love will offer little more than temporary gimmicks.

6

Inner Work: Re-Programming

Change yourself and you change the world.
                                        —The Tao

Having explored the spiritual foundations of self-love recovery, we are ready to begin working on building its structure. Beginning with this chapter, we will investigate the principles and practice that activate self-love recovery. Many steps have brought us to this point. With wisdom we acknowledge that we are not "in control" of life and its unfolding. With humility we accept that it will take a Power greater than ourselves to heal us and to help us achieve the love for ourselves we need. With a decision to surrender to that Higher Power and with trust in that Higher Power's loving will for us, we are on our way to truly taking care of ourselves and loving ourselves as we need. We leave it to our Higher Power to lead us to achieve the potential and destiny for which we were made. We leave it to our Higher Power to help us achieve the happiness we were made for. On our part, we continue to surrender "control." Day after day we prayerfully offer our willingness to surrender to a higher wisdom, a higher power, a higher love to connect with us, lead us, and guide to the love for our selves that we cannot assuredly find or maintain totally on our own.

"Surrender" does not leave us off the hook, however. We are not in total control, but neither are we helpless. We have given up illusionary power to control what we want, in exchange for real power to do what we need. For our part, we must cooperate by letting our Higher Power's will be done.

God expects us to work with him in self-love recovery. We

must be responsive and responsible. In practical language, this means that we must dig in and begin our work, our inner work—not to change the world and people, but to cooperate with our Higher Power in changing our selves. Our biggest and basic need for change is learning to love our selves adequately and appropriately. This is our inner work for now. This is what we dedicate and commit ourselves to in all the insights and exercises that follow in this book.

As we learned in the last chapter, there is a "self," our self, which we have been developing all our lives so far. It is through that self that we "embody" ourselves, that we "flesh out" our "I." It is through that self that we are connected to the world about us. Everything our selves have experienced has repercussions on their development. If our development has been more abusive than supportive, more negative than positive, more full of doubts than assurances, more in the hands of King Baby than in the hands of our Higher Power, more cynical than optimistic, then we are wounded and our self-love is likely to be radically deficient.

But from now on, in self-love recovery, we will begin a new program to build and enhance our self-love. We will do that by working with our selves as special friends and life-long companions whom we will treat with affirmation, devotion, caring and nurturing. Love for our selves will grow as we take loving actions on their behalf.

INNER WORK NEEDED

Whenever we feel that "enough is enough" in feeling bad or "empty" about ourselves and make a firm decision to do something about it, our first inclination is to clean house, change jobs, get a divorce, move the kids out, tell someone off, buy a new wardrobe, move to a new apartment, enter a recovery program, go back to school, et cetera. There may be benefits for us, emotionally and psychologically, to choose any of these, or other, options. However, all these choices usually have one thing in common: they are all directed *outward*. Our first inclination when we have been hurt, let-down, disappointed, and frustrated beyond what we are willing to bear is to blame something outside of us, and to "fix" something outside of us.

As we have already seen, blaming and "fixing" something outside of ourselves does not solve our problems. No matter what we change on the outside, we still carry our wounded selves with us on the inside. As will be indicated again and again, our real work of self-love recovery is *inner* work. "Change yourself," wise men say, "and you change the world."

Change yourself and the world will look different. The world becomes what we are. Our world gets better when *we* do. Improving our situation, therefore, means changing our selves— changing something within.

Changing our selves will mean changing attitudes, assumptions, and fundamental stances we have toward reality. Changing our glasses will mean seeing the world in a new light. What was threatening may now be seen as opportunity. What was frightening may now appear comic. What was self-defeating may now be seen as self-challenging. People who were seen as enemies may now become friends.

Marion has maintained her low status in a secretarial pool since she began working in a bank five years ago. She has seen six of her co-workers elevated to higher rank as personal secretaries to bank officers or managers of other departments. There is no doubt in her mind that she is as skillful, if not more so, as most of the secretaries who received promotions ahead of her. She is beginning to hate her job. She is bitterly resentful of her floor manager for skipping over her with recommendations. She insists that the manager "hates" her, is "jealous" of her, and is "always picking on" her. "Nobody appreciates" her.

From the day she began working at the bank, Marion had a "me against them" attitude, which has literally been the story of her life. In a company scandal, her father lost a high-paying job when she was a young teenager, and he was never again able to provide the family with the affluent comforts to which they had grown accustomed. After their move to a "lower class neighborhood," Marion had to take a job with a fast food chain to give herself spending money, and her hopes for entering a big name university gave way to her attendance at a local community college.

She has never forgiven her father, her "fate," or herself. She feels chronically sad, deprived, and depressed. She has a quick temper and is hyperly-sensitive to any criticism, no matter how constructive—which is precisely why she has not advanced out her secretarial pool. In tears, she tells me that she needs to "get away" from "that bitch" of a manager, to get a new job, to move to a new apartment, to find some "decent" friends, and maybe go to night school for a degree.

What Marion needed most, however, was inner work on her poor self-image, her depleted self-esteem, and her fundamental self-loathing. She needed to free herself from shame over something for which she was never responsible. When she finally came to analyze the genealogy of her self-defeating behaviors and began to work on her self and her attitudes, "lights began to turn on" for her. When she was able to adequately grieve her losses, accept her self, and love her self for being basically the good person she was, her life turned around. Her whole world became different. She saw life in a new light and she began to behave in a new light. Within six months she became an executive secretary to a bank vice-president. Her former manager is becoming a close friend. If she would have taken her own advice and had left for "new pastures," there is little doubt that her traumas would have continued. She would have to have had taken her self along with her. Only the new location would have been different. She began her inner work, however, and it paid off richly.

Blaming and "fixing" are also attempts to get us off the hook of having to work for what we need in self-love recovery. I am always amazed how the libraries of friends who are seeking greater self-fulfillment are well stocked with a variety of self-help books. One friend blatantly asserts, "They (the books) didn't work." The truth is, of course, that books never "work"; we work. Seeking help in books, authors, and programs is futile if the moment never comes when determined inner work begins. A book of itself is never a remedy; it is only a guide.

We have a tendency in self-love recovery to read *about* our issues or study *about* remedies for recovery, while avoiding the actual work necessary to make those remedies effective for us. This is an indication of how subtle and deflective the power of King Baby is. We want the "cure," the good feeling, the spiritual enlightenment, all in a flash of insight, now, this instant. We want to feel better as soon as we can. We want what we want, but we don't want to make efforts to get it. As soon as suffering abates, or we get distracted, or we feel a little bit better about ourselves, it is back to business as usual—until the next time, when the cycle starts all over again, this time, perhaps, with another self-help author.

GET A LIFE

A good friend has a favorite expression he uses on anyone who is weighed down with self-defeatist attitudes or is sitting too long on a self-"pity pot." He tells them bluntly to "get a life." Somehow it gets their attention. It gets mine.

What "get a life" means is that we start living "for real." That we take our self-love recovery seriously. That we begin choosing goals for ourselves and finding the resources to achieve them.

Live your life. Get invested in your own living. Act rather than react. Stop moaning and complaining about what is happening to you and take steps to *do* something for your self. *Take the initiative* where your life is concerned. Don't sit back like a spectator watching it all happen. Life is not something you *have*; life is something you *do*.

Surprisingly enough (or perhaps not surprisingly at all), people who actively live their lives are in the minority. The majority of people don't live life, they endure or survive it.

For all the admonitions we may hear to the contrary, our culture actually trains us for passive living. In our society, our primary role is to be a consumer. The whole idea of the American Dream is that we be consumers. When a recession hits, America weeps. We are terribly dependent on money and what money can buy. We are terribly dependent on being taken care of.

Most foreigners consider Americans to be very spoiled. And we are. We grow up feeling that we should be taken care of, that somehow life owes us. Many editors in early 1992 took up the cudgels against a leading Japanese executive who challenged American workers, in general, with being fundamentally lazy. Many were stung by this "insult." The point is, we normally don't get stung to the quick unless the shoe fits. All Americans may not be lazy, but it is part of our upbringing to get the most for the least. To make the most money with the least amount of effort. To get whatever we can, for nothing. We want service. We expect service. It is almost as if we had an unconscious attitude that we didn't ask to be born, but now that we find ourselves here, someone (other than we) had better do something about it. We have a passive and expectant attitude toward living. King Baby knows his rights.

In many years of ministry to the dying, I have observed that the people who were most afraid of dying were those who didn't feel that they ever really "lived" at all.

Choosing life is the only way to begin living life. Choosing to live is the only way to develop a more assertive attitude toward living. We will never learn to esteem and respect our selves enough unless we commit ourselves to get out of a "survival" mode. We need to challenge our passivity. We will never learn to love ourselves as we need unless we are committed to make a project of our own living. True, we have been given life without our leave, but our Higher Power asks us to "choose life." Choose our life as our own. Own it and use it. Take it to the limit. Get a life! Live!

SELF-LOVE IS NOT A FEELING

A great part of professional therapy today is often invested in helping a client get in touch with his or her true feelings. The client is encouraged to acknowledge, own, and express feelings, especially those that are buried, out of shame, in the deep cellars of the psyche. The client needs to learn that having feelings is perfectly O.K. If there is one lesson that took me a long time to learn and assimilate, it is that feelings are perfectly OK, that all feelings are perfectly legitimate.

Feelings tell us something about our selves. Feelings are like thermometers that indicate what is going on within us. Feelings are neither moral nor immoral. They are legitimate simply because they are. *Acting* on our feelings can raise moral issues, but the feelings themselves are normal, natural, and perfectly acceptable.

On the other hand, a misleading piece of cultural propaganda would have us believe that feelings are all that matter. "If it feels good, do it!" summed up a philosophy of the 1960s. "If it doesn't feel good, run from it as fast as you can," is implied. This philosophy has succeeded in becoming etched onto our contemporary souls. We live in our feelings. We test all waters with our feelings. In much conversation, "I think" has given way to "I feel." There is no greater offense that someone can make against us than to hurt our feelings. How we *feel* has become for many of us the primary consciousness of life itself.

While feelings are indeed legitimate, believing that they are all that count is not. There is more to life and reality than feelings. Unfortunately, we often use feelings as a barometer of what is right and wrong for us, or to authenticate what is true, good, valid, valuable and meaningful for us.

"Authentic," however, is what will stand on its own with or without feelings. Feelings do not necessarily indicate what is in our own best interests. Feelings are unreliable; they tend to come and go. Feelings shift by the hour. The weather alone can change our feelings. To base our lives, and the way we handle our lives, on the shifting sands of feelings is a predictably unstable and precarious way to live.

Nowhere are feelings more dramatically an issue of what "counts" than when we speak about love today. There is nothing more ingrained in us by our culture than that love is a feeling—a romantic feeling. If you feel you are in love, you must be. If you feel you are not in love, you must not be. Most couples enter a friendship or marriage because of "that loving feeling"; most terminate friendships and marriages because, as the Righteous Brothers once sang, the feeling is gone, gone, gone.

Most authors who write about love and relationships today, however, take great pains to emphasize that love is not a feeling. Love for our selves is not simply a matter of feeling good about our selves. The good feelings that are generated when we love our selves or someone else are reasonable, and it is reasonable that we should enjoy those feelings. But the feelings accompanying love cannot, and should not, be identified with love itself. When loving feelings wane or dissipate, it is not of itself an indication that love is no longer present. As a matter of fact, it is only "after the honeymoon is over," only after we have fallen in love with others, or our selves, that, most authorities believe, real love can begin.

Our inner work in self-love recovery is not simply to make ourselves feel better. Our goal is to recover the love for our selves that we need, not just better feelings about our selves. It is wonderful if good feelings accompany our self-esteem and self-love, but those feelings are a bonus. They are not to be identified with love itself. I may feel like king of the hill on a day off at the beach with friends, when the sun is shining and summer is in the air. I feel terrific, but do not love myself at all. On the other hand there may be days when I feel particularly down and depressed and nevertheless take some active measures to take proper care of my self. That's love! And, as we will see, there is often no better way of showing genuine love for our selves than by taking care of our needs in spite of some very contrary feelings.

LOVE IS AS LOVE DOES

"Love" has been defined in a hundred ways by scholars, song-writers, and poets, but one of the best definitions of love I have seen comes from M. Scott Peck in his continuously popular

best-seller *The Road Less Traveled*. Peck defines love as "the will
to extend one's self for the purpose of nurturing one's own or
another's spiritual growth." "Love is as love does," says Peck.
Love is not a feeling, but an *action*, an activity, we take on our
own, or someone else's, behalf. Love is not an emotion, but an
act of the will. Love is a commitment, something we choose to
do, rather than simply a feeling we have. Identifying love with a
feeling, Peck asserts, "allows people all manner of self-decep-
tion" about being in love or not being in love.

Coming to love ourselves as we need will not be a matter
of feelings, therefore. Self-love is not a matter of feeling good
about ourselves. We cannot assume we have "arrived" at appropriate self-love just because we feel better. It is important that
we recognize and accept this, especially when cultural inputs
may be telling us otherwise. Self-esteem is something we possess, but self-love is something we do for our selves. "Love" in
our context is a verb, not a noun. Loving our selves is not something we feel; it is something we do for our selves.

*Self-love is a choice and a commitment to extend ourselves for the
purpose of nurturing our spiritual growth. Love for ourselves is an
effort to take care of our selves and nourish our selves in a way that
will continue growth and development of our fullest potential.*

Self-love is a commitment to work on our own behalf—a
commitment to heal, take care of, and nurture our selves, as we
would anyone that we truly loved. Not simply wishing to feel better, but to do something for our selves that may well result in our
feeling better. Not simply desiring improvement, but being willing to make an improvement. With no commitment, no willingness, no work, there is "no way" to succeed. Love is what love
does.

BECOMING AWARE/OBSERVING

One of the most important goals in self-love recovery is to
become more conscious. One of the first things we *do* in self-
love recovery is to struggle to become more *aware*. Self-love is

based on a foundation of self-knowledge. Self-love is based on being aware of who and what we are in the depths of our being. Self-love grows as we become more aware of what we need to do to love ourselves as we need.

The greatest gift we have as conscious beings, a gift that sets us apart from all the rest of creation, is awareness. Anthony De Mello in his book *Awareness* demonstrates that awareness is both a gift and a challenge. According to De Mello, awareness is our highest potential as human beings. Becoming more and more aware is the great spiritual journey to which all of us are called. Awareness, becoming more aware, is our greatest, and most difficult, inner work. According to De Mello the majority of human beings are fast asleep—and apparently want to stay that way.

Most of us live by momentum. We are set in motion and continue merrily on our way until some unforeseen person or event (usually painful) either makes us stop to consider where we are going, or causes us to deflect immediately and mindlessly to another path, much like a mouse bouncing its way through the corridors of a maze. Inner work will demand that we become *aware* of our momentum, our motion, and our direction.

A commitment to love our selves is a commitment to make awareness of our selves a way of life. Awareness of who and what we are. Awareness of where we are going and why we are going there. Awareness of our thinking, feelings, options, and choices. Awareness of how we are reacting to the world around us, and why we react the way we do. Awareness of our belief systems, our mind-sets, our possibilities and our limitations. Awareness of our behavior and how it might need to change. Awareness of what we need to reprogram within our selves.

The struggle to become "aware" just might be the most formidable task before us. If we are to love our selves adequately and appropriately, we must be prepared to become more self-conscious. We love our selves best when we are aware of what we are doing, why we are doing it, and what will be the consequences of our actions.

To become more aware is to deliberately expand our consciousness. We resolve to open our eyes to the bigger picture. I am reminded of here of a motion picture show I once saw at the Smithsonian Cinemax exhibition. The show began with a message and credits on a screen not much bigger than a large television. And then, with a fanfare of "surround sound" music, the screen enlarged from floor to ceiling and from wall to wall, until viewers felt engulfed in the show. The expansion of visual perception was exhilarating. The expansion of consciousness will be equally so.

CHANGING THE "TAPES"

Once we accept that self-love recovery will mean inner work; once we accept that love for our selves is something we do for ourselves; once we commit ourselves to grow in awareness and self-consciousness, our next long-range goal will be to reprogram our selves for a much more self-loving life style. And to do that we will need to *"change the tapes."*

Changing the "tapes" means changing the mind-sets that, along with King Baby, control so much of our lives. If we can agree with what has been said so far in this chapter, and if we commit ourselves to the affirmative action program that follows in the next, changing those tapes will be of major significance in the way we come to love our selves. To explain what "change the tapes" is all about, however, I must first address the fascinating topic of computers.

One of the greatest technological advances of this century has been the development of the computer. We are living in a Computer Age. We see the impact of computers everywhere we look. From the space shuttle in orbit to our groceries being scanned in the check-out line, computers are making a significant impact on the way we live life at the turn of the century. Science fiction writers have foretold that computers will inevitably match or surpass the intelligence of human beings. Is it possible? Is it just wild speculation? Who knows? It is amazing, however, how much computers can resemble human beings. But it is even more amazing how much human beings resemble computers.

Two years ago I purchased a personal computer as an aid in writing, speech making and record keeping. Then I added games and an assortment of specialized programs until now my computer is a world in itself with all kinds of possibilities. Computers fascinate me. But what fascinates me most is how they are *programmed*. All computers operate dependent on their programs. Ultimately, everything about a computer, what it does, and how it does it, depends on its programming.

One thing that human beings and computers have in common is that ultimately they *act out their programming*. Following its programming is essentially what a computer does. Following out our programming is essentially what human behavior is all about.

Our selves, like the largest computers, are composed of an enormous amount of "programming." We "run" according to "tapes." Popular names for these tapes are "mind-sets," personal "blueprints," or what Eric Berne calls our "scripts." We can also call our tapes our "assumptions" or our "beliefs." These tapes, mind-sets, blueprints, or scripts may be of our own making or they may have been programmed into us by others. These tapes may have been programmed into us by genetic endowment, by our parents, by teachers, by peers, by cultural and political propaganda, by advertisers, etc.

Why did we believe we were right to go to war with Iraq? Why do the people of Iraq believe we had no right to interfere in Kuwait? Why do I hate mushrooms on my pizza, but love anchovies? Why do you like a full size car, and your husband will drive nothing but a jeep? How come you can graciously accept any criticism, while your wife starts to cry over the slightest criticisms? It's all a matter of "programming." It's all because of our "tapes."

Our minds are one of the most powerful tools we have. But, maybe strange to say, our minds are essentially mindless. They don't think on their own; they simply process data. "Reasoning" is data processing. Our minds process data in fairly predictable ways, but they can only work according to a program.

Whenever our minds are confronted with a brand new task (especially when we were young children), they do their best and then program a tape to handle similar tasks in the future. Whenever our minds are confronted with a problem that has occurred before, or even comes close to looking like a challenge that was met before, our minds first search out their "computer banks." They search for a tried and tested "tape." They have no way of knowing whether the tape is actually appropriate or not, only that it has been useful before in a similar, or vaguely similar, situation. As a matter of fact, our minds will draw up an old tape whether a situation is real or not.

The mind is only a highly specialized tool. You can actually fool the mind with your imagination. Try it. Try visualizing, for example, an angry situation where you are a protagonist. See yourself being harassed and insulted by someone you dislike intensely. Get into the scene. Try to make it look real. If you are good at it, the mind, confronted with the image, immediately locates your anger-response tape and plays it with venom. It might even get your body into the act by raising your blood pressure. And it's all going on in your mind. It's all going on in your mind, but you really *feel* angry. (Talk about the unreliability of feelings!)

You can get angry just by looking at certain people. A total stranger may have "a look" that automatically activates one of your tapes. What's happening here? What's happening is that a program has been "accessed." The "action," of course, goes on completely in your head. The mind rarely distinguishes real life from what goes on in your imagination. This is what makes us create a "tempest in a teapot" and "mountains out of molehills." The mind is only a smoothly functioning tool we possess that receives complex data, sorts it out like any computer, and finds a suitable "tape" to handle the data. As I say, the mind is, for the most part, mindless. That is why our tapes can also be called our "blindspots."

Experiment further to test the validity of this assessment.

Visualize, for example, all kinds of sad things that have happened to you recently. See all those sad things in full color. Watch how quickly your personal grief tape turns on. You might even be able to bring yourself to real tears, all from your mind.

Or imagine all kinds of terrible things that might happen to you in the future. Think how dangerous it might be for you to change, even love your self more. What might others think? What might others say? Within seconds, your anxiety-coping tape will turn on and you might feel real fear. And it's all in your head.

Or visualize happy times, or something erotic. Even your body will be convinced that something real is going on. It's amazing what joy or anxiety you can create for yourself, just by using your imagination. (We will be studying the use of the imagination as a self-love recovery tool in Chapter Thirteen.) The tape is turned on and away it goes.

But there's more. Our minds also have another remarkable talent. Our minds will also filter, or screen out, what doesn't fit into its current programming. My computer sometimes tells me: "not found" and refuses to process further. Our minds tend to reject outright what doesn't "fit" a tape. Unless we are aware and make a conscious "override," they will not process further. This again is where our "blindspots" come in. This screening process is what accounts for the fact that we most often reject advice to change and improve ourselves. If we don't have a program for initiating self-growth and change in our mental computer banks, "it goes in one ear and out the other." We don't "hear" because we can't. If a suggestion or criticism, no matter how constructive, doesn't "fit" with an old tape of our self-image, our mind will tend to reject it as "incompatible," "not found." Most of us are not programmed to accept change; we are programmed for "resistance."

Our tapes are generated by our "needs" of the moment. As infants and children we learned what it took to be approved by our parents, teachers and other caretakers. Most of us simply accepted the tapes and programs of our parents because that was a way to make sure we would be loved and cared for. We adopted the tapes of our culture, especially those displayed by our peers, so that we wouldn't feel "strange" and isolated. We adopted the tapes of our churches, our political party, our bosses, and our spouses, all out of concern to "fit in" and be acceptable. Some of these tapes are helpful to us to this day; some of them are definitely not. Some of them are defeating our best interests. Some of them are inadequate to our present stage of development. Some of them are inappropriate to our ambitions for a better future for ourselves.

It's tragic that most people aren't even aware they are "programmed." They aren't aware that they feel this way or that, believe this or that, prefer this or that, or behave in this manner or that manner, simply because of their programming. Our self-love has been impaired, perhaps severely, because somewhere along the line we were programmed with a tape that told us that we were insignificant, inadequate, helpless, or defective in comparison with others. Our self-love has been impaired because we have been programmed with a tape which Matthew McKay and Patrick Fanning, in their book *Self-Esteem*, call the "pathological critic." This critic puts us down, tells us we haven't got what it takes, asserts that we are losers, and emphasizes, without constraint, that we are stupid, incompetent, and ugly to boot. The power of the tape is that, when it is playing, it sounds so reasonable, justified, and true. The point is that it's not true; it's just a tape—a dangerous, self-defeating tape at that.

Most of us think we are dealing with "real life," when all we are dealing with is tapes and programming. Most of our programming was arbitrary. With a different set of parents, teachers, cultural inputs and experiences, living conditions, peers and friends, there might just as well have been a whole other set of programs that would have made for completely different consequences in the way we live our lives.

Much of our problem with other people is a programming problem. Fundamentally, we are equal and alike. It is our programming that sets us apart and makes us different from one another. If you think about it, it is always unlikely that we know people as they really are. If you think about it, we rarely communicate with other people as they really are. What happens is that our programs interface with their programs, and their programs interface with ours. All of us are basically actors. We "act out" our programming. Programming is normally all that is revealed. We think we are dealing with real life, but we aren't; we are dealing with programs. Programming is so much part of us that, when I am talking to someone, I can never be sure I am interfacing with a person directly, or with their programming. Confusing programs with people is the major cause of most problems we face in our social relationships.

Not too long ago I pulled out of a parking lot at the same time another driver was pulling in. He turned wide and lightly clipped the edge of my front bumper. Instantly my programming kicked in. I lunged out of the car, steaming with adrenalin, ready to take the other driver on. His programming kicked in too. He lunged out of his car, defensively-aggressive, calling me all kinds of nasty names. He looked bigger than I am, so another program kicked in telling me to ease off a bit or I might get hurt. Other drivers kept beeping at us to get out of the way, and since no real damage was done, we ended up driving off, full of anger at each other, each fully self-righteous, each fully "convinced" the other was a moron. Two human beings, basically alike down deep, not knowing each other one bit, one program interfacing with another. A comedy.

It is obvious we can be victimized by our programming. Tom is one of the unfriendliest people I know. He once told me that the greatest lesson he ever learned in life was that "you can't trust anybody." And he doesn't. He doesn't know why he feels that way; he just does. He can recite a hundred examples of how people, even those closest to him, family members and co-workers, can never be trusted. He is a chronic complainer. He is always "getting burned." He is a lonely and bitter bachelor. I know his loneliness is a terrible burden to him. He doesn't want to be lonely. He just is. I was never able to convince him that his "tape," "you can't trust anybody," is a program that is victimizing him and defeating the possibility of any happiness he might find in life. That one simple tape has made, and continues to make, his life miserable.

Consider the many educational dilemmas we are facing today, because some children have been programmed to believe that "school is for the birds," or that reading is for "nerds." Consider how many young people flock to gangs because they are programmed to believe that the gang is "real family." Consider how many marriages fail today because young couples are programmed to believe that love is a feeling, and when that feeling goes, so does the marriage.

If we study our selves any day, we can come up with a hundred examples of how our various programmings work. What is really us, and what is really our programming? What is really programming in other people? All of us are programmed and mind-set in countless ways. Fortunately, as I said, all of these programs are relative and arbitrary. The good news is that our programming can be challenged. The good news is that our programming can be modified to our advantage in self-love recovery. What is no longer useful or appropriate can be changed.

If our old tapes were generated by needs of the moment, new tapes can be generated by needs of this moment. It is the hope offered by this book that we do have the power to reprogram our selves. We do have the power of "override." We are not stuck with our programming. With awareness and effort we can change any program we wish, especially a program that is responsible for our not loving our selves enough. A program is only "software." We can change our software if we find it is keeping us from loving our selves as we need. To care for our selves and love our selves as we need, it is important that, from now on, *we live by our conscious choices*, not out of automatic tapes and programming.

Awareness, and the willingness to confront and change our programming, will carry us into the affirmative actions for our selves that we will address in the next chapter. The next chapter will give us an assortment of new tapes for conscious insertion into new programming.

7

Inner Work: Affirmative Action (Part I)

Primary Principles

The great end of life is not knowledge but action.
                                        —T.H. Huxley

To discover how "programmed" we are is a big step in awareness. To discover how we got to be programmed and how our programming operates within us (sometimes requiring help from a therapist) is another big step. To discover that we can change our programming to make life more satisfying and fulfilling is yet another big step. To actually *change* our programming is the biggest step of all.

Self-love recovery is dependent on actual changes in our attitudes and behavior. Most of us have become addicted to self-defeating attitudes and behavior: denial, blaming, avoidance of responsibility for what happens to us, self-pre-occupation, co-dependency, procrastinating, depression, etc. We need to give up our addictions. We need to change. These addictions need to be overridden with program changes on our behalf.

In this and the following chapter we will examine affirmative actions that loving one's self demands. These affirmative actions indicate what changes we need to make. In this chapter we will examine some primary principles of affirmative action; in the next chapter we will examine the corollary actions that flow from these principles.

We are learning to take affirmative action on our behalf. We emphasize again that love is not a feeling, but basically an *action*, something we *do*! "Love is what love does." Love is commitment and action we take on another's behalf. Love is commitment and action we take on our own behalf. For us, "love" is a verb, not a noun. Love is something we do for our selves. Love is demonstrated by the affirmative actions we perform for our benefit. And we do them often enough until they become a way of life.

If we have already come to believe that we are "beloved" by God as we understand him, all these affirmative actions will seem natural and logical, and easy to perform. But if belief in our belovedness is yet too difficult to embrace, it does not discount that we still need to take loving actions on our behalf. Many in self-love recovery inform us that very often we first need to take loving actions on our own behalf before we can come to appreciate that we are beloved. We need some healing first, before we can see ourselves as truly lovable.

We approach all self-affirming actions in a spirit of "surrender." Our continued willingness to surrender our lives and our wills to our Higher Power will help us avoid a self-defeating impatience to achieve "quick cures." We are not expecting "cures"; we are content to be "in recovery." Self-love recovery will be a lifetime project of continual learning to live in more self-loving ways. Life will always include fear, self-doubt, anxiety, worry, and problems. They are an integral part of normal human living. We cannot escape them. But we can learn to take care of our selves in a more self-loving way, despite our fears and despite our problems.

Our Higher Power wills that we come to our fullest potential and achieve the destiny for which we were created. But we cannot do it alone. We are not expected to do it alone. We work *with* our Higher Power in co-creating our selves. We are happy and grateful with any results our Higher Power designs to come our way. But we are patient over "results." Thus we come to love, esteem, and appreciate ourselves as our Higher Power does: as we are, for what we are, however we are. Our Higher

Power never judges us as more or less worthy. Our Higher Power looks upon us, as we are, and finds us delightful to behold at whatever stage of development we may find ourselves in. We need to look upon our selves in like manner.

All the affirmative actions that follow are geared to helping us love our selves as we need. *Any one* of them, if acted upon, would work significantly to help us achieve the love for our selves that we need. All affirmative actions on our behalf work synergistically. Acting on any one of them constellates and energizes all the other affirmative actions. But adequate self-love can only come about if we actually *perform* affirmative actions on our own behalf. Reading *about* affirmative actions and agreeing with their logic will not do the trick. Love for our selves is the specific affirmative action we take on our behalf.

In each of the affirmative actions we examine I would ask the reader to struggle for "awareness." Try to be an impartial observer of your self in action. Notice how your self is affected by, and reacts to, everyday situations. Observe to see if the affirming actions presented actually fit in with your current attitudes and behavioral patterns. If so, so much the better. If not, a decision needs to be made to override the "old tapes." A decision needs to be made to consciously insert a new tape (the affirmative action) which will enhance self-love.

Deliberately performing a self-loving action, deliberately choosing the new tape, demonstrates to our selves that we love them. We will play the new tape again and again until our minds, as situations arise, will automatically pick the positive tape from its store of options rather than the negative.

ASSERT YOUR SELF: *A RIGHT TO BE*

There is no need to assert yourself, but there is need for you to assert your "self." Think about that. The inner you, the observing "I," the I that says "I," needs no justification, needs no affirmation, needs to make no case to prove lovableness. You share being with the eternal creator Self of the universe. You need never make excuses to yourself or anyone else for that honor we all share.

Your self is your gift. Your self is your specific embodiment. Your self is your extension into the world. Your self is your means of experience in the world. Your "self" is what makes you "you." Your self is the composite of your genetic endowments, all your experiences to date, all your thoughts, memories, physical attributes, attitudes, presumptions, feelings, "tapes," all your potential for the future. That self, for its own uplifting and well-being, needs to feel asserted by you. That self needs to feel that you approve its existence.

It is you, the observing "I," to whom your Higher Power offers co-creatorship of your life. You are encouraged to honor your existence by taking charge of your self and its programming. You are urged to be invested in your self's condition and development. You are encouraged to guide and nurture that self with all the love you can give. You may need to make some changes in that self, but only that you may esteem and love it all the more.

Your self feels loved when you *assert its right to be*, when you consciously and affirmatively approve your self's very existence. As we have already noted, people who do not love their selves not only deny their selves' right to exist, but wish that self was replaced by another's. This is utter torture to your self. Your self needs approval from you. Your self is your embodiment. It makes you who you are. Your self is the only self you will ever have. To disown, discredit, or despise that self is psychological suicide.

For all your warts, limitations, sins, mistakes, and failings, you are basically a good person, and always have been. You've always wanted to do the right thing, and most often you have. You see yourself as a loving person and you want to love your self as much as you can. It's time to take steps to ensure that.

None of us chose to be born. We didn't choose the circumstances of our upbringing. All of us were handicapped in that we didn't receive all the love we needed, when the need was there. We were brought up therefore not feeling very self-assertive. Perhaps we were specifically trained not to be self-assertive. Not being self-assertive, or wishing we had someone else's life, has hurt us. We're sorry it happened that way, but we cannot change that. We can only take responsibility for what we do with our selves from now on. You are as worthy as anyone else on this Mother Earth to exist in the self you have. No one can take that from you. Your self has just as much right to be loved for what it is as anyone else's.

It's time you made the best of the self you have. It's time you lovingly worked on developing it into the best self it can be. It's time you asserted your self's right to be and told it that you find it "beloved," a pleasure to behold.

BE WHO YOU ARE: *UNIQUENESS*

An old and wise maxim proclaims a philosophy for a happy and satisfying life: "*To Thine Own Self Be True.*" Depending on what part of the maxim you place emphasis, this piece of wisdom can be understood in two ways: always be honest and true to your self, or always be faithful and devoted to your self. Both understandings are valid for self-love recovery. Being honest with, and devoted to, the selves we have means that we honor and love our *uniqueness*.

Society as a rule is pledged to modify our uniqueness. Society, for its own survival (often aided, abated, and imitated by dogmatic religious institutions which have the same agenda), tries to maintain a status quo by demanding all its members become "adjusted." Society needs order and control. Society is always threatened by non-conformity.

Some conformity is necessary of course for social order, but for most of us in self-love recovery conformity tends to go too far. All of us need to grow and become independent as individuals. Our personal maturity depends on it. An independent respect for our individuality is critical to self-love. Carl Jung asserted that maturity is only completed in "individuation." We are meant to be unique.

"Rebellion," therefore, might be something we should expect, if not welcome. And yet from birth we are trained by our parents and other teachers to conform to one rule after another of what and how we are "supposed to" be. Being "different" was shamed. We were led to believe that our selves did not have the right to exist in their uniqueness, that social acceptability was more important than we were.

People who do not love themselves much are more typically "conformist" than not. I am not encouraging criminal behavior, but I think we need consider well what a terrible price we pay for rigid and unquestioned conformity and living up to someone else's expectations. Lack of respect for our uniqueness, or feeling that we have to conform to the judgment and expectations of others, is primarily what gives us an all-pervading sense of hopelessness to do things for our selves and accomplish what we need. Pessimism is the offspring of conformity. If our happiness depends on conformity, we are always at the arbitrary mercy of powers beyond our management.

Boredom and apathy inflict so many at the price of "adjustment." Consider how many never achieve a sense of personal integrity because they spend their lives living up to someone else's standards. Consider how much creativity has gone down the drain, especially with promising young students, because educational norms demand only what is "acceptable" to an arbitrary grading system. Consider how many find life listless and dull because nothing stimulates them to "stand out" or "push on."

We need courage, not to fly in the face of rules of social harmony and good ethics, but to be who we are without shame. Closely aligned with asserting your self's right to exist is allowing your self its *uniqueness*. Be who you are.

Some years ago, talk host star Oprah Winfrey very publicly went on a stringent diet to give herself a model figure. It worked. With an enormous outlay of will power, she slimmed down to a figure the cameras took a great liking to. A new Oprah was born, and she looked terrific. But the weight loss didn't last. After some months, she was back again to her "average" weight. Not without choice, however. She decided to give up fighting to be what she wasn't. She decided to be who she was. And I believe she received more admiration for her choice to be herself than for fighting to attain an image that was glamorous to the media, but just wasn't her self.

Be who you are. Accept your self. Allow your self its uniqueness. Love your self by allowing it to be as different as it really is. Everyone of us is unique. The universe relishes variety in creation. The differences in plant, insect, bird, and animal life stagger the imagination. The differences between all of us as individuals are overwhelming. Those differences, and their right to exist as differences, should be accepted and honored. Like a snowflake, there never was, is, or will be someone exactly like you. Why try to defeat that design? Why browbeat your self by making it feel it "has to" be this or "has to" be that or it isn't worth your love? Your self wants to know it is lovable just as it is, for its own sake.

With every person you envy and with everything you covet, you are telling your self it is inadequate and not worthy of your love. Allow your self to display its own colors without putting it down with critical old tapes or by harassing it with "have-tos." Be who you are. When the fox tries to be a bluegill, it is only asking for trouble.

Being who you are means accepting all that you are, angel wings, warts, and all. Your limitations are uniquely your own as are your assets. All that makes you "you" is simply accepted and validated. This means acknowledging that you are not perfect and are not expected to be. You have your limitations like anybody else and you do not "have to" pretend you are better than you are. This means that your outer life expresses the inner you. And this is what personal integrity is all about: "What you see is what you get!"

OWN YOUR SELF: *INDEPENDENCE*

Owning our selves goes a step beyond being our selves. Being our selves honors our uniqueness; owning our selves honors our *independence*.

Owning our selves means that we embrace our selves as

our own. Our selves are to be taken care of, nourished, support-
ed and loved by us. Owning our selves means that we fully take
possession of our selves and do not leave ownership of our
selves to the possession and handling (manipulation) of others.
In other words, with regard to our selves, we act as owners, and
not as someone who rents.

At this very moment, as I write these words, I am hearing
in the background a song that very plaintively moans, "I can't
live without you, baby ... I can't go on without your love." That's
what much of modern music moans about all the time. Much
contemporary music mesmerizes the minds of our youth with
"dependency." I like country music, but I rarely hear country
music lyrics that aren't about someone being abandoned by his
or her "baby" and can't find meaning in life anymore. It seems
that contemporary songwriters are hell-bent on making sure we
hand ownership of our selves over to "baby."

M. Scott Peck in *The Road Less Traveled* defines dependency as "the inability to experience wholeness or to function adequately without the certainty that one is being actively cared for
by another" (p. 98). It is estimated that nine out of ten of us are
co-dependent to some degree. Co-dependents don't feel ownership of their selves. Co-dependents have significantly low self-
esteem and manipulate others to bolster their crippled egos.
Co-dependents spend their lives worrying about what someone
else thinks or living up to what someone else expects. Co-
dependents continually reach out to others for acknowledgement, approval, love, and direction. Co-dependents can appreciate themselves only as mirrored in the eyes of someone else.
They can only feel alive if someone else affirms and approves
them. Co-dependents will put up with enormous amounts of
abuse just to win a tiny measure of approval from someone
whose own life may be falling to pieces.

Perhaps you are in a toxic relationship. Maybe you have
been taking abuse of your self-esteem all your life. Maybe abuse
is all you know. Maybe your parents are still putting you down.
Maybe your spouse is doing his or her best to refashion you in
his or her image and likeness. Maybe those who are in authority

over you are still putting you in your place. It is important to realize that other people can only abuse us as we empower them to do so. People can only manipulate us insofar as we hand our selves over to them.

No matter how "romantic" it sounds, to put our selves into the hands of another is not a definition or sign of love. It is evidence of abdication. Living off the approval of others is not a sign of humility; it is evidence of parasitism. Dependency is not a virtue; it's a disease. When we hand ownership of our selves over to another, our selves cannot help but sense that abdication. Even if those to whom we have abdicated our selves are the "most wonderful and loving" people we know, we inevitably suffer for it, because our selves will not feel they are worthy enough of our own care. Furthermore, nobody is perfect. Sooner or later others are going to bungle the job of being our selves' landlords. Nobody can ever give us all we need. Everyone is as limited as we are. Everyone has his or her own problems, agendas, and handicaps. Everyone is governed by King Baby just as much as we are. Giving our selves over to another is usually a set-up for getting "burned."

Our selves feel loved when we care enough to assume full ownership of them. Own your self. Don't cut your head off and present it to someone else on a platter. Don't offer your self in sacrifice to anyone else's approval. We want to be loved so badly that we often degrade ourselves by putting our selves into the hands of someone who simply cannot give us the care we need. We sometimes devote all our energies to taking care of "monsters" who reciprocate with nothing but abuse. We live in the pathetic hope of being liked a little by people who get their kicks out of kicking us.

The hunger of wanting desperately to be loved will never go away or be satisfied until we love our selves as we need. Nobody else can fill us up. No other human being, no matter with how much love and feeling he or she has to share, can ever fill up the emptiness we might feel inside. Nobody really wants to. Nobody wants to be "used" in this manner. It's ironic, but no one can love us until we love our selves.

Own your self by asserting and working on your independence. Be the author of your life story. Risk following your own leads. Trust your own intuitions. Relish your uniqueness. Fight the inclination to owe your being to social pressures, public opinion, and conventional thinking, which may or may not be good for you. You have to decide what is in your best interests and then be willing to live with the consequences.

Own your own beliefs, values, ideals, standards and principles. Don't simply swallow what has been projected onto you. "Faith" is never authentic unless you personally work through your beliefs and own them because you have personally seen their validity. Don't live with hand-me-down beliefs or second-hand values. Test them out. Do they fit your needs? Are they of value to your happiness? Do they enhance your self-love?

Own even your "dark side," your limitations, your imperfections. They are part of you as are your assets. It is the "shadows" of your personality that are needed to bring out the vivid colors in the tapestry of your self that you are creating. They need to be respected too.

TAKE RESPONSIBILITY FOR YOUR SELF: *MORAL ACCOUNTABILITY*

Taking responsibility for our selves goes one step beyond owning our selves in that it adds the dimension of *moral accountability* for what we do with our lives. Taking responsibility for our selves means just what it says: we just don't *have* responsibility, we actively and positively *take* it. We consciously and proactively assume it. Assuming responsibility keeps us off the "pity pot" and helps us avoid the perennially self-defeating posture of blaming. "Responsible" means that we fully expect to "make a response" for our actions. We take responsibility for our selves by holding our selves accountable for what goes on in our lives. We hold ourselves liable for the consequences of our actions or inactions. At the bottom line, taking responsibility lets our selves know we mean business in our self-love recovery program.

As much as we might hate taking responsibility, it is thrust upon on us whether we like it or not. Responsibility is something every court in the land believes in. Responsibility is something the IRS believes in. Responsibility is something that anyone who is disappointed in us believes in. The difference between those who love themselves and those who don't is that self-loving people *take* responsibility rather than just have it thrust upon them. Consequently, they are more willing to say, "I have no one to blame but myself."

Avoidance behavior and denial, however, seem to come naturally to human beings. We don't like taking responsibility. Consequences can be scary. We would rather blame. Deep down in our unconscious we remember how wonderful it was to be cuddled, rocked, cradled, fed, and cleaned as infants. We want that euphoric state of someone else taking responsibility for us to continue.

A common way we avoid taking personal responsibility for our selves is living our lives from our "supposed to" tapes, rather than from conscious, personal choices. When we live off our "shoulds" rather than conscious, personal choices, we are responsible (responding) to our programming rather than to our selves.

Marsha Sinetar, in her excellent book *Do What You Love, The Money Will Follow*, gives special treatment to how we need to deal with *the Big S*: the "shoulds." According to Sinetar, the "shoulds" are "all types of rules of living that we learn from parents, teachers, peer groups, religious dictates, the media and a variety of other social sources." They are "subliminal programmings that strongly condition what we think we are supposed to be, do, have and look like." In reality they are little more than a "constricting prism through which we see ourselves as limited, defined and controlled by others" (p. 102). If we are to live responsibly, we need to devote our selves to dissolving our dependence on the "shoulds." We need to take responsibility for our selves by living according to our conscious, personal *choices*.

Taking responsibility for our selves will mean facing the fact that we are governed by an immense variety of "shoulds" and "suppose tos." Some are productive for our well-being, but many bind us to self-defeating attitudes and behavior. Taking responsibility for our selves will mean we begin making conscious choices. We begin making conscious choices about what injunctions we intend to live with. We weigh our own values. We do not uncritically live our lives with hand-me-downs.

Obviously, not all "shoulds" and "should nots" are bad. Taking responsibility for our selves, however, means that they will not have arbitrary or automatic censorship over us. They will be used insofar as they foster love for our selves and they will be rejected insofar as they don't.

Most of us wish that our parents and significant others would have done more for us in our early years of development. In self-love recovery, we are learning to take that responsibility upon our selves. From now on we will act toward our selves as we wish others would have acted toward us. We will take responsibility. We will "parent" our selves.

Taking responsibility for our selves means that we fully take the praise or blame for what we do with our lives. We accept compliments graciously, we take criticism constructively, and we accept the consequences of our mistakes. Taking responsibility means that we are willing to make those mistakes. Acting "responsibly" does not mean that we don't make mistakes, but that we accept their consequences.

It is a universal truth that most of us learn only by our mistakes. Any growth and development we hope for ourselves will often mean making a lot of mistakes. And that's perfectly OK. As imperfect human beings we have a right to our mistakes. It is often only in seeing where we can do wrong that we learn where we can go right. All real growth is normally a hit-and-miss activity. When we make a hit, we accept the applause. When we miss, we go back to the drawing boards. The only way to develop our fullest potential is to learn to make better choices. We cannot make better choices unless we learn first-hand what the less effective choices are.

All religions teach that there will be a "judgment day." All religions teach that we are responsible for our actions. We are ultimately answerable for our selves. No excuses, no blaming, no lawyers will accompany us as we make our final accounting. All religions teach that the Creator holds us accountable. We show love for our selves by embracing that responsibility consciously and full-heartedly.

Finally, taking responsibility for our selves means taking care of our selves and our needs. It's important to note the selection of words here. It is one thing to *care about* our selves. Most of us do that quite well. We're sensitive about our selves. We worry about our selves. We desire good things for our selves. But it is quite another thing to take care of our *selves*. Most of us often do not do that well. We don't follow through on the actions that would make caring a reality. "Caring" is a general attitude of good will toward our selves. "Taking care" is putting that good will into action. Caring is something that goes on in our hearts. Taking care is following through on caring. "Taking care" makes "caring" a reality.

BELIEVE IN YOUR SELF: *EMPOWERMENT*

Our attitudes and behavior will never change unless we believe in our selves and our possibilities. Belief is empowerment. Every success story I have ever heard proves time and time again that "faith can move mountains." Success stories mean that "mountains" were moved. "All things are possible to him who believes," wrote the evangelist Mark. Norman Vincent Peale brought a message for positive living to millions. He encouraged his listeners to tell themselves everyday, "Every day, in every way, I am getting better and better." This act of faith, with just a slogan, was enough to turn many people's lives around.

Belief is the energy that puts us into action. Belief is the energy that gets us what we need for our selves. Belief in your self is a confidence that your self will thrive on. Belief keeps your self alert to its amazing possibilities. I took my first steps as a baby solely on the faith my mother had that "you can do it." I took my first job in grammar school as a paper boy solely on the power I received from my father that "you can do it." My courage to dive off the high board came from a coach who believed I could do it, and led me to believe the same about myself.

Claude Bristol entitled his book *The Magic of Believing* because there is magic in faith. Faith is the magic that makes things happen. We literally *become* what we believe about our selves. If you believe the best for your self, you are already on your way to success. If you believe the worst for your self, you are already on the way to defeat.

All our "tapes," all our inner scripts and mind-sets, are little more than beliefs. Those beliefs either build us up or tear us down. They either help create us or help destroy us. What is most enlightening, however, is that most of our beliefs are completely relative. We could just as easily have been raised, trained, and educated with different belief systems, which would likely have made our entire development different. Our beliefs about our selves, as with our tapes and mind-sets, are not set in stone. For a self-loving person, beliefs are a matter of choice. They can be changed by a conscious confrontation, evaluation, and decision. Beliefs that affirm us and help us grow need to be strengthened; those that keep us from being all that we can be need to be eliminated or *reprogrammed*.

We create reality for our selves by what we believe about our selves. As Anton Chekhov wrote, "Man is what he believes." If you really believe someone can do you in with voodoo, your life is endangered. If you believe, on the other hand, with Dr. Bernie Siegel in his *Love, Medicine, and Miracles,* that you will recover, you have a good chance of recovering from even the most life-threatening illness.

Dr. Wayne Dyer entitled one of his latest books, *You'll See It When You Believe It*. Dr. Dyer explores "The Way to Your

Personal Transformation" and demonstrates that "seeing is not believing." On the contrary, *believing* is the only way we can see our reality for what it is. Life is run on faith. Change, modify, and increase belief in our selves, and our lives will be transformed accordingly.

I accept my self and assert my self's right to be.

I honor and respect my uniqueness.

I assert and will work on my independence.

I hold myself fully accountable for the consequences of my actions or inactions.

I believe in my self and my possibilities.

8

Inner Work: Affirmative Action (Part II)

Self-Loving Actions

Love is as love does.

—M.Scott Peck

In the previous chapter, we examined some primary principles of self-love recovery through affirmative action that we need to take on our behalf. Love is as love does. Self-love is action we take on our behalf. In this chapter we will explore self-loving actions. These affirmative actions flow as corollaries from the principles already presented. They should be accepted with the same conditions we used with the primary principles: awareness of how they are operative or non-operative in our lives and how, in terms of the affirmative action, we might need to replace old negative tapes with more positive ones.

It is useful to remember again that any and all of the affirmative actions presented are part of a self-love recovery program because in general they are all part of a self-loving person's life. Any one of the affirmative actions, while appearing separate, contains in a sense all the rest. We need not look upon self-love recovery as a formidable program with an overwhelming number of affirming actions to be performed. Practicing any one of the affirmative actions will constellate or energize the others. These actions are treated separately because each of us is different, with different needs at any given moment. One or more of these affirmative actions will appeal to one individual reader in a way that they might not appeal to another. In covering them all, it is my hope to offer something for everyone.

We all want to be loved. While we are loved unconditionally by our Higher Power and are lovable just as we are, we very often cannot appreciate our lovableness until we do things for our selves to increase our sensitivity to our lovableness. In this sense, we work to make our selves lovable to ourselves. We make an act of faith in our lovableness and then take affirmative, loving actions on our own behalf. Those loving actions themselves enhance our lovableness. They help us to grow in appreciation of how lovable we are. In turn, feeling more lovable, we are likely to increase and expand those loving actions we take on our behalf. They become easier for us to do. In time, a wonderful cycle of action—appreciation—action begins. This growth cycle, combined with our willingness to surrender our lives and our wills to our Higher Power, establishes us firmly in self-love recovery.

LIVE NOW

Taking care of our selves means living in the NOW, living in the present moment. "Now" is the only reality that is. The past no longer is, and the future is not yet. And yet what countless hours we waste in anguish over the past which no longer exists, or in worry about the future which doesn't exist either. What needless abuse we subject our selves to with worry and anxiety. Worry and anxiety are phonograph needles stuck in a groove, endlessly producing the same jarring sound and going nowhere. Worry and anxiety are King Baby in paralysis over a control issue. Worry and anxiety are about the most useless, non-productive, self-abusing and toxic actions we can subject our selves to. What have worry and anxiety ever done for us but make us miserable?

We might argue that living in the NOW is impossible

because it goes by so quickly, or that anguish over the past and worry about the future are actually part of our "now." (I feel anxious, now!) I would respond by asserting that living "now" is all a matter of focus. We have no control over the past or the future, but *we do have control of where we direct our focus.* When we worry about some future event it is because we are focusing on the future. When we anguish over the past, we are focusing on the past. When we live in the present moment we focus on the events that are transpiring at the given moment. We focus on the here and now.

Focusing is a self-loving action because it reduces stressful worry and anxiety by drawing attention away from the past and future. Focusing is a self-loving action because it draws attention and energy into the present moment where alone joy can be experienced.

We don't have power over the past or future, but we do have power over where we direct our attention. It may take some discipline and determined effort, but we can limit our attention range. When we acknowledge that worry and anxiety are functionally fruitless and potentially toxic, we can diminish their toxicity simply by not giving them the attention they need to exist. When we are focused on the present moment and on present activities, it is quite amazing how quickly worry and anxiety begin to dissipate. Worry and anxiety thrive on attention and focus. The mind, however, can generally only handle one focus at a time. Focus on the present and anxious thoughts and worries cannot be energized.

GROW UP

One of the greatest disservices we impose on our selves is inhibiting them from achieving maturity. Adulthood does not come to us with chronological age. Maturity is not a given on our twenty-first birthday. Adulthood is earned. Maturity is developed. The first step in developing your potential in self-love recovery is simply to "grow up."

Perhaps you are successful in business, but have never succeeded in making a healthy psychological split from your parents. You still feel and act like a child—their child. Perhaps you still face adult challenges with the emotions of a teenager. Your clownish sense of humor got lots of laughs on dates, but is seriously harming your relationships with co-workers and preventing you from being treated with respect. Maybe you need to take mature action on an upcoming marriage, or maybe you need to end a toxic relationship, and you approach these important decisions with the fear of a five year old. Maybe you are an affluent socialite still fending with the self-absorbed mind of a nervous debutante, whose every minute is absorbed in impressing peers with the "right" clothes, throwing the "right" parties, eating at the "right" restaurants, and being informed of the "right" gossip. Maybe you are still living your life with behavior that is more appropriate to children or teenagers.

You cannot love a self you allow to remain immature. It is true that sound religious philosophy teaches us to "become like little children." The need to "grow up" does not discount this important maxim. This wise teaching presupposes that we have become adult enough to become like little children again, that we are grown up and secure enough to take on the child-like virtues of awe, curiosity, innocence, openness, simplicity, joy, and playfulness. This wise teaching is not advocating regression or, much less, making an excuse for infantilism. We are encouraged to become child-like, not childish. We can only take on child-like qualities when the adult self feels confident enough as an adult to do so.

Act like an adult. Be an adult. Your self will never feel safe until it feels it is under the direction of you as a capable adult. To a child, the adult world is fearsome. If you are content to act and react like a child all your life, you will always live in fear. Your self will always feel unsteady, threatened, and insecure in the hands of a child. It will only feel safe and ready to advance in the hands of an adult. Self-love is doing your self the favor of growing up: thinking and acting like an adult.

DISCIPLINE YOUR SELF

We show love for our selves by setting goals for our selves, by taking affirmative action on our behalf, by standing up for our selves, and by guiding our selves in paths of growth and development. To accomplish these aims will inevitably require discipline on our part. Discipline is a self-loving action because it assures the self that we will do whatever is necessary for its survival and flourishing. Discipline is a self-loving action because it assures the self that someone is firmly in the driver's seat.

"Discipline" is a word reeking with negative connotations for most of us. Discipline for me has always meant something punitive. When I was "disciplined," I was normally punished. Or else it meant some grueling exercise I had to endure, like mid-summer work-outs for football players shaping up for the fall season. In truth, discipline is neither punishment nor an endurance test. In truth, discipline is a loving action we take on behalf of our selves.

In truth, discipline is a *commitment to do what needs to be done*. There are certain things we simply need to do to achieve our goals in life. There are certain things we need to do to achieve adequate love for our selves. However, most of us are committed to personal comfort and passivity. Our culture trains us to be "comfort junkies." It is difficult to commit our selves to effort and achievement, even when it's in our best interest. It feels uncomfortable to discipline our selves. It feels difficult to make efforts.

Discipline is our effort to do whatever is needed despite what feels uncomfortable or difficult. Love cannot exist without discipline. Love for our selves cannot exist without self-discipline. Discipline allows us to perform for our selves despite our feelings.

Discipline is a *willingness to postpone gratification*. Despite the protests of King Baby, we cannot have what we want whenever we want it. Life doesn't work that way. We set ourselves up for endless disappointment and frustration to demand that it be that way. The ability to delay gratification has always been considered one of the classic indications of maturity. As we have seen, timing is important in the unfolding of our development. Nothing can be pushed or rushed. "Everything in its own time," says the book of Ecclesiastes. There is a time to hold back, and a time to push ahead. Discipline is the capacity to work for what we need, but to allow our Higher Power to work out the timing of "results." Discipline is "letting go" of control.

Discipline is a *conscious effort to be aware*. Discipline is making a determined effort to think. It is a determined effort to use our minds to figure things out, to make sensible judgments, and to set reasonable goals for our selves. Discipline is a willingness to learn.

Discipline is honesty in saying "yes" when we mean yes, and "no" when we mean no. Discipline is courage to take risks to do what we need to do for our selves. Discipline is guarding our boundaries by not allowing others to run herd on our emotions. Discipline is studying how our old tapes are affecting our attitudes and behavior. Discipline is a conscious decision to reprogram the tapes that are not working in our own best interests. Discipline is expressing our needs directly and asking for what we need and want. Discipline is a conscious effort to see and embrace discipline as a loving action on our behalf. Discipline is an act of self-love.

DO YOUR OWN DRIVING

Respecting our independence and taking care of our selves means that we *don't leave what would be in our best interests up to others*. We make the decisions about what we need for our selves and we follow through with our own action plans to secure what we need. In self-love recovery we reject the Greyhound Bus Company slogan: "Leave the driving to us." If we need to do something important for our selves, we do the "driving" ourselves.

Taking care of our selves in this manner is an act of self-love because the self feels stimulated and empowered by the confidence we give it to get a job done. Accepting responsibility for our own care stimulates our minds to find the resources to do so. Our minds thrive on challenges. They love to demonstrate their alacrity. Stories are told of hapless and "helpless" victims of boating accidents who become stranded for years on some remote island. They not only survived, but often thrived, in seemingly hopeless situations. It is amazing how enterprising and imaginative we become when our survival depends on it.

It is also amazing how enterprising and imaginative we become when we decide that our well-being is up to us and not dependent on others. We might surprise ourselves about how resourceful we can become to take care of our selves as we need.

Do your own driving. Take charge of your life. Honor your self by giving it a chance to show its true colors.

MAKE YOUR SELF "ADEQUATE"

People who don't love themselves very much are usually well-acquainted with the words, "I can't!" Self-loving people on the other hand, are usually well-acquainted with the words, "How do I get this done?"

Taking care of your self *means making your self "adequate."* Many who did not experience enough love in their formation somehow never feel "adequate" to life. Many never feel competent to handle the everyday challenges of living. Perhaps they were told time and again that they were helpless and hopeless, and the old tape keeps on playing "their song."

Taking care of your self means taking whatever steps are necessary to become adequate. You don't just sit on a pity pot, you take action to make your self adequate. If the gas tank is empty, you don't complain that the car won't run, you fill the tank.

You may need more schooling, more intensive self-study,

more time for meditative and inspirational reading. You may need to get in touch with your unconscious sources of wisdom and energy. You may need to become better acquainted with the mysterious energy of your dark side. You may need to explore your dreams. You may need the help of a professional therapist, mentor, spiritual director, or teacher to guide you on the road of self-love recovery. You may need the power of sharing that comes from attendance at a Twelve-Step meeting.

But whatever it takes, you are willing to do it. You don't sit with "inadequacy." You search out and implement whatever it takes to make your self adequate. And your self cannot help but feel loved, affirmed and energized when it knows you care enough to give it your very best shot.

FACE AND SOLVE PROBLEMS

One of the most dreadful abuses of your self is to keep your self paralyzed in the face of problems that need solving. There are many things we have no control over in life, but there are many problems that can be taken care of, if only we put our minds to it. Our self is abused and tortured by needless worry and denial, but also by our failure to put our problems to rest.

I know people who waste endless hours of time and energy worrying about problems that don't even yet exist. When the problems do come, they are too exhausted to handle them. I know people who spend weeks and months worrying over current problems. All that time and energy would be better spent in simply working on solutions. I know others who spend copious amounts of psychic energy in denial that any problems exist. I know still others who will put up with suffering for years, with an addiction, with a stressful job, with an insufferable marriage, with untreated back pain, with loneliness, with impossible living conditions, etc. For some reason they will not take the necessary steps to bring their problem to a satisfactory conclusion. And in most cases a satisfactory conclusion could be achieved with a little determination and effort.

Every day everyone of us faces problems of varying degrees of severity. No one alive escapes problems. Even isolated people who live imprisoned in their little shells have problems. Problems, however, only become "problems" when we feel we should not have them. When we feel we shouldn't have problems, all our resistance issues come into play. We lose the energy we need to solve problems to the antics of King Baby.

Problems are meant to be dealt with, not resisted or lived with. The very idea of a "problem" is that it is meant to be handled, not empowered to make a mess out of our lives. A problem by nature is an opportunity. Problems become harmful when we sit with them. Problems become dangerous when we react to them with fear, rather than solve them with courage.

One young woman complained to me about how lonely she was. I asked her what she was doing about it. She responded, "What can I do? I'm all alone!"

It is an abuse of your self to wallow in misery, or to sit on the "pity pot" feeling sorry for your self all the time. Your self often needs compassion, but it does not need to be felt sorry for. It needs to feel that you love it enough to ensure that problems are being faced and resolved.

Problems can be handled and resolved only if we believe that we have more power than they do. All of us in self-love recovery have learned to look at problems negatively. They become signs reinforcing our sense of being failures. They are looked at as evidence that we are inadequate. "If I wasn't bad, I wouldn't have so many problems"—which, of course, is nonsense, because, as we have pointed out, everybody has problems. The president has problems. The pope has problems. Mother Teresa has problems. Our favorite "pop" singers and movie stars have problems.

Let me repeat again that problems only become real "problems" when we feel we shouldn't have them, or that we have no ability to handle them. Either premise is false: everyone has problems, and no one gets a problem that he or she cannot handle. As a matter of fact, a problem becomes our problem precisely because we *can* handle it. I have no problem over the operation of the space shuttle because I am not involved in its operation. I have no problem with the weather because I like all kinds of weather and don't feel I need to control it. A problem is only felt by us because it "fits" us.

Once we begin to look at our problems more objectively and positively as opportunities, they will take on a whole new dimension for us in self-love recovery. Once we embrace our problems as growth stimulants and opportunities for growth, they will become stepping stones in self-love practice. Self-esteem is earned by working out our problems, day by day. Self-love is worked on specifically by handling the problems our selves need to face. In self-love recovery we need to see ourselves as being on a "hero's journey," with every step and every problem simply a means to fulfill our quest.

The mind thrives on problems. Problems are exercise for the mind. Problems give the mind a chance to flex its muscle and to access resources. It is a great boost to the self to allow it the experience of problem-solving. Problems test strengths and weaknesses. When we learn our strengths, we have power to live on. That alone is a great feeling for the self. When we learn our weaknesses, we know what to avoid or correct. That again is a great assurance to your self. Solving problems lets the self know it is in trustworthy hands which are willing and able to handle whatever comes along.

Solving problems also allows the self to build up its resources. The self is appreciative of the confidence we place in it to solve what needs to be solved. We feel better and much less threatened. Solving problems on a consistent basis lets your self feel safe and confident to rise up to any occasion. If problems are too big for us at the moment, we take care of our selves by asking for help. If the problems are impossible for us, as some are, we surrender them to our Higher Power. One way or another, however, our self feels the security of knowing that problems will be handled, not ignored, denied, or put up with—which is a very loving affirmative action.

BE DIRECT

People with inadequate self-love tend to be "pussy footers." Full of self-doubt, they feel they have no right to be assertive of what they might need and want. Unsure of themselves, they are often unaware of their real needs. Feeling inadequate and undeserving, they are hesitant to express whatever needs and wants they have. If they do so, they usually do it in a roundabout way.

One way they approach what they need comes out very passively. They may cry, or moan, or look pitiful in the hopes that someone will take notice and come to their assistance. They may talk a lot about their pain and suffering, and what they have to put up with. They hope, above all, that someone will take the initiative and come to their rescue.

Another roundabout way to get what they want is to become inappropriately aggressive. They might show a great degree of rage, or become excessively demanding, or employ an assortment of insults. To all appearances, their aggressiveness may indicate that they are strong, overly confident, and arrogantly self-sufficient. But aggressiveness is normally an indication of a fearful and cornered animal. Feeling the flush of anger is a display of pseudo-strength. And, of course, it doesn't work. Those whose help is needed either are driven away or react defensively to the perceived aggression.

One of the best self-loving actions we can take on our own behalf is simply to be *direct, firm and assertive.* Not making excuses or disclaimers ("I know I shouldn't be so forward, but...") but directly asking for what we need ("I need to hear from you more often"). Not going into a rage over what we aren't getting ("I don't deserve to be treated this way!") but firmly making a request ("I think we need to talk this out"). Not hoping to be noticed in a pitiful condition ("Nobody cares about me") but assertively expressing a feeling ("I feel abandoned when I get spoken to this way").

Self-loving actions are neither passive nor aggressive; they are assertive. We have a right to what we need and even a right to what we want. We may not always get what we need or want, but we certainly have the right to ask for it.

ASK FOR WHAT YOU NEED

It is ironic that people who need something the most are often the least inclined to ask for it. Jesus once made a point by saying, "Only those who ask, receive." Taking care of your self means *asking for what you need, when you need it*. It means taking the initiative of asking rather than assuming that others should know what you need. It means asking rather than sitting and stewing in hopes that someone will notice your plight.

I can appreciate reluctance to ask for what might be an extravagance. I can appreciate reluctance to put other people on the spot. But we are speaking here about a "need." Why are we reluctant to express our needs? Does the need itself so sap the soul that we are rendered incapable of asking? Are we embarrassed to appear "needy" or weak? Were we programmed to believe that other people's needs come first and that our needs are dispensable? Do we fear rejection in our requests? What is it that prevents us from asking for what we need? A wife may need more affection from her husband but is afraid of raising the issue. A student needs extra help in class but is fearful of approaching the teacher. A friend needs the comfort of another friend's presence but is afraid of "imposing." An employee needs arbitration in an office conflict but is reluctant to "bother" the boss. Why is this?

Not loving our selves as we need, we feel making any request for help to be an intrusion and imposition. Our reluctance to ask for what we need is caused by an old tape that tells us we are unworthy of notice and that our needs don't count.

In self-love recovery we need to learn and acknowledge that our physical, intellectual, emotional, social, sexual, and spiritual needs are perfectly legitimate. We need make no excuses for having them. They do count, because we count. They come with the package of who we are and what our

Creator meant us to be. In many respects, we are dependent on others for our needs being answered. "Individuation" and our need for independence in our self-love excludes needing others to assure us of our self-worth, but does not exclude a healthy dependence on others to supply for our legitimate needs. We need make no excuses for our need to ask for what we need.

Even our "wants" and desires are perfectly legitimate. We can feel free to ask for what we would like to have, even if it doesn't qualify as a real need. We may not get what we want, but that does not disqualify us from asking. We may get refused, but that does not mean our asking was invalid or inappropriate.

Our Higher Power promises to give us what we need, but not necessarily what we would like. What we like may not be in our best interests. But even with our Higher Power, we should not be timid about asking for what we want. As long as we are willing to surrender control and submit to our Higher Power's will for us, we can ask for whatever we desire and not feel guilty about it.

Knowing *how* to ask for what we need is important also. Making requests for what we need and want often comes down to an art and a craft. Anger, for example, is identified by many therapists as needs/wants being unexpressed, or being expressed badly. In their book *Self-Esteem,* Matthew McKay and Patrick Fanning offer sensible rules for making a request: keep it small to avoid massive resistance, keep it simple so as to be understood and remembered, don't blame or attack the person you are making a request of, be specific about what you want, don't hedge, but be assertive in a self-confident way (pp. 234-235).

Requests can always be refused, and our knowledge of that may make us hesitant and reluctant to ask for what we need and want. However, our willingness to surrender to the will of our Higher Power prepares us for that. We don't "have to" get what we want. Surrender does not make our requests inappropriate, but saves us from devastation if they are not granted.

People with good self-esteem have little trouble asking for

what they need: advice, a few kind words, a returned phone call, a pat on the back, help in moving, a ride to the store, a loan, time off, consultation with a doctor or an attorney, better care from a landlord, more police protection, better service, etc. I suspect that asking for what they needed helped give them self-esteem in the first place. When the self realizes that provisions are being made for its needs, it knows it is cared for and loved.

AFFIRM YOUR SELF

One of the most self-loving actions we can take on our behalf is the practice of affirming our selves and learning to graciously accept affirmations from others.

Starting with the latter, many of us in self-love recovery know how difficult it is for us to accept compliments graciously. Getting an affirmation makes us tongue-tied, uncomfortable, and deflective. Receiving a commendation may even make us embarrassed and ashamed. "Oh, it was nothing," we say, when we may have broken our backs to do what we did. Blood rushes to our faces and we attempt to change the subject.

Why do we do this? Why is it so difficult to accept applause? Why do we shut down in front of the very caring affirmations we need and want? What is happening is that an old tape, our "pathological critic," becomes accessed and tells us that we are really no good, inadequate, "show offs," prideful, fooling ourselves to think we have done something admirable. The old tape plays louder than the new tape. The compliment confronts the old tape and loses.

Affirming your self means deliberately replacing the self-defeatist tape with one that allows you to embrace compliments you receive from others. Affirming your self means that you deliberately stop automatically reacting with a disclaimer.

Accept the compliment. Say "thank you." Eliminate any self-disparaging commentary. Take the compliment into your heart and relish it. Tell your self that it deserves the compliments you get. Few of them will ever be exaggerations. And what does it matter if someone is trying to "butter you up"? Your unconscious won't know the difference. As it gathers more and more compliments, as you continue to lift the restrictions, it will feel better and better about itself and begin to take affirmations in stride.

The other side of the coin is to give your self affirmations. A friend told me that her recovery from depression accelerated when she accepted a suggestion from her therapist that three times a day, morning, noon, and night, she was to find one thing she could compliment herself on. Sometimes it was as simple as "How well you wash dishes," or "How nicely you handled that." When we have spent a lifetime hearing put-downs, it does us good to balance our selves out with self-affirmations. We need to balance the scales of self-appraisal. You matter, and everything you do matters. You count, and everything you do counts. There is much for you to be complimented on.

Never discount the power of affirmations. Melody Beattie, in her book *Beyond Codependency*, calls affirmations the "most important recovery tool we can embrace" (p. 125). "Affirmations are how we charge our battery...how we change the rules, change the messages, deal with shame, and travel the road from deprived to deserving." For Melody Beattie, "affirmations aren't optional...they are the core of recovery work" (p. 126). Affirmations are ways we "empower" ourselves to love our selves as we need. (We will give special attention to self-affirmations in Chapter Eleven.)

It does not matter how insignificant you might think the action is—affirm your self. Bombard your self with compliments. Tell your self how much you love it, many times a day. Look in the mirror and make it more personal. Tell your self what a good job you do in driving, taking care of your appearance, keeping the house in shape, paying your bills on time, answering phone messages, getting your work done neatly, keeping your language decent, performing some service for your church or local charity, etc.

A friend of mine has little Post-It stickers on her bathroom mirror, the refrigerator, and her night table which say: "Hey, good-looking!" "You are good!" "You look great, kid!" It works because they keep her positive about her self. We never tire of hearing how lovable we are. Affirmations are one of the most loving actions we can perform for our selves.

STAND UP FOR YOUR SELF

I recall a day in the sixth grade when I was being badgered by a couple of eighth grade bullies on the school playground. Just when the going was about to get rough, another eighth grade boy stepped in and took my side. I have forgotten his name, but in all these years I have never forgotten how great it felt to have him stand up for me.

It is often said that we are our own worst enemies. The reason this is said is because we so often treat our selves so badly. Almost daily we confirm old tapes that tell us we are not worthy. We not only don't stand up for our selves; we often play a major role in putting our selves down. We murder our selves a little bit more each time we let our selves be bullied, or, worse, each time we bully our selves.

A new restaurant has opened close to the residential area where Helen lives. The restaurant has little parking of its own, so customers take the liberty of parking on the side streets where she lives. Helen is resentful every day that she can never get a parking place right outside her own home. A call to the alderman could set things in motion to get "residential parking only" signs posted on her block. But Helen can't imagine calling up her alderman. "Who am I?" she argues, "He would just think I was a crank."

Helen has never stood up for her rights. She has never defended her self. She apologizes when a waitress spills coffee on the sleeve of her new dress. She has never been able to ask for a raise. When a benevolent new boss took over her company and doubled her salary, he said she should have been getting a doubled salary years ago. She simply could never ask. When her husband divorced her, she received a fraction of what was owed to her because she refused to allow her attorney to fight for more. Helen was well taken care of physically as a child, but her parents were never there for her emotionally. She never felt loved enough. To this day she honestly believes she doesn't count.

Your self cannot help but feel loved when you take its side. Show love for your self by standing up for your self. Refuse access to that old tape that tells you that you really don't matter. Defend your self from those who would abuse you or make you dependent on their good will. Don't pay the price of self-abuse. Hold your self in positive regard. Protect that self. Let it know that you intend to stand up for it, no matter what. You are its champion. You are its lawyer, advocate, counselor, guide, manager, and coach, all wrapped up in one. You will never let that self be damaged, bullied, or abused. You will stand up for its rights and never allow it to be taken advantage of.

BE ALL YOU CAN BE

I get a significant lift from reading biographies and anecdotes of people who, despite handicaps or extraordinary limitations, made great successes of themselves. Some grew up in the worst of living conditions, some never completed formal schooling, some had extreme physical handicaps, and yet they made significant contributions of themselves to the improvement of society. What this proves is that we are all born with enormous potential—a potential which, because of our negative mind-sets, we might never look at.

Robert Schuller, pastor of California's Crystal Cathedral, entitles his popular Sunday service television program: "Hour of Power." Dr. Schuller promotes an affirming brand of Christianity urging listeners to become all that they can be. Dr. Wayne Dyer entitled one of his many best selling books *The Sky Is the Limit*. The title says it all in Dr. Dyer's observation that most of us sell ourselves terribly short on our possibilities.

Being all that we can be means that we develop our selves to their fullest potential. All of us have the potential to become towering evergreens, and yet, because of our unconfronted tapes and self-defeating mind-sets, we most often settle for being bonsai dwarfs.

Self-love is bringing our selves into more and more be-ing. In self-love recovery, we show love for our selves by urging them to their limits. You cannot help but love a self that is on an upswing. You cannot do your self a bigger favor than to commit your self to its highest and broadest potential. You cannot help but be proud of a self that is unfolding and blossoming under your benevolent, nurturing, and conscientious direction.

On the other hand, we cannot be proud of a self that we keep "under wraps." Our old tapes keep us trapped in negative mind-sets. They keep us stuck in prejudices and out-dated values. They keep us narrow, petty, and "small."

Whether we think about it or not, we are changing all the time. If we do not consciously direct that change for the better, we are likely changing for the worse. If we are not swimming, rest assured we are sinking little by little. "Not to advance is to retreat" is proven every day by people who have given up on making anything out of themselves.

Being all you can be therefore means being committed to *expanding* your self. It means getting out of the isolation of a small restrictive world and becoming part of the bigger world at-large. It means getting out of self-absorption and egocentricity. It means stretching your boundaries to new sights and new sounds, new relationships, new experiences, new cultural and educational opportunities, new foods, new forms of recreation and entertainment.

The more you extend the boundaries of what you are "at home" with, the less your self has to be afraid of. Perhaps in time you might even again achieve the ecstatic "one-ness with all that is," which deep in your soul you still remember from early babyhood. M. Scott Peck in *The Road Less Traveled* speaks about the "gradual but progressive enlargement of the self." He sees this enlargement as a stretching and a thinning of our ego boundaries until the distinction between the self and the world becomes blurred, and we become identified with the world. He calls this identification a "mystical union" (p. 95). When the self has expanded to feel "at one" with the world, its fears can turn into an ecstasy of union.

DISCOVER YOUR SELF

Being who you are, of course, is impossible if you do not know who you are. Many of us travel through life unaware of who we are. As we saw previously, many of us don't give our selves much thought. We become so immersed in everything and everybody else that we never have taken the time to discover our selves. Consequently, in self-love recovery, we need to be open to self-discovery. We need to be aware of what makes us unique. We need to be aware of what makes us tick.

We already have seen how significantly our lives could change as we come to identify with how our loving Higher Power looks upon us, as infinitely lovable. Life would change significantly for us if we could accept in our hearts that we are beloved in the eyes of a loving Creator. Millions of people over the ages have had their lives transformed, and have come to love themselves, by the recognition and embracing of this universal truth.

But we can also discover many things about our selves by reflectively watching our selves in operation from day to day. We all have our unique ways of handling life. We think and behave in ways that are uniquely our own, and we have every right to be that way. We have our own way of talking and presenting our viewpoints. We have our own obsessions and preoccupations. We have things that bother us and ways we bother other people. All these behavioral patterns reveal something about us.

It can be fun observing our selves in action. Spend a week in self-observation. Play science researcher and write down your observations. Don't judge or criticize your self. Simply observe, and record your observations. Record your thoughts and reactions in a variety of situations. What makes you happy? What makes you sad? What puts you in a good mood and what turns you sour? Itemize your good moments and your bad moments. Record your impulses, your feelings, what triggers off your emotions. A week of playing detective with your self should reveal quite a bit of biographical material about your self. Upon review, many things about your self may be pleasant surprises.

We can also discover a lot about our selves by exploring what we want out of life. We might ask ourselves pointed and self-revealing questions: What do you want out of life? What are your goals and ambitions? What do you have to offer life? How would you like to be remembered? What accomplishment would give you a sense of fulfillment that your life has been worthwhile? What are the times when you are "at your best"?

Self-discovery is self-loving activity because, coming to know our selves better, we know what to affirm or what to change about our selves. Self-discovery leads to other loving actions on our behalf.

DEFINE YOUR SELF

Being who you are means not only discovering more about your self, but that you take the initiative to define yourself. You determine who and what you are and who and what you will be. You do not swallow definitions of yourself suggested or imposed by family, friends, superiors, or much less, enemies.

Definitions of our selves most often come about from the expectations of others and from the "labeling" others impose on us. (Think of the nicknames you may have been given.) Definitions given to us by others are most often impositions rather than accurate descriptions. People normally see us the way they want to see us, irrespective of who and what we really are. They impose "labels" on us and anticipate that we will wear those labels without question. Many of us go through life without questioning or challenging hundreds of labels that have been pasted on us without our full knowledge or consent. In a self-defeating manner we live by those labels rather than by who and what we really are.

Others, even those near and dear to you, may not like you to be your self. They may prefer to deal with the image they have, or want, of you. You might inconvenience their agendas by not conforming to that image. Some may not like you as you progress through self-love recovery. They might have to work to readjust to a more honest you. You might discover that friends will leave you because they are not growing themselves and wish to remain attached to the "old" you.

But that is their problem, not yours. You continue to do your self honor by refusing to accept any label or definition of your self that is not of your own determination. You honor your self by living up to your own expectations. You do not accept labels of your self offered by authority figures, acquaintances, or co-workers. If there is a label to be given to your self, you, and you alone, will bestow the honor.

Self-definition is a spiritual exercise that answers four basic questions: Who am I? Where do I come from? What am I doing here? Where am I going? Self-definition is acquired when you determine what counts for you in life and what doesn't count, what matters and what doesn't. Self-definition is acquired when you abandon haphazard living and become "grounded" in something solid, when you abandon aimless wandering through life and establish some clear directions for your self.

One of the greatest gifts you can give to your self is definition and direction. A self which lives at the mercy of the definitions and directions of others will always live insecure and afraid. Defining your self will set up perimeters and parameters to assure your self's safety. Self-love is always self-defining.

DETERMINE YOUR PERCEPTIONS

One of the biggest illusions we can live by is that "reality" is something substantive and objective and that somehow we can understand and get a hold on it. In that illusion we believe with the beverage commercial that there is "the real thing" and that we can get our hands on it.

In truth, "reality" is the most nebulous and porous idea in the world. In truth, we do not live in, or by, reality; we live in, and by, our *perceptions.*

We see what we want to see and we hear what we want to hear. There is never a "grip on reality"; there are only perceptions. Our perceptions create "reality" for us. I create mine and you create yours. Everyone creates his or her own. It is absolutely remarkable that for all our uniqueness, there are times when our perceptions actually coincide. It is at those times that we presume we are in touch with reality together. But it is only that our perceptions are temporarily in sync.

With the use of our five senses we make our perceptions. Our minds further interpret those perceptions with their own filtering processes. This is why it is so difficult for us human beings to ever get to "the truth." Our senses can easily be impaired and our mental processes are rarely up to par. That is why twelve people can look at an accident and tell twelve different stories of what "really" happened. We don't know "reality," we only know our perceptions. We don't know how things "really" are, we only know how we represent them.

One thing for sure, therefore: *perceptions are relative.* What we hate today we may love tomorrow. What turned us off yesterday may be turning us on today. Clarification from a sympathetic advisor can help us see things in a new way. "Yes, I see!" Greater awareness and self-consciousness may help us "see the light." We are forever "waking up to reality" and forgetting that present "realities" are little more than new perceptions.

In self-love recovery we need to critically examine our perceptions. We need to stop pretending and experiencing our perceptions as "reality." We need to acknowledge that perceptions are relative and that in any experience we can determine our perceptions to fit our needs. We can determine whether a half glass of water is half full or half empty.

We do our selves a terrible disservice by limiting our perceptions to what is negative and self-defeating. If perceptions are relative and conditional, we can just as easily look at what is positive and uplifting. If I am stopped for a traffic violation I can get angry at myself and frustrated with the policeman or I can acknowledge that safety in driving is important to my self's security. Getting stopped for speeding could well give me a message that could save my life. I can be grateful for the citation.

We do have manage-ability over our perceptions. We can see what we want to see. We do it all the time anyway. If this is so, why not show love for your self by perceiving and representing "reality" to your self in a more self-empowering way. Why not chose the positive? If your perceptions are relative, why not choose a perception that will pick you up rather than put you down?

Self-loving people see "problems" as stepping stones. They see "failure" as a temporary set-back. They see "illness" as a time to recoup. They look at strangers and see potential friends. They look into the dark sky and see stars. They look at clouds and see silver linings.

Self-love is adopting perceptions and representations of "reality" to serve our best interests.

LIVE OFF YOUR ASSETS

Taking the initiative to define our selves and making a conscious effort to adopt perceptions that are more conducive to self-love prompts us to question whether we live off our assets or our limitations.

Taking care of your self means *living off your assets* rather than off your deficits, or limitations. Again, it's all a matter of *focus*. There a very few things over which we have any control, but we do have manage-ability over our focus. We can choose, and do choose, to see what we want to see. To enlist an example already given, we can look up at a dark sky and see the darkness or we can see the stars.

When we do not love our selves adequately, we generally live off the tapes that, one way or another, continue to defeat us and our best interests. Our old tapes are usually negative and down-playing. They tell us we are untalented or that our talents don't count. We have believed these tapes so long that we may be grossly unaware of what talents for self-care we do possess. Self-love recovery encourages us to search out our talents and to focus on our assets. If we want to develop "blind-spots," let them be over our pathological critic.

It is helpful to realize that assets exist; limitations technically don't. Assets are part of us, whereas deficits aren't. Assets are powers we possess. A "deficit" is an abstraction for something we *don't* have. Technically, even though we frequently speak about them, we can't actually "possess" a deficit. That is why living off negative tapes is so fruitless and makes us feel so "empty." Living off the down-playing messages of our negative programming is like trying to breathe in a vacuum. Constantly focusing on limitations is wasting energy in a hopeless attempt to give them a reality which in fact they do not possess. And our minds witlessly accommodate our focus. They automatically put us in a slump to match the "vacuum" of the focused deficit.

This is not to deny that we are indeed limited by our limitations. Jumping off a cliff and thinking I can fly will quickly make me clear about that. The key word here again is "focus." In self-love recovery we deliberately and consistently focus on what is: our assets; not on what isn't: our deficits. We empower what is helpful and not what is self-defeating.

INVEST IN YOUR LIFE

"Being all you can be" implies being invested in your life, being invested in *living* your life. Investment in life means living in a way that is *vital*.

The late Joseph Campbell, who was an expert on the great myths of humanity, concluded that people don't so much crave "meaning" in life as they hunger after *vitality*. According to

Campbell we all hunger for a simple *experience of being alive.*
What we seek most is an experience of the rapture of living.

Boredom is the great enemy of vitality. Boredom is an
indication of the absence of vitality. Boredom is our Higher
Power's way of telling us that we should be on the move.
Boredom is an indictment that we are not using our talents and
are living off our assets. Boredom is a warning that we are stuck
in a rut. A great disservice we do to our selves is to condemn
them to a life without vitality.

We can only experience our life as being vital by keeping it
in dynamic motion and growth, by rising in greater awareness
and consciousness, by expanding our horizons and opening our
selves to new experiences. As we will shortly see, experiencing
our life as vital will necessitate taking some risks.

A vital life gives the self a sensation of living. A "vital" life
will conclude: "I've lived a full life...I've done my best with all I
had!"

INVOLVE YOUR SELF

"Getting involved" is giving your self a vote of confidence
that it is fit to become invested in the lives of others. Getting
involved is giving your self a vote of confidence that it is fit to
become invested in the broader interests and needs of society.
Self-loving people love other people. Self-loving people readily
devote themselves to humanitarian causes.

"Being involved" rests on an acknowledgement that all of
us as human beings are threads in one fabric. We are all part of
each other. Our destiny is held in common. What affects one
affects all. The prayer of the Hindu mystic affects the cabdriver
in Manhattan. The death of an AIDS patient in Iowa City
affects the CEO of a firm in Japan.

Being involved means working to bring others to spiritual
advancement. Being involved means building the self-esteem
and self-love of others with your care, affirmations, and nurtur-

ing. Being involved means challenging them to accompany you on the road to greater self-love.

Many people in self-love recovery find that doing "for others" is one of the best ways of doing for themselves. There comes a time when inner work "shows." Success in developing self-love can be multiplied a hundred-fold when we use that success to make others successful in self-love. It is part of human nature to share. I have written this book because I wanted to share the principles and practices that are so helpful in my own self-love recovery.

Involvement and sharing with others is a natural impulse. We want someone with us to view a magnificent sunset. We want someone with us to share a painful loss or let-down. Self-esteem and self-love are built in sharing joys and sorrows. That is part of the success story of the Twelve-Step movement. Self-esteem and self-love grow in the acknowledgement, compliments, appreciation, and gratitude we give and receive. We always enjoy being on the receiving end, but our selves also take great pleasure in feeling useful and needed. "Getting involved" may mean work, but it will also mean significant gratification to our selves.

RISK YOUR SELF

Taking risks with our selves is an affirmative action that follows from the principles of believing in our selves and being all that we can be. Risking our selves appropriately is a self-loving action we take on our behalf. Most people who love themselves adequately have little problem with taking risks to achieve their goals and ambitions. Risks are considered obvious and unavoidable stepping stones to growth and development.

Risk-taking is not so easy for those of us in self-love recovery. Risk-taking, daring to do something new, can be very threatening. Risk-taking involves change, and change does not come easy to those who feel inadequate, worthless, or insecure.

Even our willingness to surrender to our Higher Power can feel risky.

All change and growth, however, involves taking risks and daring to do something new. We have learned that the most difficult thing we can do for our selves is to change. Our internal system is programmed to prevent new tapes from entering. Fear is what the program uses to bar access. Fear of change, therefore, is understandable. Fear of risk-taking is predictable. Nevertheless, in self-love recovery changes need to be made, risks need to be taken, and fear needs to be confronted with courage.

It might be helpful to understand something about the psychology of fear and change. Fear of change and fear of risk is not so much about what might be awaiting us in the future, but about losing something with which we are familiar in the present. Fear of risk and change is actually fear about losing something we have now. We don't want to disassociate our selves from what has become habitual. Ironically, it is in this sense that we don't want to part with what is harming or hurting us. Even our miseries become familiar companions.

Change also makes us feel as though something is dying in us. And something does die in us when we change. That is what the discomfort and pain in change is all about. The old must die for something new to be born. This is the story of life. Spring follows winter. Dying to give birth to something new is the rhythm of the natural world.

But few of us are comfortable with the natural world and its paradigm of change. We spend most of our lives chasing after guarantees, predictability, and security. We want control. We feel safe with what's familiar. Real life, however, is fairly unstable, unpredictable, and insecure. Real life is a series of endings and new beginnings.

We are not being encouraged to be foolhardy and jump into a pool without seeing if there is water in it, but we are encouraged to confront and overcome our desire for immoderate security in what is a very insecure world. In reality things are changing all the time, and to "be real" we need to change all the time too.

One of the most common sayings recorded of Jesus is, "Do not be afraid." Accepting the teachings of Jesus at face value called for significant life changes for his followers. His disciples were called upon literally to live a new life. For Jesus, change meant "dying to one's self," which was potentially a very fearful thing to do. "Do not be afraid," in the face of this kind of radical change, needed to be heard often.

"Do not be afraid" is a message we also need to give to our selves often. Life is risky business. But we need not be afraid, because our Higher Power will never ask us to change more than we are capable of handling. We will not try to force our selves to change what cannot be changed. We will not risk something for which we are not yet ready. That would not be taking care of our selves.

Taking risks will not destroy us. A butterfly is not destroyed by leaving its cocoon. It is transformed to a new and better life. In coming to love our selves, we are entering a new and better life for ourselves. We need not be afraid. And if we are afraid, we need to prime our selves with courage. In self-love recovery, courage is not an absence of fear; courage is doing what we need to do in spite of fear.

Our fear of risk and change can also be tempered by being *cautious.* Caution means that we take appropriate measures for our safety, both physical and psychological. A little child will run around boldly, and fearlessly explore new sights, as long as mother is somewhere nearby. He may climb on the sofa for the first time and enjoy the strength he feels in his arms and legs, but from the side of his eye he is aware of his mother's presence. Now and then he will run to mother for assurance that she is still there. A little child needs to feel safe.

We always need to feel safe. Survival is our primary instinct. We need our safety nets. We will rarely take risks that could jeopardize our lives. We will step forward only if we are assured that we can step back if we feel ourselves falling. Our need for safety and security has kept us out of many dangerous situations.

But it may have kept us out of many opportune situations also. While respecting our need for safety, we still need to take care of our selves and continue to grow into our fullest potential. As we have already indicated, that will involve change and risk-taking. We need therefore to have the best of both worlds: to be safe, and to able to take risks. Using caution and courage, we achieve both these goals.

It is not only fear, however, that prevents us from taking the risks we need. Marsha Sinetar, in *Do What You Love, The Money Will Follow*, reminds us again of the power of "the big R": resistance. In describing the patterns of unsuccessful and unfulfilled people, she says: "They prefer comfort over challenge, safety over growth, invisibility over visibility. The ideal set of circumstances for such persons is a womb-like environment: warm, safe, secure, with all their needs met. They avoid confrontation and risk at all costs. Thus, professionally and personally, they back away from what would help them become more useful to themselves and others."

We need to understand, therefore, that risk avoidance does not stem from risks themselves, but from a resisting mind-set which prefers to keep us in the "womb." It's the tapes, not the risks themselves, which frighten us off. Taking the risks we need for our self-love improvement will not only take courage, but a conscious resistance to our own resistance.

I was delighted this past weekend to see a sixty-two year old grandmother, who had never ridden a bike before in her life, screaming in delight as she learned to ride for the first time. It took a lot of courage and effort, but after she achieved her balance and got control over her motion, you could not get her off the bicycle. She conquered her fear of risking (falling and looking silly), and resisted her resistance to try something new.

Appropriate risking of our selves is a self-loving action. It can bring our selves to a better life. All of us in self-love recovery need to take some risks, to dare to do something new and out of our ordinary. All of us can experiment with some new behaviors in safe, little steps.

Geraldine had a self-effacing habit of saying "I'm sorry" a hundred times at day. It was more than asking for forgiveness or being exceptionally polite; Gerry felt that her whole life was an imposition on others. Her old tapes told her that, at best, she could only be in someone's way. She apologized, automatically, for anything and everything. She apologized when someone bumped into her, or walked in front of her, or pushed past her to get a better place in the grocery line. She agreed to experiment for one week with not saying she was sorry at all. This change in behavior made her very uncomfortable at the beginning. She almost had to bite her tongue at times. However, just performing this experiment with her self helped her become more aware of how self-put-downing she was. Not apologizing anymore felt risky, but it gave her a new handle on life, and new appreciation of her self.

BE GENTLE WITH YOUR SELF

One way to insure caution and the need to feel safe is to *be gentle with your self*. Treat your self kindly and lovingly. Your self does not need to be threatened or scared into action. It does not need to be abused by severe discipline. It does not need to be scolded or shamed. Treat your self gently. Your self will only respond to gentle coaching. When it feels threatened or abused, it is likely to withdraw into its shell. It is likely to regress into old and self-defeating behavior as a means of self-protection.

Be gentle with your self by *treating your self with compassion*. Compassion is like love: it is not a feeling, it is something we do for our selves. Compassion in self-love recovery often requires a whole new mind-set for us who have not loved our selves as we need. Compassion often requires a whole new attitude of how we understand our selves, of how we accept our selves, and of how we forgive our selves. No judgments. No harsh words. No stringent demands. No persecution. No put-downs.

You are basically a wonderful person, faults and all. You generally strive to do your best with what you have, just like everyone else. So take it easy on your self. Take affirmative actions on your behalf, but do them with the calm and forbearance that are indicative of your willingness to surrender. Be leery of any obsessive behavior, no matter how noble it appears. Forgive your self for your sins, mistakes, and failings. In time you will rise above them. Let go of the past.

Be gentle with your self by *respecting your timing*. Give your self time. Timing is very important in self-love recovery. It has taken us years upon years to come to where we are at this point of our lives. Change for the better will not come about with a moment's decision. We cannot change by simply "wanting" to. We cannot change our selves by "trying harder."

In self-love recovery we are attempting to radically change fundamental attitudes and behaviors. This is not impossible, but it is a monumental task of transformation for most of us. It will take time for us to acclimate our selves to a new world view and a new self-evaluation. Self-love recovery takes practice, practice, and still more practice of the affirmative actions we are outlining here. Self-love recovery takes time, persistence, and perseverance. Habits are difficult to change and replace. There is no "quick fix." Every day, in "baby steps," we make progress, and affirm our selves every step of the way.

Our motto in self-love recovery is *"one day at a time."* Do not add more anxiety to your life with impatience. One step at a time. If you fall down, you pick your self up and start again, with no self-chastisement or self-recrimination. Recovering the love you need for your self is a life-long task. Be content to be "in recovery." At times you will make great strides; other times you will regress. Accept that. Do not badger your self. It has been hurt enough. Be gentle with your self by recognizing your need both to feel safe, and to grow at your own pace.

A friend of mine decided to give up smoking, as a way of enhancing his self-respect. Over a course of two months he broke his resolution twice with one cigarette each time. In the fourth month, he broke his resolution with his third cigarette, and with that breakdown he decided that he had "no will power at all," and went back to smoking again. He berated himself mercilessly for being so weak and became quite depressed over the whole matter. What he needed was not more will power but more gentleness with his self. A life-long habit was not going to be broken with one act of the will. He needed to keep his resolve, but give his self all the time it needed.

ACCEPT YOUR FEELINGS

As we have already indicated, all of us commonly authenticate reality with our feelings. We validate reality with the way we feel. What is true must feel true. What is good and valuable must feel good and valuable. We identify authenticity with our feelings. In self-love recovery, however, we learn that, while feelings are perfectly legitimate in their own right, they are very unreliable norms of what is right and wrong, true or false.

Feelings can block the truth as well as present it. I may feel like striking out at you in anger, but that does not make it all right to do so. We need to learn that what is "authentic" is what will stand up on its own as true, good, or valuable, independent of our feelings. Love is proven by actions, not by feelings. I show love for my self by doing something beneficial on my behalf, whether I feel like doing it or not. As a matter of fact, some of the most loving actions we can perform for our selves will likely happen when we don't feel very good about our selves at all.

This is not to discount the importance of feelings, however. There is no question that we live in our feelings. There is no question that many psychological difficulties are experienced by people who deny their feelings or cannot express them appropriately. There is no question that feelings give zest and excitement to life. We would be bored to death without our feelings. Loving our selves means that we permit our selves to have our feelings, whatever those feelings might be. Loving our selves means that we accept our feelings as perfectly legitimate, whether they are good feelings or whether they are bad feel-ings. Feelings simply are.

We actively accept our feelings by *naming* them. Naming a feeling allows it to surface fully. Naming a feeling limits its chances of being suppressed in our unconscious where it can do us damage. Naming a feeling can also take away its negative edge, if it has one. When we feel angry, it is important that we are able to say, "I feel angry!" When we are upset, it is impor-tant that we are able to say, "I feel upset!" All our feelings should be able to surface in a simple declarative sentence: "I feel sad," "I feel let down," "I feel depressed," "I feel frustrat-ed," "I feel unappreciated," etc. Naming the feeling allows us to take ownership of it, and disallows the feeling from taking own-ership of us.

Feelings need to be accepted as symbols of our selves. We can learn a lot about our selves and our needs by observing our feelings as they arise in any given moment. Feelings give us insight on what make us "tick." Feelings tell us what we need to do to take care of our selves.

Again, as we have seen previously, feelings themselves are neither moral nor immoral. Feelings of themselves are neutral. Feelings need not be hidden or despised. No feelings are "shameful." And yet I have often heard people express shame and self-disdain for "despicable feelings." "I can't believe I feel this way!" they might say. "I can't believe I got so angry." "It's awful the way I feel." "I can't believe I got a feeling like that in church."

There is no need for such self-abusing reactions. Feelings may be passionate, but all feelings are basically neutral; they simply are. We may need to be cautious about the way we express or act out our feelings, but we have no need to apolo-gize for them. Acknowledging and accepting our feelings, with-out judging our selves or putting our selves down because of them, is a way of showing love for our selves.

As we learn to allow and accept our feelings, we can also learn to use them as an important source of energy in our self-love recovery program. Feelings can provide the horsepower necessary to get our inner work into practice. Success builds on success. The good feelings that accompany success motivate us to go after more. Think of how much easier it is to perform a difficult task when we are flooded with feelings of enthusiasm. Feelings used to advance self-loving actions on our behalf can be used for all they're worth. Even anger, impatience, boredom, resentment, sadness, and fear can provide us with the stimulus and energy we need to take care of our selves. The important word here is "used." We use our feelings, we do not allow them to use us. We own our feelings; they do not own us. We do not work for our feelings; they work for us. Feelings are our servants. We use their services on our behalf.

TREAT YOUR SELF SPECIAL

Loving our selves means *treating* our selves as if they were special. We treat our selves as special simply because to us they are. Treating our selves as special is no different from treating someone we love very much as special or treating something we treasure very specially. Couples very much in love will often tell each other, "I would do *anything* for you."

I once had a neighbor who absolutely treasured his vintage car. I have never seen anyone handle an object more lovingly. He kept it in a garage, under a large comforter no less. He washed and waxed it every week. The engine under the hood was spotless. He ran a water line to the garage and had the garage heated so he could wash it even in mid-winter. He literally beamed when he received compliments on the car's classic lines and upkeep. He was a shy young man and didn't seem to have any friends to take riding in his "pride and joy." I often wondered if he loved himself as much as he loved that car. I wondered how his life might be different if treated his self as specially as he treated his automobile.

Treating your self as special means *rewarding your self*. Compliment your self when you've done something well. Give your self a treat now and then. Buy your self a gift—not something you need, but something a little extravagant. Pamper your self a little. Take a bubble bath. Send your self flowers. Take your self on that vacation you have been talking about for years. Get your self a new set of clothes. Try a body massage. Get a year's subscription to the local opera. Get your hair done professionally. Go to a fancy restaurant. Try snow-skiing. Do something just for fun.

I am not advocating materialism or excessiveness. We do what we can afford. The point is that people who have little self-love rarely, if ever, treat themselves as special in the first place. Habitual extravagance or "going to extremes" will not likely be their issue, unless they are dependent on possessions to artificially bolster their self-images. The self feels loved when it is treated as special, and this just might mean going to a little extreme now and then.

When adequate love is felt by the self, it will have no need of "extremes." But in the beginning of our self-love recovery, we may need to go a bit overboard to show our selves that they are special to us. We do this because everything we do makes an impression on our selves. The self at the unconscious level notices everything we do. When you do something special for your self, even in some small token ways, it is picked up by your unconscious. Your self feels affirmed, worthy, maybe even flattered that you would care enough to give it special treatment. Self-love often comes in many such roundabout ways.

ENJOY YOUR SUCCESSES

I have served and ministered in highly affluent communities, where residents seem to have all that one's heart could desire: beautiful and well-furnished homes, spacious grounds, luxury cars and boats, extraordinary vacation opportunities, and country club memberships. And yet I would regularly run into people who were terribly unhappy and unable to enjoy the fruits of "success." In counseling sessions, it quickly became apparent that the inability to enjoy affluence stemmed from a self-perception that they did not "deserve" to be where they were, or to enjoy what they had.

If we do not love our selves enough, we tend to believe that we do not deserve *anything*. We cannot feel successful because in the depths of our being we feel unworthy of the good things that life has to offer. If we feel basically unworthy, no matter how little or how much of the world's largess we possess, we will not feel we are deserving. Happiness or unhappiness does not stem from having or not having possessions, but from whether or not we love our selves as we need.

We take steps in our favor and show our selves the love they need by rejecting the old tapes that tell us we are unworthy and undeserving. We reject the old tapes that tell us we shouldn't have good things in life. We reject the old tapes that tell us we shouldn't be successful. Quite the contrary we show love for our selves by deliberately enjoying the fruits of our work and industry. Our Higher Power has made us for abundance. Our natural desires are infinite. It gives joy to our Higher Power to see us enjoying the good things we possess.

We also work on our self-love by rejecting the old tapes that would hint that by having what we have, we are *depriving* others who are not as fortunate as we. Some of us may have been raised not to leave food on our plates, or not to enjoy eating too much, because "there are children starving all over the world." We cannot take personal responsibility for what others don't have. We cannot take personal responsibility for the lack of industry in others. We cannot take personal responsibility that our Higher Power has other plans for other people. I am not discounting the importance of compassion and sharing, but our enjoyment of what we have is not a deliberate act of depriving anyone.

Enjoying the merits of our industry does not mean that we "cling" to our successes and possessions. "Clinging" is a sign of desperation, not self-love. Clinging is evidence that we have not surrendered control as we need in self-love recovery. Life could take away our health and wealth in a moment's notice. It happens all the time. If we have identified with our possessions, we risk self-destruction when they are lost or diminished. We enjoy what we have when we have it and are grateful to our Higher Power for all that we enjoy. If it is meant to be lost, we give it up freely. It was all part of a gift to begin with.

Gratitude for the gifts we enjoy actually prompts us to share with others. Generosity is an indication of progress in self-love recovery. When we share our talents to help others in their self-love recovery, when we share of our means to relieve the needs of those poorer than we, when we reach out to help build a better society, we are extending our selves beyond the confines of our individuality. Better, we are extending our individuality to become more and more inclusive of the larger world of which we are a part.

PRESENT YOUR SELF APPROPRIATELY

Taking care of your self means *presenting your self appropriately*. We are affected and easily hurt by the reactions of others. Often we unwittingly and unnecessarily cause our selves grief by not being sufficiently aware, and taking into account, how our actions impact others.

Taking care of our selves means we love our selves enough to present our selves in their best light. Taking care of our selves means we love our selves enough to be sensitive and caring for the feelings of others. We will neither take offense nor give it.

TAKE CARE OF YOUR HEALTH

Studies have been made proving the devastating effects of poor nutrition. Inadequate nutrition has even been linked to a variety of personal and social disorders, including delinquent behavior. Proper health care may seem obvious, but it is surprising how poorly people lacking adequate self-love take care of their health. Not loving themselves enough, they don't seem to care.

Taking care of your self means that you take a *vigilant* attitude toward your health. Vigilance includes proper nutrition and diet. An old adage states that "you are what you eat." That should scare us into vigilance. Eat junk food and you will feel like junk. The book market is replete with information and programs for proper nutrition. Read them and beware what you put into your mouth. Vigilance also includes exercise, regular medical check-ups, dental care, time-off for vacations and recreation, etc. The market is equally full of data on these topics.

As self-loving people, we will not put our selves at risk for illness and disease. We will not work our selves to death. We will guard our emotional lives by avoiding toxic people and relationships. We will modify stress by not exposing our selves to unnecessary stressful situations. We will learn to have fun.

ALLOW YOUR SELF FREEDOM

In our American culture, "freedom" is most often understood as the ability to do whatever you want to do, whenever you want to do it. This kind of "freedom" is the favorite theme of King and Queen Baby. Nothing, however, is guaranteed to bring more chaos, frustration, and misery into our lives than unrestricted "freedom" of this type. The reason should be obvious. If everybody in our highly populated world did whatever he or she wanted to do, whenever he or she wanted to do it, we would destroy one another.

In self-love recovery, we define "freedom" as *having the wherewithal to do what we need to do to love our selves adequately and appropriately*. Freedom is being able to do what we need to do to love our selves as we need.

All good psychotherapy is empowerment to seize and utilize freedom. "Recovery" is learning to be truly free. There is great freedom in being rid of the handicaps of our self-negating tapes. There is great freedom in being able to use our feelings as our servants rather than be subject to their unstable domination. There is great freedom to be able to work on our own initiative, in our own behalf, and not be subject to the mercy, whims, and opinions of others. There is great freedom in not having to rely on public opinion of what's "best" for us. There is great freedom in setting up and maintaining our personal boundaries. There is great freedom in the refusal to be a "victim." There is great freedom in owning our selves, being our own person, and taking responsibility for bringing our selves into fuller being.

There is no greater freedom than "surrender" of our lives into the hands of a Higher Power. There is no greater freedom from fear and anxiety than conscious surrender of "control." There is no greater freedom from insecurity than not needing security anymore. There is no greater freedom from the uncertainties of life than surrender to life's fundamental ambiguity.

There is no greater freedom than independence from "logic" to solve all life's problems. There is no greater freedom than trust in our unconscious and "irrational" forces.

There is no greater freedom than being able to love our selves as we need.

GIVE YOUR SELF WORK YOU LOVE

One of the most tenacious dogmas of the Judeo-Christian tradition comes from the book of Genesis where God casts Adam and Eve from the garden of paradise and condemns them to earn their bread "by the sweat of thy brow." Work is cast as a punishment upon mankind for the "original fall."

Is work a blessing or a curse? A response might come quickly from a majority of workers that all work is a curse. Studies show that the majority of Americans are not happy with their jobs. (Is it any wonder that American products have begun to lag behind the competitive market?) Living with a job one does not love is tragic because work consumes such a major portion of one's life.

Studies also show that unhappiness with work follows the worker home and enters into his or her relationships. If dad is miserable at the office, he is likely to bring that misery into his marriage and life as a parent. If a woman feels degraded and unfulfilled in an eight-hour-a-day job, it can't help but affect the way she handles her primary relationships. I'm not suggesting that all work has to be fun and games (although for some it certainly is), but if we are to love our selves adequately and appropriately, we will have to confront the issue of how we earn our living. We are not self-loving if a major part of our lives is spent in unfulfilling and self-negating work.

If we are to love our selves as we need, we need to have work that promotes self-love. We deserve work that helps make us happy. We don't deserve work that slowly and inevitably eats away our souls. We deserve work that is "right" for us.

We are limited here to only a brief discussion, but this topic alone would make up a whole book. The reader is highly encouraged to read Marsha Sinetar's excellent book *Do What You Love, The Money Will Follow*. A point Sinetar makes is that "any talent we are born with eventually surfaces as a need" (p. 10). Any talent we have is one of our assets. A self-loving person lives off his or her assets. A self-loving person will make a living off his or her assets. Talents or assets will surface as "needs." In self-love recovery our needs need to be addressed and responded to. If we feel that our talents (needs) are not being addressed and fulfilled in the work we do, it might be time to consider a job change.

Not long ago I read a sad story of a man dying on a commuter train on his way home from his retirement party. He had worked hard all his life in hopes of being able to retire in comfort. In a week, he and his wife were to have moved to a community of "sun and fun." They had many plans.

I wondered if he loved his work. Life is so full of shocks and surprises. Did his fulfillment come from his work, or only from his dreams of retirement? What a tragic story (which I know is repeated in the lives of many others) if he only planned to love himself as he needed *after* retirement.

Loving your self will mean listening to your inner voice about what you would love to do, and then finding the courage to "follow your bliss." If it means a career or job change, you make it. Life is too short. You will never be helping your self or anybody else by "sticking it out" with what makes you unhappy on a daily basis. "Stuck" people have a way of being miserable, and making others miserable that is all their own. Better to work, as Marsha Sinetar advocates, at discovering your "right livelihood." Do what you love, and you show love for your self.

SPEND TIME ALONE WITH YOUR SELF

One of the greatest pleasures for special friends is to be in each other's company. Some chapters back we discussed that the pain of loneliness is not so much being alone, but being alone with someone you don't like, namely your self. Imagine being stuck alone on an island with someone you have always resented, put-down, made fun of, deliberately ignored, manipulated and abused. How many months, days, hours, would it take before you totally lost your mind? Imagine being stuck with a self you have always resented, put-down, made fun of, deliberately ignored, allowed to be manipulated and abused, a self from which you can never escape.

We fear being separate from others, but in truth we are. Despite what the poet Blake says, we are islands. We are separate. We are significantly separated from each other by our bodies. We are separate from each other by our uniqueness. Our differences of thinking, feeling, and relating our differences in tastes, likes and dislikes, make each of us a breed apart.

We really are individuals. While we have healthy dependency needs; while we need each other as social beings; while we can indulge in the joy of "sharing;" while we share being with all that is, even the being of the eternal Self, we are basically alone, in and by ourselves. If we cannot come to love our selves as we need, if we cannot enjoy and like our own company, we doom our selves to a very lonely and painful existence, whether we are in the company of other people or not.

Coming to love your self through affirmative action will take time and effort, but come to love your self you will. As you come to love your self more, you will find how enjoyable your self is as a special friend and companion. As you learn more about your self and how fascinating that self is, you will have much to enjoy in that self. As you come to see how beloved and beautiful you are, you will come to take great pleasure in your own company.

This is not delusional thinking. Self-loving people relish being with others, but they also relish being alone. Self-loving people can enjoy their solitude—not just to get away from the noise and bother of the world outside, but to commune with their selves in private, and find joy in their own company.

It is pleasant to be with other people, especially those you love, but you don't "have to" to be happy. It is a wonderful thing to have relationships, but you don't "have to" have them to be at peace with yourself. It is fun to be out with the crowd and having a great time, singing, dancing, making gossip, but you don't "have to" be with a crowd to enjoy yourself. Once you make your self dependent on a "have to" half the pleasure is gone anyway. Once you "have to" your freedom is radically diminished. When you "have to" be in the company of others to be happy, you are telling your self that it is inadequate. Loneliness is only experienced when you fall victim to "have to."

When you "have to" be in the company of others, or when you "have to" be in a relationship, all the fun goes out of it. The trouble is that you cannot leave that inadequate self at home when you go out in the company of others. You bring that inadequate and little-loved self with you into your social relationships. Little wonder that so much of our socializing, partying, getting together with "friends," is so half-hearted and wearisome after a short time. Little wonder that relationships go on the fritz so quickly. When you "have to" use others to escape loneliness, it can't be a joy anymore to be in their company.

Do your self the honor, now and then, to keep it company, alone. Deliberately put aside time to be alone with your self. Give your self the pleasure of feeling respected and cared for. When it knows you are interested, it will respond creatively to make your time with it enjoyable. Get to know your self as a friend and life-long companion. Relish the time you save for your self. Your self will appreciate it and make you feel very good.

ALLOW YOUR SELF TO LOVE EVERYBODY

Is it true, as all the great spiritual masters advocate, that it is possible to love everybody? I am not speaking about the special love we have for a spouse, children, and intimate friends. It is quite impossible to love everybody with the intensity of love we have for those who are special to us. But is it possible to expect us to love *everyone*?

I bring this up only because love is such a powerful force for healing in self-love recovery. "Love covers a multitude of sins." Much of our stress arises from the demands, expectations, judgments, and condemnations we ourselves place on other people. "Hell is other people," proclaims Sartre. But there is a fallacy here. People don't actually make "hell" for us. No one can "make" us happy or miserable. We can only do that to our selves. It is our own mind-sets and programming that create hell for us by setting our selves up for hell in the first place.

To be able to love everyone is obviously an advanced state of spiritual development, but not such an advanced state that we cannot develop an attitude of sensitivity, understanding, compassion, forgiveness, and loving care for others. Love for everyone comes from a frame of mind that includes *everyone* in our caring and compassion.

When we love our selves enough, we will be able to love everyone. When we love our selves enough, we will realize that we are our brother's, and sister's, keepers. On the other hand, having love and compassion for others will, in turn, help us be more loving and compassionate to our selves. When we love "everyone," we will not be able to exclude our selves.

Loving "everyone" is easier to accept when we come to appreciate something about the dynamics of love. When you are genuinely "in" love, you are not simply attached to another person; *something significant happens to you* in the process. Something changes in you. For proof of this, you need only observe someone who has recently fallen in love. Love does something to the soul. Love radically transforms you, as water transforms a desert. Love opens and expands the mind and heart. In love you see things differently and you act differently. You are different because love substantially changes your perspective on life and people.

People don't change; *you* change. That's what the nature of love is. Love opens you up. And the more you open up, the more others can be allowed in.

Furthermore, the less you can identify with King Baby in the love you have for others, the more you become identified with everyone and everything else in their own right. The more you can become united with your Higher Power, the more you can see everyone from your Higher Power's perspective, that we are all one. That from CEO to shoeshine boy, we are all equal, with the same hopes and dreams, with the same fears and despairs, with the same heartaches and struggles. The more we appreciate this, the easier it becomes to love everyone.

The more we can come to love others, the more we come to love our selves. The more sensitive we become to others, the more sensitive we become to our selves. The more forgiving we are of others, the more inclined we are to forgive our selves. The more we can accept the defects and faults of others, the more we will accept our own. Trying to understand where others are coming from makes it easier to understand where we are coming from.

We can come to love our selves by loving others. The more people we can encompass in our love, the more of our selves we can embrace in our love. Those who are most difficult to love are symbols of what is most difficult to love in our selves. Loving them can result in our loving what is most difficult in our selves.

You can give your self a great gift of peace and joy by allowing it to rise above conditional love into a surrender to unconditional love. No one is consciously left out; everyone is accepted as part of you. You remember that from babyhood. You re-identify with all that is. You love everyone "as your self."

ALLOW YOUR SELF TO BE LOVED

In self-love recovery we discover how much we have blocked our selves off to love from others. Feeling deeply unworthy in the depths of our souls, we find it difficult to believe that others could love us if they really knew us. Feeling unworthy, we are not open to being loved. Feeling unworthy, we assume offers of love from others to be misguided or potentially manipulative.

Perhaps we learned conditional love from the earliest years of our lives. Our significant others may have used love to control us. Love "depended" on how good we were in the eyes of others, or on how well we performed for their approval. Or we simply may have lived and associated with people who had no love to give. We learned to downplay our need for love so that the pain of our love hunger would go away. We became used to not being loved. Consequently we don't trust love as we need.

Allowing our selves to be loved, therefore, is a big step in our recovery program. We need to take a risk and deliberately open the doors of our hearts. It is a fearful thing to do, because we leave our selves wide open. We become vulnerable. And that is why the willingness to "surrender" continues to be so important for us. Without the courage to surrender even our hearts, they will remain closed—closed even to our own love. Loving our selves means allowing our selves to be vulnerable. We need to be loved. We need to remove the blocks that prevent it from happening.

It will take time and baby steps before we gain enough confidence to trust love again. But as long as we are taking care of our selves and continuing to perform loving affirmative actions on our behalf, we will be safe. As our confidence grows in our ability to take care of our selves, we will become more open to the love of others for us. We will begin to trust their love.

In opening our selves to love, we need to caution our selves that we cannot control that others will love us as we need. As with all "control" issues, any attempt at manipulating the love of others for us will always be self-defeating.

Even more self-defeating is expecting others to love us *unconditionally*. No one but God can love unconditionally. Expecting unconditional love from another human being may sound wonderfully romantic, but is little more than a set-up for guaranteed disappointment. As human beings we all have our limitations. Being able to give only conditional love is one of them.

Whether others will love us, or will love us as we need, we leave up to our Higher Power. On the other hand, our Higher Power assures us that we will find the love we need in our self-love recovery program. As we come to love our selves and take affirmative actions on our behalf, we do in fact become more lovable. Being more lovable, we attract the love of others. When we don't love our selves the way we need, we don't feel lovable, and other people pick that up. If they feel we are desperate for their love, or that we are dependent on their love, healthy people are inclined to pull away. Ironically, as we have indicated before, it is only when we don't depend on the love of others to make our selves complete that we begin to receive all the love we need. People are drawn to self-loving people. When we love our selves as we need, others will love us too.

BE GRATEFUL

I recall once going through a very bad period. I was very depressed and facing an onslaught of personal problems, so I took care of my self by consulting a wise counselor. I spent almost an hour pouring out my soul with long lists of concerns, anticipated hardships, and an overwhelming sense of powerlessness to get through it all. As I waited, desperate for wisdom and strength, for the help I needed, she ended the session we had together with a brief, "Tell God how grateful you are."

That was it? That was going to help me get through the problems I was facing? Be grateful? Be grateful for what? Was this some sad attempt at humor? I was inundated with problems that I would give anything to be rid of, and she is telling me to be grateful. I left feeling disappointed and even sorrier for myself.

It has taken me a long time to appreciate the value and power of gratitude. Gratitude is an act of loving acceptance. Gratitude goes further than acceptance and is thankful for whatever our Higher Power allows to come our way. Gratitude takes the edge off our problems by further neutralizing our resistance.

Resistance to "what is" is the major source of our emotional turmoils. When we defy "what is," when we feel we don't "deserve" the bad things in life that come our way, we set our selves up for despair and depression. Life isn't fair and we are beating our heads against a brick wall by expecting it to be. Of course we don't deserve the bad things that come our way. But deserving or not deserving is not the issue. "What is" is. Gratitude allows us to be thankful for whatever is, as part of a our Higher Power's loving plan for us.

Gratitude is a direct confrontation with King Baby. Gratitude is a humble acknowledgement that we are not "entitled" to anything. Gratitude is seeing everything in life, our life itself, as pure gift. Even our trials and tribulations are accepted as part of that gift. Gratitude can bring great peace of soul, because our troubled waters are calmed by the wider perspective of giftedness.

What is a gift is freely given and is just as freely able to be taken away. If we demand "entitlement," we are habitually set up for frustration. Only by surrendering any idea of entitlement can we perceive life as basically a game of give and take. We win some; we lose some. Gratitude brings us tremendous freedom to win or to lose with equanimity and tranquility, thereby freeing our selves from the torture of "loss."

Live Now

Grow Up

Discipline Your Self

Do Your Own Driving

Make Your Self "Adequate"

Face and Solve Problems

Ask for What You Need

Affirm Your Self

Stand Up for Your Self

Be All You Can Be

Discover Your Self

Define Your Self

Determine Your Perceptions

Live Off Your Assets

Invest in Your Life

Involve Your Self

Risk Your Self

Be Gentle with Your Self

Accept Your Feelings

Treat Your Self as Special

Enjoy Your Successes

Present Your Self Appropriately

Take Care of Your Health

Allow Your Self Freedom

Give Your Self Work You Love

Spend Time Alone with Your Self

Allow Your Self To Love Everybody

Allow Your Self To Be Loved

Be Grateful

Enjoy Your Successes

9

Inner Work: De-Programming

The fault, dear Brutus, is not in our stars, but in ourselves that we are underlings.

—Shakespeare

To study the abnormal is the best way to study the normal.

—William James

In the previous two chapters we have seen a number of affirmative actions we need take on our behalf to reclaim, nurture, and enhance self-love. These affirmative actions are all part of re-programming negative mind-sets that prevent us from giving our selves the love they need. In self-love recovery it is particularly important that we monitor our inner programming. We all have self-supporting and self-negating tapes that pre-condition our attitudes and behaviors. People with low self-esteem and who do not love themselves adequately have an unusually large library of self-negating tapes. In this chapter we give added emphasis to actions we need to take to de-program some of the most common negative tapes whose replacement is of particular necessity in self-love recovery.

REFUSE TO BE VICTIMIZED BY OPINIONS, EXPECTATIONS, AND CRITICISM

Maturity is indicated by the level of independence we have attained in our development. Maturity is attained, and maintained, by making our own decisions, by making our own mistakes, and by taking responsibility for their consequences. There are times, however, that we need to take care of our selves by asking for help, by consulting an authority, or by seeking advice from a friend. This is sound policy. What must be avoided, however, is putting our selves under anyone else's control.

We can respect the opinions of others, but this does not mean that we allow our selves to be a victim of opinion. The media, advertisers, and anyone giving us unsolicited advice, for example, are trying to sell something. They are not philosophers seeking the ultimate truths of the universe, which they hope to share with us. When we are being persuaded to buy a certain product, or to buy into a certain way of thinking and acting, it is likely that we are also being persuaded that there is something unacceptable about us if we don't act on the suggestion. And that is simply not true.

I am not advocating anarchy by suggesting that everyone should follow the suggesion to "do your own thing." Those who truly love themselves will be able to "do their own thing," and it will be the right thing, and not be at odds with the broader needs of society. Self-loving people are never anarchists. Self-loving people typically display a high degree of altruism. As we noted earlier, Abraham Maslow has demonstrated that self-interest in highly actuated people runs hand in hand with altruism. Nathaniel Brandon, in his many fine books on self-esteem, makes clear that rational self-interest is the only guarantee that society itself can flourish in peace and harmony. Living by one's own lights is the beginning of living in "enlightenment." Our enlightened life will serve society. A harmonious society will come about only with self-loving people acting in their best self-interests. What is honestly in our own best interests will be in the best interests of society at large.

Base your beliefs and behavior, therefore, on what will enhance self-love recovery. Refuse to be at the mercy of public opinion or human respect. A great disservice was likely done to us as children by creating a mind-set in us that put us at the mercy of "what will others think!" This tape has often been destructive to our self-love. It has shrunk our development.

While adjusting to ethical and orderly social living is appropriate, we are learning to follow a moral and ethical code because we are conscious of its validity and benefit to us as well as others. In self-love recovery, we learn to "own" our code of conduct rather than uncritically follow the persuasion that "everybody does it."

As we have already noted, the expectations of others are very often "impositions" of their viewpoints. Criticism is often an imposition of a particular viewpoint. Therefore, be sensitive to criticism, but never be self-condemning because of it. Criticism can be helpful to us in self-love recovery only if we calmly accept its validity for us. Criticisms are based on perceptions. Everyone looks at life with a particular set of eye glasses. With different eye glasses we see the same things differently. We see things in a different "light." When people tell us they are disappointed in us for one reason or another, all they are saying is that they are disappointed in something they perceive about us. They perceive us as disappointing *their* expectations in behavior *they* perceive as disappointing.

Perceptions are always open to calm evaluation and negotiation. There is never an "objective reality" to perceptions. No critic has an unassailable viewpoint. No critic can really see us as we truly are. To accept a criticism as an accurate description of our selves, or, worse, to go into an aggressive reaction or depression over it, is to renege on loving our selves as we need. We respond to criticism of our selves by calmly maintaining our self-respect before all else, and addressing the criticism's validity for us on emotionally neutral grounds.

REFUSE TO BE VICTIMIZED BY THE "SHOULDS"

"Why do I have to do this, mommy?" "Because you 'have to'!"

Most of us grew up developing behavior patterns based

not on what we truly believed was intrinsically valid or beneficial to us, but on what we "had to." The "shoulds" began early
in life when we discovered certain things we "had to" do in
order to gain the love of our parents and significant others.
When we did things "their way," we received the applause and
love that we wanted. When we didn't, we got stung by disap-
proval and put-downs. We learned to do what we "had to" do to
get the love we needed. We sacrificed self-love at the price of
"buying" the love we needed.

Again, I am not discounting the importance of social
order. "Ought," "must," "should," "have to" are part of life and
necessary to law and order in a harmonious society. On the
other hand, they can be serious obstructions to self-love recovery when they indiscriminately and unwittingly condition how
we live our lives. In self-love recovery we learn to *own* our codes
of conduct rather than uncritically follow a "have to" or
"should" mentality.

The "shoulds" develop in us as universal principles and are
tyrannical in keeping self-love to the minimum. Raised on
"shoulds," we are conditioned to believe that we should never
show our anger, have bad feelings, or ever be afraid. We might
believe that we should do everything perfectly, that we
shouldn't let anything bother us, and that we should never
make mistakes. We might have been trained that we should
make a lot of money to prove our success, or that we should
always put work before pleasure, or that we should never trust
anyone other than family. Needless to say, none of these rules,
or others like them, are true or even realistic. But they still have
tremendous power over us—until we directly confront them.

We need to monitor and examine the "shoulds" that motivate our lives. More than likely they are motivating attitudes
and feelings about our selves that are not very self-loving. Our
"shoulds" need to be confronted and challenged. If you notice,
words like "should" and "must" are deliberately avoided in this
book. From the beginning we have emphasized that self-love
recovery begins in "surrender." We surrender not to "shoulds"

but to a Higher Power that has more in mind for us than perfectly executing a chain of "have tos."

There are few "shoulds" more handicapping to our self-love recovery than thinking that life should be fair, that we should not have to struggle to regain the love for our selves that we need, that we should never have problems, or make mistakes, or get sick, or suffer. Problems, struggles and suffering are part of life. They are inescapable. With self-love and a proper mental attitude we grow and develop through our problems, struggles and sufferings. Adopting an attitude that problems, struggle and suffering should not be part of our lives is ultimately unrealistic and self-destructive. Jung found that neurotics basically deny the inevitability and legitimacy of suffering and struggle. For Jung, "neurosis is always a substitute for legitimate suffering."

If we can accept that life is not fair, we are in for less disappointment. If we can accept that struggle is simply part of life, struggles will lose their fearsomeness for us. If we can accept that pain cannot be avoided, pain will lose its cutting edge when we have to endure it. Denial and resistance put our emotional shackles on edge and actually double and triple our struggle, pain and suffering.

Embracing the struggle, embracing the ambiguity of human existence, accepting that life is not fair, helps us to achieve serenity in the challenges we face in life, and are therefore very self-loving actions we take on our behalf.

DON'T STAY STUCK IN SELF-DIMINISHING OR NON-NOURISHING RELIGIOUS SYSTEMS

There is a central or core experience of *"enlightenment," "awakening," "conversion," "salvation," "redemption,"* at the heart of all religious systems. It is an experience which "believers" may or may not actually come to achieve. The reasons for non-experience are many, but the primary reason is that "religion" most often gets in the way.

Just as we are embodied in our selves, any religion is embodied in a system of beliefs, codes of conduct, and rituals, all preserved by some form of bureaucratic institution, usually clerically controlled. "Beliefs" are dogmatized theological tenets of what a particular religion is all about. They may or may not be directly connected with the founder's initial teachings. Many sectarian "beliefs" are a particular religion's defense system against non-subscribers.

Beliefs, codes of conduct, and ritual practices quite commonly become the very means by which the ruling bureaucracy maintains control over membership. The fact that so many believers have suffered from religious "guilt trips" tends to confirm this. The ruling bureaucracy is established to maintain the institution (and itself) in perpetuity at all costs. It is easy to see (especially in practice) that, over time, religion can develop far from the original perceptions and teachings of the "master." There are too many other agendas operating for self-preservation.

All religions may not be the same, but all have only a piece of the "truth." Some may have developed far from the "truth" as experienced by the original founder. Some may get sidetracked by everything but the founder's core teachings.

Studies show that we pick and choose our religious preferences in accordance with our needs. For the most part, our personal religious beliefs and practices are highly relative. Most of our religious beliefs were likely learned as part of our automatic enculturing process. If we were raised differently, we would likely have had different beliefs and practices. Honest reflection will show that we pick and choose what we want to believe, how deeply we want to believe it, and for how long we want to continue believing. In time, we actually create beliefs to serve our needs. Ask any ten people for their ideas about God, and you will likely get ten different understandings and approaches. We all create an image of God that suits us. We follow certain belief systems because they suit us. We believe that our belief system is the only "true" religion because it suits us to do so.

Being relative, our religious beliefs and practices may need to be modified or changed if they no longer serve our best interests. In self-love recovery, they may need to be replaced if they no longer respond to and nurture our spiritual needs. If we find our religious systems are abusive, self-diminishing, overly moralizing with "shoulds," productive of guilt trips and scrupulosity, condemning of the freedoms and beliefs of others, they are dangerous to self-love recovery and should be avoided.

But we also need to pursue religious systems that help to raise our consciousness, that help us to become more self-loving, that help us become one with the Source of all being. Self-loving people are predictably spiritual and religious, even if their forms of spirituality and religious practice are not always conventional. Self-loving people search out and utilize belief systems that actually stimulate and nourish love for themselves and others.

While this topic alone could make a whole book's worth of analysis and exploration, let it suffice here that we accept that religious systems are for our use, and not vice versa. In self-love recovery, we modify or change our religious practices when they no longer serve us as we need. We don't get stuck in religious systems that do not provide input and outlets for our expanding consciousness. We resist any religious institution's claim to have the final word on "salvation." We suspect any religious institution's claim that its current teachings are "objective" and binding forever.

"'Objective' to whom?" we might ask. God and his benevolent will for all creation cannot be "bound" to any particular religious system. "Salvation" is not restricted to any particular form of belief or worship. God reads the heart, not a spreadsheet of beliefs and practices. An all loving, benevolent Creator has room in the kingdom for each and every Christian, Jew, Hindu, Moslem, Buddhist, Shintoist, and any other variety of belief practiced with a sincere and searching heart.

This is not "pure subjectivism." Our aim is not to "conveniently create" the whole world, religion, and God in our own image and likeness. Rather, we need to actively search for a "way, truth, and life" that we can *make our own,* a way, truth, and life that will uplift and enrich us. And that faith may just be the faith in which we were raised.

All too many "believers," however, have never gone on a personal religious quest. They do not *own* their faith. Their beliefs have been pre-digested for them. Answers were provided for questions they were never really asking. Little wonder that "religion" has so little effect and carry-over in their everyday lives.

Even more sadly, other "believers" may have found in a particular religious system a support for their own dysfunctionality. We have all met "strongly practicing" Christians, for example, who just might be some of the most uncharitable, if not vicious, people we will ever come across. A religious system which has not coped adequately with its own dysfunctionality will be a haven for souls who do not love themselves as they need.

To be fruitful for us, our religious beliefs must be the fruit of our own conscious search and decision. A religious quest for our way, truth, and life may be painful and painstaking. We need to be true to our selves. We need to be rigorously honest about our belief systems and how effective they are in our day-to-day living. Are our religious systems holding us up or holding us back? Our aim, in developing appropriate love for our selves, is to disengage our selves from *dependence* on religious authority figures and religious systems that would keep us dependent by their restrictive or non-nurturing prescriptions for "redemption."

REFUSE TO SIT IN JUDGMENT

We have said before that we are our own worst enemies. No one can ever abuse or put us down as well as we can. Your self never feels an insult more than when it comes from you. Your self never feels more betrayed than when you betray it. And those insults and betrayals come so easy when we don't love our selves as we should. A little while ago, I mistakenly deleted part of this chapter on my computer and caught myself judging my self: "What an idiot! What an idiot!"

It is one thing to discover a mistake, even a very foolish one, and quite another to judge and shame the self for performing the mistake. What good does it do to judge the self? Is the mistake corrected in the shaming? Do judgment and shaming guarantee that the mistake won't be made again? Or does not the very act of judging and shaming cut down the self's confidence and thus guarantee that the mistake will be made again?

As the recovering alcoholic goes "cold turkey" in respect to all alcohol, we need do the same with any negative self-judgments. As a matter of fact, those of us in self-love recovery need to go cold turkey with any judgments whatever, of our selves or others.

Jesus, with other spiritual masters, was emphatic about avoiding any judgment making. He did not advocate that we judge wisely, or judge according to the law. He said simply, "Judge not." There is great wisdom here. Judgments are always relative. Judgments are always based on biased perceptions. Judgments are rarely, if ever, identifiable with "the truth"— which means they can be dangerously unreliable.

Judgments always proceed from a particular perspective. Judgments coming from those with poor self-images or from those who are lacking in adequate self-love are particularly unreliable, if not distorted. Poorly self-loving people make awful judges of themselves or others. Their perspective is highly impaired from lack of insight, balance, and love.

Furthermore, judgments are generally a waste of time. Judgments of any kind rarely if ever change others or our selves. Experience daily proves this. If anything, judgments diminish us. Judgments enhance our control issues. Judgments make us arrogant. Judgments put us on a throne where only our Higher Power belongs. We need to tell our selves that we simply cannot afford to sit on that throne anymore. And, in truth, we can't.

NEVER HARBOR ILL-WILL, HATRED, OR UNFORGIVENESS

Dorothy is a seventy-one year old recluse, whose bitterness not only is etched in the lines of her face, but comes out in her quick, savage temper. Halloween is the worst day of her year because of the vandalism done to her property by trick-or-treaters out to rile up the "neighborhood witch." Twenty years ago, she took some brief psychiatric treatment on the advice of her doctor who was treating her for ulcerative colitis. She left treatment after three visits when the therapist confronted her with being "misanthropic." She didn't need to be told something about herself that she already well knew: that she hated everybody.

For close to fifty years, Dorothy has been in the grip of a resolute hatred for people in general, because three months short of her wedding date, almost a half-century ago, her financé ran off with her best girlfriend, who was to have been her maid of honor. And, short of a miracle of conversion, Dorothy will go to her grave eaten away by her lack of forgiveness and her desire for vengeance.

It might seem hard to believe that someone could live so long with so much bitterness. But it shouldn't surprise us. Millions of people live with ill-will, hardness of heart, spite and resentment for decades upon decades. If we search our own souls, we might discover many long-buried resentments that still fester, deeply hidden within.

What we fail to appreciate, however, is that resentments don't just lie buried in the depths of our unconscious; they *work* there. If we haven't let them go, they are still preventing our attainment of self-love, harmony and happiness.

Why do we harbor hatred? Why do resentments keep us in such an iron grip? Why is forgiveness so difficult to come by? Is it pride, or standing up for our rights? I don't think so. I think that somewhere within us there is a tape from early childhood that tells us that wishes somehow come true—that if we hold a wish long enough and hard enough, it will be fulfilled. When we have been hurt by someone, we want to hurt back in like or worse manner. We want to get even. If this becomes impossible, we keep the wish alive in our hearts and hope that somewhere, somehow, our desire for vengeance will have its effect—something like our own version of voodoo.

The only problem with hatred, ill-will and lack of forgiveness, however, is that it is psychological suicide. All religious masters have urged as one of their primary teachings that we forgive, absolutely, with no reservation. You might think they were fanatic about it. Jesus said we should forgive, without limitation ("seventy times seven times"). He went to an excruciating death openly forgiving his enemies. What is it these masters know that we don't know?

What they know is that hatred and unforgiveness are extremely toxic to self-love. What they know is that *we* are the only ones actually hurt by our lack of forgiveness. Vengeance consumes the avenger. We falsely assume that we are hurting someone we hate, when we are only hurting our selves. Dorothy destroyed herself, her whole life, all her potential for happiness, with fifty years of hatred and unforgiveness. Who was affected by her festering bitterness? Only her self. She punished her self for someone else's actions. Her fiancé and maid of honor went on their merry way, probably never again giving Dorothy a moment's thought. Dorothy's life is a classic example of tragicomedy all of us unwittingly play into.

Self-love is incompatible with hatred and unforgiveness. Never hang on to grudges and grievances. Think of them as malignant cancer cells that can eat away your heart, because psychologically that is exactly what they do. Empty your self of your hostilities, judgments, and condemnations of others. They harm no one but your self.

For Jesus, forgiveness was so important that he advised his followers to even "love your enemies." Someone can only become an enemy when you do not love your self enough. An "enemy" is perceived as someone who is stealing from one's self-image. Self-loving people are not vulnerable to that. Their self-image is not subject to others. If you love yourself as you need, you will not even perceive an "enemy." If you love your self as you need, forgiveness will flow as the most natural thing in the world.

"Letting go" is never more important than in dealing with our angers, resentments, and hatreds. "Hanging on" to our grievances is another doomed attempt by King Baby to control people and events. It doesn't work. "Hanging on" to our spite for others is another foolhardy attempt to change others to suit our needs. It won't work.

We forgive best by letting go our desire to change anyone else. We forgive best by refusing to be over-sensitive to their thoughts and actions. We forgive best by allowing others the same pre-occupations, self-delusions, problems and agendas that we allow our selves. We forgive our parents for being far from perfect. We forgive God for creating such a messy, mysterious, paradoxical world.

We show love for our selves by forgiving ourselves also. We forgive ourselves for our mistakes. When we made them, we were doing the best we knew at the moment (as does everyone else). If we made wrong decisions, we have already paid the consequences, and have no need to hang on to self-resentments. We forgive ourselves for the abuse we have put our selves through, for simply being human, for failed opportunities, for not forgiving as we needed to.

Forgiveness of our selves for our mistakes also means that we let go of our guilt and shame. Guilt is something we feel when we have gone against our personal code of conduct. Guilt is our conscience's way to make us conscious of an error in behavior. Guilt leads naturally to remorse and energizes us to make amends. Once amends are made, we go on.

Unfortunately, for many of us in self-love recovery, guilt turns into shame. Our errors and mistakes convince us that there is something fundamentally wrong with us. Instead of energizing us to make amends for our mistakes, shame paralyzes us and makes us sit and stew over how rotten we are. Guilt is feeling bad over something we have *done*; shame is feeling bad about our *selves*. Guilt is normally temporary; shame can remain with us a lifetime. Guilt is healthy as long as it remains only temporary; shame is never healthy. Forgiving our selves allows us to let go of our guilt and shame. We accept the consequences of our actions and then get on with taking care of our selves as we need.

DON'T ISOLATE

As we have already noted, a tendency we share with all animals, when we are wounded, is to retreat into a dark corner, alone. This is a logical survival technique. We need time to heal our wounds and recoup our strength. In a dark corner we are less liable to more attack.

This survival technique however, can also backfire on us. One talent we have, which animals don't, is that we can *reflect* on our injuries. We can brood and stew over them. Isolated in our dark corners, we can work our selves up to a frenzy of self-pity. We can catastrophize about the future. We can brood and stew so much that we miss the healing that could make us whole again.

Isolation breeds inferiority feelings as nothing else can. Isolation ferments our fears and irresolution. Isolation nurtures our sense of inadequacy.

Isolating, when we are hurting, may be an impulse, but it is also an old tape we need to confront. There is never a time we need to take better care of our selves than when we are hurting. There is never a time we less need isolation than when we are enduring a personal tragedy. If there is ever a time we need to reach out for support and healing from others, it is when we are depressed and down on our selves. If there is ever a time to "talk it out" and share with others, it is when we feel that our world is coming to an end.

Self-love recovery means taking the courage to step out of our dark corner and getting the help we need. We recover by opening our selves to healing from others. The power of the Twelve-Step program, for example, is found in the sharing that takes place at meetings. There is nothing better for us, when we are in our doom and gloom, then to challenge our impulse to retreat and to talk to someone who can see things from a different and broader perspective. I have often been raised from the dumps by friends who saw those dumps as playgrounds of opportunity, and helped me to see things that way too.

There is no safety or security in isolation. Isolation is not a self-protecting device for human beings; it is a self-defeating defect. Isolation inevitably brings us even more misery and depression than we already have. Our own experience proves that to us time and again. Stepping out of our dark corner lets our selves know that we care enough to bring them the healing they need. We reach out for the help we need.

DON'T AMPLIFY

Being members of a narcissistic culture, we are likely burdened with the disorder of "grandiosity." I am inclined to grandstand almost everything about my self. I am aware that my conversations are peppered with superlatives. "This is the greatest." "This is the worst thing that could ever happen." "I have never felt worse in my life." "This is the best meal I have ever had." "This is the worst cold in the world."

Whenever King Baby feels threatened about anything, his immediate defense is to magnify our perceptions of "danger," accelerate our attempts at "crisis control," and amplify our negative thoughts. If I am slightly late for an appointment because of a traffic jam, I feel frustrated to the boiling point. If I inadvertently left out an important part of a lecture I was giving, I feel that I "disgraced" my self completely. If I have put in superhuman efforts to get an assignment done on time and fail to do so, I end up feeling like a "total failure."

The problem with amplifications is obvious: they make mountains out of molehills. They also set off a cycle of self-defeating emotions.

I remember the embarrassment I felt at a formal dinner

party when I discovered that I had on two different pair of socks. I feel "absolutely mortified." The more I thought about it, the worse it got. "I should never have come." "How will I ever live this down?" "What a fool I will be taken for." "What a fool I am!" The thoughts made me feel even worse, and, with worse feelings, even more negative thoughts come to mind. "I will never be invited again into polite society." "I'll be the laughing-stock of the community for months." "I will never be able to walk with my head up again." And then even more bad feelings came, and the cycle went on and on, until I actually made myself ill. Laughably enough, no one even noticed.

When we love our selves enough to accept, with humility, that we are just human beings, with no superman or super-woman about us, we can save our selves from self-wracking amplifications of our failings and short-comings. Refusing to exaggerate our selves from the start allows us to retain a proper perspective of what it means to be the human beings that we are. Allowing our selves to see the humor in our humanity can bring that perspective to a fine point.

Nothing works better to keep us in perspective than observing others more disadvantaged than we. I remember feel-ing particularly sorry for myself when my back went out on me recently. I was angry and disgusted with myself for moving fur-niture in a way that almost guaranteed that I would sustain some injury. Sitting in an easy chair with a heating pad pressed onto my lower back, I spent some time scanning the daily news-paper. There is nothing more enlightening about the sufferings of human beings than the daily newspapers. I noted one feature after another of major accidents, suicides, crushing political defeat, murders, rape victims, incest, job losses, increasing instances of communicable diseases, on so on. After fifteen minutes of pondering the calamities of other people, I put my back pain back into perspective. It was amazing how the pain itself began to subside as my compassion for those much worse off than myself increased.

"FEAR NOT"

Fear is a very natural response to a perceived threat. Fear can be a powerful tool and ally. It can keep us out of a lot of trouble and danger to our selves. Fear can also be very self-destructive. It can paralyze us into inaction. Fear, therefore, is only helpful as long as it is managed.

Fear is a feeling. We have learned that feelings belong to us as servants. Never is the need for exercising management over feelings more appropriate than in dealing with fear. Fear, without reins, will invariably run wild and cause us untold and unnecessary misery. Fear under discipline can actually turn into excitement. As a matter of fact, fear and excitement are two sides of the same coin. Fear is the negative energy of excitement.

Fear is especially debilitating to all of us in self-love recovery. Constant fear indicates how poorly self-loving we are. Fear arises out of our attempts to protect a self-image that we feel is extremely fragile and insecure. Somehow we misguidedly feel we have the power to "control" our own protection when the only real "protection" we have, paradoxically, is to continue in our willingness to surrender and be vulnerable. Fear diminishes only as we increase our willingness to surrender to our Higher Power.

Fear also loses much of its edge when we respect it as an ally. Once fear is "named" ("I feel fearful") and accepted as a tool, its paralyzing qualities diminish. Fear puts us on notice of "danger ahead," and that is where its job ends. We acknowledge our fear and use its energy to take positive steps to remove our selves from the danger. If there is nothing we can do to eliminate the perceived danger, we take the positive step of surrendering it up to our Higher Power.

On the other hand, we abuse our selves by letting fear run wild or by focusing too much on whatever could magnify fear's negative energy, such as permitting our fertile imaginations free rein to speculate about a future we cannot know or control. Once we let our feelings go, once we allow fear full and free rein, self-paralysis is inevitable.

Observe fear. Observe where the fear is coming from.

Name the fear. Acknowledge its presence. Fear is not there to harm you, but to warn you. It can only harm and debilitate you if you allow it to run wild. Speculate on how you can take care of your self using fear as an energy source. Reflect how you are going to protect and stand up for your self in face of a threat. Determine what discipline you will take to prevent fear from running amok and threatening your self further.

Look upon fear as a tool. Use fear as your servant to energize actions on your behalf. Muster the courage to do what is needed. Remember that courage is not the absence of fear, but taking action on your own behalf, in spite of fear. Self-love is using fear as an energy source for positive action.

DON'T WORRY

Nothing seems more glib and less helpful to someone who is worrying than to be told, "Don't worry." (In a future book, I hope to address what is helpful and not helpful to people in need.) If we hear it a thousand times, worry is predictably the most non-productive activity we can ever engage in. Worry produces nothing but emotional pain and calamitous feelings. Worry creates nothing. Worry solves nothing. Worry profits nothing. Worry never works.

Worry is what happens when fear alerts us to some kind of danger. Worry is fear kept on alert. Worry is another misguided method we adopt for handling problems. We mistakenly presume that by using energy in worrying, somehow our problems are contained and controlled. Of course it doesn't work that way. Worry therefore needs the same self-discipline that fear requires.

It is easier said than done, but the point is: it can be done. The trouble with most of us in self-love recovery is that we tend to sit with worry rather than positively confront it. We *react* to a perceived threat with worry, rather than *take action* to neutralize the threat or eliminate it.

Worry is best managed and diffused when we actually do something tangible to take care of our selves and our problems.

Worry is not diffused by *thinking*. Worry begins to evaporate as we take *action* to have a problem solved. Any action we perform on our behalf will use energy and tap into the energy of worry itself. Even if we can only "surrender" a problem over which we feel helpless, the action will suffice to use the energy on which worry depends.

"Worry" is a *struggle against surrender*. Worry is the energy of resistance. Worry, like fear, is a form of sustained panic that our fragile and insecure egos are inadequate to confront a perceived threat. We feel we are incapable of controlling our own protection. And, of course, we are incapable of "control." We are not helpless. We can take action on our behalf. But we are not "in control," even of our own protection. Once we are willing to surrender ourselves to a Higher Power and willingly surrender up the problem we are facing, worry is greatly modified.

Either we "put up, or shut up." Either we perform an action on our behalf to take us out of a perceived danger, or we surrender. We do not abuse our selves with interminable languishing over something we don't have control over anyway. If we act, our minds are energized to find solutions. If we surrender, we allow our Higher Power to help us with a solution. And the solution will come, if we listen and are open.

Worry is also a *distortion of focus*. I have seen people, who claim to have little ability at concentration, focus in with amazing concentration on some problem over which they are worrying themselves sick. They will focus on the tiniest details of what is upsetting them and why. Consequently, they lose all sense of proportion and perspective.

"Focusing" is the magic button that activates the imagination. If we are focused optimistically on problem solving, the imagination is activated to come up with all sorts of possible solutions. If we are focused pessimistically on the "impossibilities" of a situation, the imagination is activated to dig deep into its own stockpile of horror stories and pulls them out, one right after another. It is not long before we are paralyzed with fear and terror.

Our imagination is programmed to make our focus come

true. Our imagination is programmed to validate our focusing and expectations. Expect the best, or the worst, and our imagination will do its very best to accommodate us.

DON'T RELY ON "LOGIC"

If there is one thing that will never work on fear and worry, it is "logic." There is a terrible misconception about the "power of logical thinking." Most of us were raised to "think logically" and to do the "logical" thing. Our errors and mistakes were most often pointed out to us as "illogical." Somewhere we have an idea that the world and people run on logic. If you haven't noticed by now, they don't.

If anything, life is full of mystery and paradox. Mystery and paradox are the greatest proof that we and our world cannot be reduced to some purely materialistic and mechanical theory of the origin and evolution of life. Life is not logical. If anything, life and people are extraordinarily complex. Logic seems a desperate attempt to impose order on something we don't really understand. Logic may make our thought processes more intelligible, but logic doesn't do much for reflecting the real world. In the real world, people run on their feelings, not logic. It's completely illogical for un-self-loving people to feel about themselves the way they do. But they do. Again, logic has nothing to do with it. If it did, we would be very happy people just by working out syllogisms in our heads.

"Logic" is one of our old tapes. Self-love recovery is dependent on powers that go beyond linear thinking. Our recovery is dependent upon the natural healing powers in our selves. Our recovery is dependent on our willingness to surrender to a power greater than ourselves. Our recovery is dependent on our openness to achieve greater awareness and a higher consciousness for our selves. Our recovery is dependent on faith in our selves to transcend whatever keeps us in impoverished and impoverishing attitudes and behaviors. Our recovery is dependent on trust that recovery is possible, and that we already have the wherewithal for recovery within our selves. To look for "logical" explanations of why things are the way they are, or to expect "logical" solutions and outcomes to our dilemmas, is nothing less than futile.

Giving up on logic to solve our problems means that we *surrender to the ambiguity and paradox* that is part of the essence of life. There are no clear answers. There is no "last word" on any subject. Every proverb can be matched with a contradictory proverb. There is no ultimate "cure." There is no "final solution." There may be no "solutions" at all, but never-ending steps and challenges to our growth in recovery. There is no *absolute* anything, this side of creation. Life is fundamentally a mystery. We are asked therefore to embrace a life that is fundamentally illogical. And we assure our selves that they are nevertheless safe in an illogical world.

STOP "PERSONALIZING" EVERY MISTAKE

Until we love our selves as adequately as we need, our tendency will be to personalize every mistake we make. We identify with a quality we exhibit or with an action we perform. Instead of simply solving a problem, and not identifying with it, we become addicted to recrimination of our selves. Every failure means *we* are failures. Every case of bad judgment means we are bad. Every opportunity lost means we are losers. Every setback we encounter means we are characterless. What energy we waste on these total fabrications. King Baby unwittingly demands to identify with *everything*, even our mistakes

Stop taking everything personally. An error is simply an error, not a commentary on our state of being. A mistake is a mistake, not a summary statement of our personal worth. A sin is a sin, not an indictment of our right to exist. Errors, mistakes, failings, sins, are all to be expected and anticipated because we are human beings. Even the great saints of history were never adverse to calling themselves great sinners. We are not God and no one has the right to expect us to be. We have no right to blasphemously expect divine qualities from our selves. All we are is human, and our mistakes are there to be learned from.

Loving our selves is not something we do *after* all our mistakes and failings have been corrected, but something we do *despite* our mistakes and failings. Mistakes are simply teaching tools. In self-love recovery we need to deliberately permit our selves mistakes, because mistakes are the only way we learn. They have no relation to whether we are good or bad, worthy or unworthy, adequate or inadequate. We are good and worthy only in relation to a Higher Power who already holds us as good and worthy no matter what we do. We are good and worthy by the very fact that we have come into existence by the will of One who loves us absolutely. Our mistakes are not held in judgment against us.

Taking care of our selves means we respond to our needs. But we have difficulty learning our real needs without a hit-and-miss trial of discovery. We cannot learn what will satisfy our needs without a hit-and-miss trial of attempting a variety of options. We cannot come to own our code of conduct without seeing what consequences will unfold from a variety of behaviors.

Until our awareness expands to know more options and better ways of dealing with our needs, we will continue to make mistakes. We don't deny our mistakes, because we take responsibility for the consequences of what we do. We grow by learning what mistakes to avoid in the future. We don't foolishly attempt mistakes, because that would defeat our need to take care of our selves. But we do not perceive mistakes as a norm or indication of our self-worth. Our worth is evaluated by standards much higher than the mistakes we make.

AVOID ENVY AND "WISHFUL THINKING"

Most of us are easily led to believe that "the grass is greener in someone else's yard." Those of us in self-love recovery are especially vulnerable to this persuasion. Part of all advertising strategy is to keep us sufficiently dissatisfied by displaying models of success for us to envy and emulate. The media create great fanfare around the glamor of those who have "made it."

While there is an appropriate use of modeling to urge on our quest for success in any endeavor, we can waste enormous amounts of time and energy with envy and wishful thinking. Millions of Americans are obsessed with envy. So obsessed are they that the energy they need to actually attain what they desire is depleted.

Dreams and ambitions for our selves are healthful, but love for our selves can only begin with respect for our selves as they are. Your self will never be able to work for you if it feels you are ashamed of it. Envy tells your self that it is shamefully inadequate.

Wishful thinking and envy, at best, are distractions from working on the reality of what we are and what we can be. It is important that we refuse to compare our self-worth with others. Everyone has equal worth in the eyes of our Higher Power. Discipline is required if we are to brace our selves against the urge to enter a dreamworld where, instead of living our own lives, we live vicariously off others whom we imagine better off than ourselves.

Comparing our selves with others usually results in putting our selves down. Comparing our selves with others usually results in forgetfulness that the lives of the most glamorous of successful people are very often peppered with a variety of tragedies. Comparing our selves with others is not an investment in life, but an investment in dreamland.

I repeat, ambition is healthful; envy is not. Ambition is an energy we can use to take care of our selves as we need. Ambition is seeing something we want and going after it. Envy, on the other hand, is King Baby seeing something it wants, without wanting to make any effort to get it. King Baby does not want to exert energy in getting something it feels it deserves by entitlement. King Baby wastes our time and energy by trying to convince us that we are "deprived" of something which should be ours by right. Instead of taking action to get what we need, King Baby lets us sit and stew over what we don't have.

In self-love recovery, King Baby, as always, needs to be confronted. We use what we have to go after what we need or want. We need to turn envy into ambition. Envy can then be used as an energy to get us into action. Once envy is put into action, it ceases to be envy and becomes a loving action we take on our behalf.

DON'T "TAKE" CARE OF OTHERS

We have learned elsewhere that there is a difference between "caring" and "care-taking." In self-love recovery, we are encouraged to care for, and take care of, our selves. We are also encouraged to care for others, but not to "take" care of them.

Care-taking of others is a disservice we do to our selves and to those we imagine we are helping. Care-taking is assuming a responsibility over others (usually to serve our own codependency needs) that only they can appropriately have for their selves. Taking over someone else's self-responsibility can only have the negative effect of keeping them from loving themselves, by continuing a life-style of immaturity, subservience, and dependence upon us or others.

I am not saying we should not be helpful to others. I am not denying that care must be taken for infants or children and for those who are physically disabled or psychologically handicapped. But even that caring must be open-ended so that it will discontinue when, and if, those who are disabled or handicapped will be able to assume responsibility for themselves. What needs to be decried is taking care of others who need self-responsibility to grow as they need.

It is an arrogant disservice to others to take from their hands the power to become independent, even if they offer that power to us. There are mothers, for example who hold their own children in bondage by not "letting go" or by not encouraging their children to take responsibility for their own well-being. I have known men in their forties and fifties who performed competent full-time jobs but still lived with a mother who fixed their beds, laundered their clothes, and prepared their meals. There are other parents who refuse to "let go" in more subtle fashion. They hold themselves personally responsible when their grown children choose paths of self-destruction. "Where did *we* go wrong?"

We are not in error to be caring and helpful. We are not in error in taking care of someone who is helpless. We are not in error by being sympathetic and compassionate. However, we are in error whenever we "take" the responsibility which another person needs to have for himself or herself. We cannot assume responsibility for how anyone else's life unfolds. There is something radically missing in our own self-love when we feel compelled to do so. We might well be co-dependent and only feel good about our selves as long as we are "needed." We disguise our bankrupt love for our selves as "love" for others.

It is only as we come to love our selves adequately by assuming self-responsibility that we realize that others need to do this for themselves also.

AVOID TOXIC PEOPLE

In self-love recovery, we learn that being open to loving everybody else is a self-loving action we perform for our selves. While we indeed are expanding our love for our selves to include all others, there are definitely people who, at the present stage of our development, may be toxic to our selves and should be avoided.

"Toxic" people are those who are so fixed in their negativity, so ill-disposed to any change for themselves, so manipulative and shame-inducing, so ever-ready with put-downs and sarcasm, that they are actually dangerous to the well-being of others in self-love recovery. Toxic people are not to be judged or condemned as bad people; they are simply to be avoided.

We owe it to our selves to protect them from whatever could jeopardize their self-love recovery program. We can hope for the recovery of others, but at the moment we are working

204/Falling In Love With Your Self

on our own recovery of self-love. In recovery we are particularly vulnerable to setbacks. We need to avoid anyone whose attitudes and behavior endanger our selves, or prevent us from taking care of our selves as we need.

We need also to avoid those who may not be quite "toxic" but certainly have a negative effect on our self-esteem. There may be others who, even with the best of intentions, can hold us in a bondage of dependency. There may be others, especially those in positions of authority, who can manipulate us in their best interests rather than our own.

We need to remember that no one has power over our selves except as we give them power. No one has power over us except as we empower them. Parents, spouses, children, teachers, friends, coaches, therapists, clergy, politicians, even policemen, lawyers, doctors, and the dentist with his drill, all rely on empowerment from those whom they serve. When the "service" turns to "control," it is time to cease the empowerment and take care of our selves as we need.

DON'T WAIT FOR SOMEONE ELSE TO DO IT FOR YOU

When we are hurting, we not only have a tendency to blame someone or something else for our situation; we also have a tendency to wait for someone to come along and make things better for us. We feel even more sorry for ourselves when we see no one coming to do just that. We sit on the "pity pot" and decry how little everyone else cares.

The question, however, should not be whether or not someone else cares enough about our selves, but whether *we* care enough. If we wish to love our selves as we need, we are the first ones we need to turn to. Wait for someone else and we just might wait forever.

Even relying too much on "experts" or authority figures can be self-defeating. Anytime we put our selves into the hands of another should be a well-thought-out, conscious decision.

The self feels rejected and inadequate the less it is permitted to create solutions for its own welfare. If our selves can get us into trouble, they can also get us out. Requesting help from agencies outside our selves is appropriate only after we have honored our own selves with the "first shot."

DON'T GIVE UP ON YOUR SELF

Perseverance is courage that endures. Sticking to our recovery program is difficult. It is all too easy and tempting to regress and run back to our old tapes. Fighting our natural resistance to change is a major effort. It takes time before results are tangible from practicing our affirmative actions.

Remember that in self-love recovery we are attempting to practically re-invent ourselves with brand new attitudes and behaviors with respect to our selves. We are working on a major transformation of our selves. Such a major overhaul cannot happen in short run. We have habits to modify, old tapes to re-program, handicaps to overcome. Furthermore, we might not receive much encouragement from those near and dear to us. There may be others who will not support our recovery of self-love. They might prefer us as our old selves, playing our old tapes, to which they have become accustomed.

Perseverance is possible only if we anticipate discipline and long-term effort right from the start. Setbacks are to be expected. "Two steps forward, one step back" will likely be our pace. Our recovery will mark only "one day at a time."

Perseverance is possible only as we consider the alternatives to recovery. Do we really wish to continue in the self-diminished state we were in before we began to learn how to love our selves as we need? Forging ahead in self-love recovery may produce a strain on us, but so does remaining out of self-love recovery. Either way will cost us. The "pay-off" of self-love recovery, however, is positive and productive. It can only lead us to a better future for our selves. Our selves will be delighted that we are not giving up on them.

As we have stressed before, we are not looking for "cures"; we are content to be "in recovery." Commitment to perseverance saves us from the folly of expecting the "quick fix." We are trained by the advertising industry to look for immediate satisfaction, for an immediate cure for what ails us. We want "instant relief." Recovering the love for our selves that we need is not a "fix," but a *process*—a process that needs to last our lifetime. Recovering alcoholics know that they are never cured. For the rest of their lives, they will be "recovering" alcoholics. For the rest of our lives, we will be in recovery of the love for our selves that we need. There is no end to growth in self-knowledge and self-love. The "sky is the limit" and we are ready to fly.

Refuse To Be Victimized by Opinions, Expectations, and Criticism

Refuse To Be Victimized by the "Shoulds"

Don't Stay Stuck in Self-Diminishing or Non-Nourishing Religious Systems

Refuse To Sit in Judgment

Never Harbor Ill-Will, Hatred, or Unforgiveness

Don't Isolate

Don't Amplify

"Fear Not"

Don't Worry

Don't Rely on Logic

Stop "Personalizing" Every Mistake

Avoid Envy and "Wishful Thinking"

Avoid Toxic People

Don't Wait for Someone Else To Do It for You

Don't Give Up on Your Self

PART THREE
CONTINUING CARE IN
SELF-LOVE RECOVERY

10

Twelve-Step Spirituality

It has been my contention since the beginning of this book that no program, exercise, or technique for recovering and enhancing love for our selves will have long-lasting effect without a connection to a solid spiritual foundation. By "spiritual" I do not mean "religious" in the common use of that term. I am not speaking about being pious, or about practicing any particular religion, or about belonging to any particular religious congregation. "Spiritual" is what goes beyond our physical, psychological, and emotional components, to the inner depths of our being. Our spirituality is our personal meaning system, our fundamental world outlook, and how basically we "respond" to life. In this sense, even a confirmed atheist has a spirituality.

Every religious system offers a spirituality, a way to understand and live life. It is not my position here to analyze, criticize, or discriminate between various religions and their claims. If a particular religious system gives you the help you need to enhance love for your self and others, by all means utilize its services. If you have not found a religious system that nurtures you to become all that you can be, I would offer for your consideration Twelve-Step spirituality. I suggest that Twelve-Step spirituality is as solid a spiritual foundation for self-love recovery as you could find.

Twelve-Step spirituality is not aligned with any particular religious faith, sect, or denomination. Twelve-Step spirituality is a path of spiritual growth which draws upon fundamental principles that are common to all the major religions in the history of mankind. It is not at odds or in competition with any religious system. Twelve-Step spirituality is for anyone and everyone.

Twelve-Step spirituality is the foundation upon which Alcoholics Anonymous was built. We need only refer here to the unprecedented world-wide success of Alcoholics Anonymous and its many affiliated Twelve-Step groups in handling a variety of addictions and dependencies, in bringing health, meaning, and sobriety to millions who were in the grips of addiction. There is something extraordinarily powerful about Twelve-Step spirituality to be so successful. "It works, when you work it!" While difficult to practice for some, it is simple to understand. Some contemporary spiritual writers contend that Twelve-Step spirituality is the spiritual wave of the future.

Again, Twelve-Step programs neither reject nor endorse any particular religious system. Twelve-Step spirituality can fit into the life-style of anyone, whatever their religious affiliation. Twelve-Step programs don't even promote or advertise themselves as a spiritual system. Members are drawn into programs through "attraction," mainly in seeing "recovery in action" in Twelve-Step program members.

I offer this brief commentary on the Twelve steps only to give the reader a taste of what I believe to be a solid, and universally acceptable, spiritual foundation for self-love recovery. I trust that I am not doing the Twelve-Step program a disservice by such brevity. For more detailed information and literature on the Twelve steps and Twelve-Step programs, readers are encouraged to contact bookstores, or any Twelve-Step meeting. Most metropolitan areas have hundreds of Twelve-Step meetings running on any given day. Consult the Yellow Pages for Alcoholics Anonymous as a start.

In the opening chapters of this book, we discussed in some detail the first three steps because of their importance as predispositions in our journey to recover and enhance our self-love. The first three steps are the foundation upon which the remaining steps depend. There is a reason for the order of the Twelve-Steps from the first to the last. Although all the steps work dynamically with each other, the success of each depends in large measure on working the step which precedes it.

The success of the whole Twelve-Step program depends on the openness of our minds and hearts to embrace and try it. The program is an action program. The steps need to be *worked*. The work, as we might expect, is inner work. As Twelve-Step authors indicate, most of the inner work of the Twelve-Step Program will go on in the unlogical, inner depths of our unconscious as we work each step, which is exactly where any effective work in recovery and self-transformation has to go on.

Twelve-Step spirituality is wonderfully adaptive to our quest for loving our selves as we need. Twelve-Step spirituality is a path of growth in self-love. In Twelve-Step spirituality we search for honest knowledge and appreciation of who and what we are. We search for our true center, and in discovering it we recover the love for our selves that we need.

(Please note that my summation and commentary do not indicate any official endorsement or approval by Alcoholics Anonymous or any affiliated Twelve-Step program.)

THE FIRST STEP: *We admitted we were powerless (over alcohol, sex, emotions, food, drugs, work, other people, loving our selves as we need, etc.), and that our lives had become unmanageable.*

The first step for most is the most difficult, especially for those of us who have not loved our selves as we need. Not being secure in our own self-love, we are often desperate for "control" and external guarantees or assurances. None of us want to admit we are powerless over anything. The need to control lives with us as King and Queen Baby. They never, ever want to let go. The first step presents us with our first paradox, by promising that we will win only if we lose, that we will "get it" only when we give it up, and that we will regain some power over our lives only if we surrender all of it. Recovery for an alcoholic, for example, only begins with the admission that he or she cannot recover on his or her own.

Thanks to King Baby, we have more addictions, compulsions, and obsessions than we might possibly imagine, or want to admit. But it isn't merely addictions and obsessions over which we have no control. Life offers no guarantees for anything to anybody. We have no guarantee that we will recover adequate love for our selves even if we follow our program meticulously. Life overwhelms us with its mystery and unpredictability. One microscopic bacteria can put an end to all of one's most feverish dreams and plans. Despite vociferous denials by King Baby, we "control" little or nothing in life. This step is honest and makes sense.

King Baby's incessant demands have made our lives unmanageable. For all our efforts, we are not what we want to be. We are not where we want to be. For all our attempts to control people, events, and our lives, things are not falling into place as we anticipated. We don't love our selves as we need. We are not as happy as we would like to be. We do not possess the peace we would like to have. We simply can't manage it on our own. The first step allows us finally to admit it openly.

STEP TWO: *Came to believe that a Power greater than ourselves could restore us to sanity.*

If we can silence the denials and protests of King Baby and admit our powerlessness, it won't be a very big step to admit that there must be something or someone greater than ourselves that could help us accomplish what we can't do for our selves. If we can be humble enough to look around this big, wonderful, mysterious, evolving world of ours, we can see that there are powers above and beyond us. Giving up our illusions of control, we can see that there is a Power that governs and guides all creation—a Power that governs and guides us as part of that creation, whether we like it or not, whether we choose to think about it or not—and that this Power has our best interests in mind and is more than willing to help us if we allow.

What this step comes down to is the fundamental question we already addressed in Chapter Five: Are we merely bits of cosmic dust, randomly floating in a mindless universe, or are we children of a benevolent Creator? If we are bits of dust, I shouldn't be writing these words, and you shouldn't be reading them. If we are children of a benevolent Power, we can trust that we are in good hands. We can trust that those hands will guide us to a healthier and more loving life, if we allow.

STEP THREE: *Made a decision to turn our wills and our lives over to the care of God, as we understood Him.*

"Let go and let God" is a slogan of the Twelve-Step program. "Surrender" is the willingness to give up control. Paradoxically, surrender is the supreme act of self-love. To surrender our wills and our lives to God, however we understand God, is to let our selves know that we care enough, and love them enough, to give them the very best care we can find.

It is not enough that we simply acknowledge that God is; we need to surrender our wills and lives into God's care. Surrender is only effective if it comes from the heart. And, as we have seen, this is difficult to do. That is why in the beginning all that is asked from us in this step is a "decision" to surrender—that we at least be "willing." It will take time and the grace of our Higher Power for actual surrender to come about.

Surrender is replacing King Baby on the throne with our Higher Power. And that is precisely what makes us so hesitant. King Baby does not want to give up. We always hedge. We surrender a little here, a little there, but always try to retain some little control over our lives. We desperately want to maintain some little margin of control in the illusion that it will work for us. But it never does.

It is here that we part company with many self-help authors and programs whose primary aim is to energize our will power and give us more "control." While offering many excellent strategies for building self-esteem and self-love, they offer them in a *context* that can only be found wanting. It is the faulty context that leads my friend to assert that all the self-help books he reads "don't work." The context is not surrender but marshaling our forces to gain more and more control. The context is not reliance on our Higher Power but enhancing the role of King Baby.

Twelve-Step spirituality is as effective as it is precisely

because of its context of *surrender*. We will never find the love we need for our selves by expanding and enhancing our power issues. We can work on self-love recovery through the loving affirmative actions we take on our behalf (or through the technical strategies offered by many self-help authors) as long as we are not striving to attain God-like powers and control. Only in humble acknowledgement of our finite human nature and in recognition of a Power greater than ourselves can our efforts at self-love recovery become realistic. Only in surrendering more and more of our wills and our lives do we achieve the inner peace we desire. The less we surrender, the more grief we must endure.

It will take time to learn that lesson sufficiently. And it is perfectly O.K. to take our time. Maybe we need still more time to learn that we are not doing such a great job with our lives on our own, that a lot of things we thought were good for us aren't, and that when we got what we wanted, we often discovered that we didn't really want it after all. We surrender as we are able, to admit that we have little to lose in surrender.

Surrender, however, becomes easier over time, as we come to realize more fully how much havoc King Baby wreaks in our lives. Surrender becomes easier over time, as we realize what little effect "power" and "control" have over helping us love our selves more and helping us attain the happiness we desire. Surrender becomes easier as we recognize that power and control strategies of whatever kind in self development will not "work" outside a context of surrender.

We are always less threatened by baby steps. The more we return to this step, the more we are willing to surrender, the more we come to realize that our Higher Power is taking better care of us than we could ever hope to do for our selves. God may not always give us what we want, but if we have genuinely put our selves into his hands, he will always give us what we really need. In time we will feel that we are loved by our Higher Power. We will feel cherished and provided for. And perhaps this will be the first time since early childhood that our selves will feel such safety and security.

STEP FOUR: *Made a searching and fearless moral inventory of ourselves.*

In hopes of achieving adequate love for our selves, we have to get to know our selves first. Self-discovery is an important affirmative action in self-love recovery. We cannot love what we do not know. If we are to love our selves as we need, we need to know what makes us tick. If there are things about our selves that we like, all the better to discover them. If there are things about our selves we do not like, all the better to change them.

Step four leads us to discover all we can about our selves—the good and the bad, our bright side and our dark side. This step asks us to be fearlessly honest about what we see and observe in our selves. We do not judge or condemn or shame our selves. We just want to be aware of who and what we really are, and then we will work from there.

The best way to do a moral inventory is to make lists—lists of our good points, assets, talents, potentials, etc.; lists of our bad points, deficits, faults, "sins," etc. Making these lists could take weeks and months. That's OK—just so the lists are made, just so we get to know our selves as we are, and have it down in writing.

STEP FIVE: *Admitted to God, to ourselves, and to another human being the exact nature of our wrongs.*

All of us have our closet of skeletons. There is plenty of debris in the cellars of our souls that has never been cleaned up. As long as the debris stays there, our selves will never feel as lovable as they need. Getting our "wrongs" into the light, out in the open, is one of the most soul-caring acts we can perform.

We fear opening up about our shortcomings, even to ourselves. It requires humility to do so. But opening up to God, ourselves, and another human being about our selves is most often the only way to change debilitating shame to honest guilt.

Guilt, as we have seen, is feeling bad about something we have done; shame is feeling bad about our selves. Guilt tells us we have made a mistake; shame tells us that we are mistakes.

Guilt is healthy and perfectly legitimate. Guilt helps us recognize something about our selves that needs changing. We grow in health and self-love by making the changes *we* need to make. Shame, on the other hand, is unhealthy. Shame is toxic to self-love. Shame actually enervates us from making the changes we need to love our selves as we need.

Owning up to our wrongs, and admitting them to another, gets us on the road to recovery, and gets us out of shame that is poisoning us. We may be very reluctant, however, to share our dark side with another human being. That is why we should be careful about whom we share with. It should be someone we can trust with our confidence. But share we must to relieve the pressure that "secrets" build up in us. It is sound psychology that we can only truly forgive our selves if we "get it out." It is not enough to be aware of our "secrets" ourselves. We can only feel that we are truly willing to surrender when we allow our selves to be vulnerable in sharing what keeps us from loving our selves as we need.

Perhaps sharing in this way will be our first real experience with intimacy. Perhaps sharing this way will be our first experience of embracing our humanity. Perhaps sharing this way will be our first experience of release from our own self-imprisonment.

Whatever the experience, this step is a clear message to our selves that we love and care about them, and are willing to risk anything to get our shortcomings out into the open where they can be examined, forgiven, and forgotten.

STEP SIX: *Were entirely ready to have God remove all these defects of character.*

It's amazing how difficult it is to "let go," even of those character defects that continually diminish our sense of self-worth. There is a bit of masochism in all of us. We would rather sit with what we know, uncomfortable as that might be, rather than launch out into unknown territory.

Sometimes we feel that if we give up our faults, there will be nothing left to us, or that life would become intolerably bor-ing. It happens that slaves get so used to their chains that they cannot imagine living without them. We might protest loudly that we wish to grow, to love our selves as we need, to get rid of anything that would hold us back, but "the proof of the pudding is in the eating." For the new to live, the old must die.

We do not rush in to get rid of all our defects on the spur of a one time decision. Our own inner timetable will set the pace. All this step asks is that we be "entirely ready." All this step asks is that we be prepared to have God remove our defects how, and when, he sees fit. It is a comfort to know that it is up to God to remove our defects. We don't have to go into a whirlwind of self-cleansing. We surrender our defects and even the timetable for their removal into his hands.

STEP SEVEN: *Humbly asked Him to remove our shortcomings.*

If we are truly willing to surrender our lives and our wills, we literally put our selves in God's hands. It will be up to him to remove the shortcomings that prevent us from loving our selves as we need. On our own we can't remove them ourselves. They are too much part of our selves. We have identified with them. We might not even recognize them as shortcomings anymore. It will be up to God to remove them in His good time. What we are asked for in this step is humility—humility to ask for what we need. In our humility we acknowledge that it is God who has the real power to change us for the better. We arrogate less and less control to our selves, even over our shortcomings, and thus find more and more freedom to just be ourselves.

This step also saves us from having to judge what is a shortcoming or not. Some things about our selves that we might consider shortcomings are in fact assets. And some things we might consider assets are, in truth, shortcomings. It will be up to God to decide. We are willing to surrender to his judgment. All we need do is to accept our selves—not degrade our selves, not recriminate with our selves, not put our selves down with judgment or shame. We accept our selves with our shortcomings, and leave their removal up to our Higher Power.

STEP EIGHT: *Made a list of all persons we had harmed, and became willing to make amends to them all.*

In working on recovering adequate love for our selves, we usually cannot comprehend how much we may be unwittingly harming our selves until we comprehend how much we may have harmed others. Surprisingly enough, the hurting we cause other people most often reflects the hurting we do to our selves.

Making a list of people we have harmed, being as thorough as we can, can be depressing. Most of our lists may be quite lengthy. The more people we have been in contact with, the larger our family, the broader our relationships, the more chances we have had to harm others. However depressing it may be, it is soul-purifying work. We hold our selves accountable. Our willingness to confront our wrong-doing shows that we are taking more and more responsibility for our selves.

Being "willing to make amends" to everyone we have harmed takes our accountability one step further. We are never really "responsible" until we accept responsibility for the consequences of our actions or inactions. Being willing to make amends is our way of showing our selves that we mean business about living a life of integrity.

In our Higher Power's plan for us, nothing we ever did was accidental, even our mistakes. Our mistakes of the past are part of God's plan for our future. Being open about the harm we caused others and being willing to make amends to them all takes away self-defeating shame and allows our mistakes to be part of our Higher Power's plan. What was negative can become positive.

STEP NINE: *Made direct amends to such people wherever possible, except when to do so would injure them or others.*

We cannot love our selves as we need if we are full of self-recrimination. As we come to love our selves more and more, the more likely we will be conscious of and sensitive to the injuries we have caused others. This can heap a lot of guilt-feelings upon us.

Honest guilt is healthy and can promote healthy actions on our behalf if we are willing to do something about it. What we do is make amends to people we have harmed, wherever that is possible. We need to clear our slate and repair our bridges. Unless we repair damage done, the memory of it sits in the depths of our being and continues to cause us more harm than we might imagine.

In many cases, making direct amends will be impossible. We have lost touch with great numbers of people we may have harmed in the past. If so, all we can do is "let go" and send our best wishes their way. If there are particular people with whom we can make amends, we do so. It may be just an apology, or it may mean making some substantial restitution.

If it would do more harm than good to bring up issues where we have harmed someone in the past, we refrain from doing so. Our self-healing cannot take place in a context of hurting someone else again by opening up old wounds. We do what we can to "make matters straight" and leave the rest up to our Higher Power.

STEP TEN: *Continued to take personal inventory, and when we were wrong, promptly admitted it.*

To "have our house in order" is an enormous step we make in self-healing. We show our selves that we love them enough to remove all self-defeating baggage from the past. We are changing for the better, day by day, but our journey in self-reform is never complete. Human as we are, we will continue to make mistakes.

We are not, and never will be, perfect. This step allows us to be imperfect. This step allows us to be human. This step gets us to face our limitations on a daily basis and helps us not to base our self-love recovery on the illusion of "perfectionism." We will not go into denial about our shortcomings nor will we bury our guilt. We will be responsible enough to our selves, and love our selves enough, to monitor our progress day by day.

When we have acted against our principles, or strayed from the path of loving our selves as we need, we will promptly admit it. We deal with it when, and as, the occasion arises.

There is enormous freedom in no longer putting up with King Baby's predictable denials of limitation. There is enormous relief to our selves to be able to promptly say we were wrong and we are sorry. We put an end to much of the "mickey mouse" and side-stepping that is so damaging to our sense of integrity.

STEP ELEVEN: *Sought through prayer and meditation to improve our conscious contact with God as we understood God, praying only for knowledge of His will for us and the power to carry that out.*

The great spiritual masters teach that the Creator, the eternal Self, is at the heart of our own deepest self. Some teach that our deepest self is even identifiable with the eternal Self. However we might understand God, our Higher Power is at our spiritual center. Our Higher Power is within us where we are most truly ourselves. It would only stand to reason that we would want to be in closest possible contact with this infinite resource.

"Prayer" is talking to our Higher Power; "meditation" is listening to our Higher Power talk to us. In prayer we ask to know God's will; in meditation we listen for God's answer.

In prayer we ask for power that we do not have on our own. In prayer we ask to carry out our Higher Power's will and trust that our Higher Power will help us. God wants us to love our selves. He is more than willing to effect those things in our lives which will bring us to our highest fulfillment, if only we allow Him.

There is great consolation, encouragement, and empowerment in realizing that God does have a will for us. We are not abandoned or forgotten. The Creator has a plan for us and will bring that plan about in our best interests, if only we allow it.

We will cooperate, but we will let our Higher Power carry the burden of self-love recovery for us. Our task is to be willing to surrender more and more each day. The more we let go, the more God can do. We do what we need to do, but leave all outcomes totally in God's hands. We "go with the flow." We do not demand "instant relief." We trust that whatever turns out for us is God's will and therefore is in our best interests, whether it looks that way at the given moment or not.

STEP TWELVE: *Having had a spiritual awakening as the result of these steps, we tried to carry this message to others, and to practice these principles in all our affairs.*

Any good thing we accomplish is accompanied by a desire to share the "good news." Happiness shared is twice experienced.

Working the Twelve Steps we develop our own story, our own "good news," our own "gospel." If we actually work the Twelve Steps, we will have an "awakening." Working the Twelve Steps cannot help but have a significant impact on our self-understanding and behavior. Working the Twelve Steps cannot help but transform us, and have a major impact on how we understand and love our selves.

Non-initiates or spiritual cynics may find these steps to be "simplistic." But that is far from the truth. These steps are the foundation of all the great religions known to man. They have had impact on millions. They continue to have major impact on millions who are in recovery from addictions over which few, if any, other methods have ever been as successful. It would be "simplistic" to discount their power.

"Love your neighbor as yourself." Once we have achieved a spiritual awakening, once we begin truly loving our selves as we need, we take the next important step of bringing the good news of our recovery to others who are in need of the same. Love for our selves begins to overflow the parameters of our own being and pours out to others. This is the nature of love. Loving people cannot help but share their love. Most religions teach that this is the reason the Creator created the world in the first place. The Creator overflowed with love, and the world began.

Self-love recovery is a gift. Even if we take affirmative actions on our behalf, we still surrender, because we are powerless to create adequate love for our selves totally on our own. In surrendering we receive what we need to make us whole. Gaining more self-love, we are more than ready and able to turn our love toward others in need. We do not reach out to change other people. They must change on their own in their own good time, just as we do, in our own time. No one was able to fill the hole in our soul until we had reached a point of no return, until we had come to see the futility of our own efforts to bring our selves the happiness we desired and deserved. It will work the same with others.

We reach out to share our good "tidings of joy," of the work that our Higher Power has accomplished in us. We share by telling our story, not by telling others what their story should be. Others will be drawn to us and to their own self-love recovery by the modeling of love they see operating within us, never by injunctions we place on them, urging them to change.

We never know what is best for anyone, so we oftentimes help others best by simply being in recovery ourselves. Working on our issues and finding satisfactory results impresses others and draws them into participation.

We learn another great paradox in this step: gifts can only be kept if they are given away. Our continuation in recovery depends on our willingness to share the love we receive. In the actual sharing, we learn to love our selves all the more. As we change, our attitudes change, and when our attitudes change we notice people changing around us also. We remember what we learned earlier in this book, that we change the world by changing our selves. Changing our selves, we begin to see the infinite worth of each and every fellow human being, called to the same destiny and glory with us.

The principles we have learned in these steps are principles which are applicable to all of life. That is why we commit our selves to practice them in *all* our daily affairs. The Twelve Steps are a way of life. Self-love recovery is a way of life.

A PERSONAL SPIRITUAL INVENTORY

It may be helpful in self-love recovery to explore where we stand in our spiritual development. The following statements are rooted in Twelve-Step spirituality and can prove useful in our self-exploration. We can determine where we are and what may need our greater attention. Check and see how many apply.

____ I live in the present moment, acknowledging that "NOW" is all there really is. I accept "what is" as significant for me right now.

____ I enjoy a simple life; I enjoy the simple things in life: I try to "keep it simple." "Live and let live" is a motto I can appreciate.

____ "Easy does it." I take "one day at a time." "First things first." I know that whatever happens, "this too shall pass."

____ I acknowledge there is a Power in this world greater than I. I accept that this Power loves and cares for me.

____ I believe in myself and accept as a primary directive: "to thine own self be true." I accept my self and am grateful for life and the opportunities for happiness it affords me.

____ I accept that God, as I understand him, has a plan for me. That I am on a journey to a destiny for which I have been specifically called. I am on a mission. I trust that God is guiding and directing me to fulfill my destiny in life. I will "let go and let God."

____ I look at the positive side of things and know that however things turn out for me, it will be the best for me.

____ I acknowledge that I am human and not perfect. I do not have to be. I acknowledge that I will make mistakes and that I will continue to be sorry for them and make amends where I am able. I am committed to having God remove my character defects, one by one.

___ I accept and embrace the fundamental mysteriousness of life, together with life's ambiguities and paradoxes.

___ I feel connected to all other human beings and wish for them the best I could wish for my self.

___ I forgive readily.

___ I am able more and more to detach from my self, and more neutrally view and observe my life as an unfolding drama. I can laugh at my self.

___ I meditate and pray to my Higher Power on a daily basis.

___ I seek to develop my highest potential and consciousness and call upon my Higher Power to help me transcend my self.

___ I seek union with the Creator and Source of all being.

11

Self-Loving Affirmations

One of the most important affirmative actions we take on our behalf in self-love recovery is affirming our selves. Making positive affirmations to our selves is meant to counteract a lifetime of negations that we have heard from others or from ourselves. We need to develop a habit of affirming our selves on a daily basis. In this chapter we will learn some effectively motivating self-affirmations.

Affirmations for Co-Dependents

Co-Dependents Anonymous is a national program for co-dependents that is based on the Twelve-Step program initiated by Alcoholics Anonymous. Using the Twelve-Step format, "CoDA" has helped, and continues to help, thousands of people who have grave difficulties in their relationships.

There are many definitions of co-dependency. Initially co-dependency was attributed to spouses of practicing alcoholics who, for all their suffering in living with an alcoholic, actually and unwittingly contributed to the alcoholic's continued drinking. Some inner need of the victim was being addressed as long as the alcoholic carried on his or her self-destructive behavior. How else can you explain Terry, who gravely suffered under an alcoholic father, leaving home and marrying a man who gave all the indications of alcoholism in their courtship.

Studies indicate that this is not an unfamiliar phenomenon. People who have undergone abuse of any sort as children

227

may very well end up perpetuating that abuse by getting involved with, or married to, someone who will replicate a living situation with which the victim has long become habituated.

The definition of "co-dependency" has widened over recent years. Melody Beattie, author of the best-selling book *Codependent No More,* defines a co-dependent as "a person who has let another person's behavior affect him or her, and who is obsessed with controlling that person's behavior." Co-dependency, according to Beattie, is primarily reactionary behavior to the expectations and behavior of others—reactionary, in that co-dependents tend to overreact or underreact, but rarely simply act from their own initiative.

Co-dependents are obsessed with other people and are significantly affected by the behavior of others. Co-dependents are significantly dependent for a sense of self-esteem on how other people accept and treat them. Their self-esteem depends not on self-love, but on how others regard them. Co-dependents are therefore further obsessed with controlling and manipulating other people's behavior toward them.

Co-dependents are basically identified by low self-esteem, a poor sense of self-identification, over-concern about the actions and reactions of others, and helplessness with communication and intimacy issues. Co-dependents are typically beleaguered with shame, low self-worth, suppressed anger, and a defective sense of personal boundaries. Co-dependents obviously have serious problems with loving themselves adequately and appropriately.

It is estimated that practically every one of us is co-dependent to some degree. Those of us in self-love recovery are particularly vulnerable to co-dependency. In our pursuit of loving our selves as we need, it might be very profitable to read the excellent books on co-dependency authored by Melody Beattie. It might also be of great value to attend a local Co-Dependents Anonymous meeting.

I have attended a number of CoDA meetings myself and have never failed to find them supportive and enlightening. The particular meetings I attended normally closed with the reading of a set of affirmations based on *Shame Faced,* by Stephanie E.

These affirmations were offered as a tool to aid in replacing negative messages absorbed from the past. They were read slowly and meditatively by the group leader. They never failed to move me.

I offer them here, with brief commentaries, as an aid to the self-affirmation all of us need. Each affirmation should be read in a spirit of meditation, rather than as a point of information. Read the affirmation slowly. Taste it with your tongue and take it into your heart. The affirmations have a power to help you see how perfectly lovable you are.

For beginners, it might be best to read these affirmations through, in their title form, many times a day. I find them particularly useful when I am under stress or in any uneasy space where I feel threatened, unwanted, abandoned, or misunderstood.

Loving our selves means taking care of our selves. Affirming our selves, taking positive affirmations into our hearts, is one of the best means of taking care of our selves appropriately.

JUST FOR TODAY, I WILL RESPECT MY OWN AND OTHERS' BOUNDARIES

"Live and let live," says the Twelve-Step program. Live your own life. I cannot change you and you cannot change me. I cannot control you, or your affairs, and you cannot control me, or my affairs. There are boundaries that separate us by the very fact that we are individual human beings, with our unique personalities, and with our own needs and wants.

You have your space and timing, and so do I. It is not right for me to invade your space and timing. It is not right for you to invade mine. When boundaries are broken, we both suffer. It is wrong for me to impose my expectations on you, as it is for you to impose your expectations on me.

It is wrong for me to try to manipulate you to like me. Love bought at the price of manipulation is not love at all; it is only manipulation. I cannot allow you to manipulate me either. My love is not on an auction block for sale or barter. I am learning to love my self enough that I don't need to manipulate you anymore. I hope you are learning to love your self too. We are both human beings, equal in dignity and limitation. You may invite me into your time and space and I may invite you into mine. But neither of us can be "gate crashers" and try to impose our will or control on the other.

Your personhood is sacred and inviolable. I am learning more each day that mine is too. I ask you to respect that sacredness and inviolability, as I will respect yours. Anything less than that respect is simply unacceptable.

I show love and respect for my self by keeping my boundaries intact. I would rather be completely alone than be abused. I show love and respect for you by allowing you to keep your boundaries intact. This is a pledge we give to each other, if just for today.

JUST FOR TODAY, I WILL BE VULNERABLE WITH SOMEONE I TRUST

When I make a pledge to uphold my boundaries and to respect yours, this does not mean that I wish to be isolated from you, or distanced. I need to express the fundamental goodness that I have as a human being. I also need to express my weaknesses and fragility. I do not wish to keep my honest human limitations to myself. Being human and having limitations is perfectly OK. Being in need of human companionship and support is perfectly OK. That is why we are human together, and share the same life and dreams.

To share means I need to be vulnerable. Since I trust you, I must invite you into my self to have a look around—to see my light, and my shadows. The light and the dark are both part of me. If I am to share with you, I need to allow you to see me as I am. Trusting you allows me to believe that you will not hurt me after you see me as I am. I will not allow myself to be abused or belittled. I trust that you will accept and love me as I am, good and bad, saint and sinner, God-like, yet very human.

As I learn to love my self more and more, I am more and more able to be vulnerable. As I begin to see how lovable I am, I am less reluctant to allow you in to have a look. When you see what I'm beginning to see, you will find me lovable too, even if just for today.

JUST FOR TODAY, I WILL TAKE ONE COMPLIMENT AND HOLD IT IN MY HEART FOR MORE THAN JUST A FLEETING MOMENT. I WILL LET IT NURTURE ME

When I didn't love my self, I had a difficult time receiving compliments. My image of myself was so bad that, no matter how complimented I was, it just didn't seem to fit. Getting praise or congratulations made me feel uncomfortable and I would brush it off with a disclaimer.

As I am learning to love my self as is fitting, I am beginning to see compliments as "fitting." I am not asking for flattery. I am beginning to feel more at ease with myself that I don't need the artificial inflation of flattering words. I know what is the truth. If I have done something well, I deserve to be complimented for it. I will take that compliment and not immediately disclaim it. I will hold it in my heart, and if it fits, it fits.

A compliment is a gift, and I am learning to accept gifts more graciously. A compliment, if it is honest, is a nurturing gift. It warms the soul and brings a sense of joy of being appreciated. I love my self enough that I wish to take good care of my self, and to nurture my self in whatever way I can. Compliments help, if just for today.

JUST FOR TODAY, I WILL ACT IN A WAY THAT I WOULD ADMIRE IN SOMEONE ELSE

Before I began learning to love my self, I found myself chronically envious of the talents and abilities of others. Not liking what I saw inside my self, I wanted to make up for it by wishing, unrealistically of course, that I could be someone else.

As I come to love and appreciate my self more each day, I am discovering that the qualities I admire most in others are qualities I have in my self. I wouldn't be able to recognize them in others if that were not the case. If I admire it, I have it. If I have a hard time seeing a good quality or behavior in my self and more easily see it in others, this doesn't mean that that quality isn't in me, or that the behavior is unnatural to me. It simply means that I have difficulty seeing it in my self, at least for now.

So what I will do is to imitate the behavior I admire so much in someone else, in hopes that it will feel more natural to me as time goes on—maybe the way you use gentle words even with people who upset you. I can do that. That ability is in me. I will act it out, until it becomes as natural to me as it is to you.

If I love my self, I will always act in my best interests. What I can "admire" is in my best interests. I will act in ways that I admire, if just for today.

I AM A CHILD OF GOD

I am not God. What a relief to finally acknowledge and live according to that fact of life. The weight of the world is not on my shoulders. I don't have to carry the guilt of mankind in my heart. I don't have to be perfect, or appear perfect, or pretend to be anything other than what I am. The continuation of the cosmos does not depend on how well I work things out.

But I am a child of God. What a thought! What wonders we are. I am divine offspring. My being shares the Being of all that is. My self participates in the eternal Self which is in all that is. God's life is in me.

God's love is in me. God is love, and where love is, there is God. When I love, I am in God. Whether I love or don't love, however, God is still in me—supporting me, leading me, inviting me, coaxing me, empowering me to appreciate the wonder of creation that I am.

I am not an accident in a universe that happened by chance. I am not a victim of mindless or malevolent chaos. I was planned for, and wished for, and created for eternal light and love, as befits a child of God. In coming to love myself, I become aware of my inviolable dignity. The more aware I am of that dignity, the more love I can have for my self.

I AM A PRECIOUS PERSON

It only stands to reason that I am "precious," if I am a child of God.

I remember that my mother had some cheap costume jewelry. It didn't bother her in the least that my little sister, as a child, would play with that jewelry all she wanted. But in the same drawer with the costume jewelry was a box that we all learned never to touch. In it were contained a few pieces of jewelry, heirlooms, which had been handed down for generations in my family. They were "precious" to my mother, and we respected that.

You can't handle precious china like plastic plates and cups. We handle what is precious in different ways than we handle what is ordinary or of little value. Being a child of God, I am precious because my value is divine. I need to treat myself accordingly. And I need to treat others accordingly too, because everyone shares in that same divinity. I will handle my self and others with "kid gloves."

I AM A WORTHWHILE PERSON

What determines something's worth? Why is gold worth more than tin? Why is a diamond worth more than glass? Why is caviar worth more than anchovies?

What makes a person worthwhile? Is it family of origin? Affluence and influence? Clothes, salary, position on the social

ladder? Education, breeding, degrees, talents? "Worth" arises
from the perception of those making an appraisal.

I am worthwhile because of God's appraisal of me. I am
worthwhile because God looks at me with love and longing.
God's perception of me makes me, and you, what we are: worthy beyond measure. The life of any of us is worth the price of
the entire universe. Our worthiness is in the eye of the
Perceiver. For children of God, we are worthwhile just for
being. "And he looked upon what he had created, and found it
very good."

I AM BEAUTIFUL INSIDE AND OUTSIDE

Again, all "beauty is in the eye of the beholder." If there is
a God who looks upon me with love, I am beautiful inside and
outside. There is something about me, and you, and all of us,
that has captured his eye. If that wasn't the case, we simply
would not be here. I repeat, I am not an accident in some mindless cosmic jumble-jamble. The eye of the Beholder sees something in us that attracts his loving gaze.

I am made beautiful, because God who appreciates, without prejudice, finds me perfectly attractive. I can live with that.

I LOVE MYSELF UNCONDITIONALLY

If I am going to love my self at all, why not go all the way?
Loving my self conditionally has already caused me great pain.
When I had to play up to the conditional love of others, I found
my self on an endless merry-go-round of trying to please, trying
to do the right thing, trying to say the right words. Just so that
others would like me, I never allowed myself to express my self
the way I felt. I became a prisoner of the whims of others and
felt obliged to pipe to their tunes.

If I will love my self at all, I will love my self without condition. No strings attached. I would love to feel that love from others. I have missed that kind of love when I didn't get it as a

child. It hurt, and still hurts. So I intend to give myself the works. If anyone is going to accept me as I am, I am going to be the first in line.

I CAN ALLOW MYSELF AMPLE LEISURE TIME WITHOUT FEELING GUILTY

Life is serious business, but it is not all that serious. We are endowed with humor for a reason. We need to laugh. We need to laugh at our selves and our overbearing seriousness from time to time. There is a time and place for fun. All work and no play makes everything dull.

My best moments in life have occurred when I have grown through my inner work. I want to make those "best moments" a daily habit. I need to put time aside to take care of my self and my continuing development. I owe that to my self. I would not hesitate to take time out and care for someone I loved. Shall I treat my self any less generously? I will take all the time I need to take care of what matters to me the most. I will feel guilty if I don't.

I DESERVE TO BE LOVED BY MYSELF AND OTHERS

For some reason I have grown up in life thinking of my self and my real needs last. I never even bothered discovering what my real needs were. I have not taken care of my self as I should. I talked myself out of it. There were always plenty of distractions. When I didn't love my self, I didn't think I deserved anything.

As I come to love my self more, I am beginning to appreciate my self and how gifted I am. In appreciating my self more, I know that I deserve more—all the love I can get from myself and others.

I AM LOVED BECAUSE I DESERVE LOVE

Love is the essence of the universe. Love does make the whole world go round. Love is not an accident any more than I am an accident. Love is not a take-it-or-leave-it proposition. Love is the whole purpose of life and being. It's not just "nice" if someone happens to love me. Without love I am essentially incomplete and unfulfilled as a human being.

We are talking about something so vital here, so rightful, so according-to-design, that we cannot treat love in the commonplace and often trashy way it is handled in modern music. We are talking about the essence of our being. I am loved because it is rightful that it be so. Love is not frosting on the cake. Love is the whole cake, the whole ball of wax. I am grateful for love, but it is only rightful that I have it. Love is the very destiny for which I was born.

I AM A CHILD OF GOD AND I DESERVE LOVE, PEACE, PROSPERITY AND SERENITY

Again, love, peace, prosperity and serenity are not special privileges of a select few; they are the birthrights of every human being. They are endowments to which all of us are entitled by the fact that we are born human. My love, peace, prosperity and serenity are not "bonuses" for successful living. They are an integral part of my life, and I need to work to make them an integral part of my life, on a daily basis.

I FORGIVE MYSELF FOR HURTING MYSELF AND OTHERS

This affirmation stings a bit—stings, because it brings back memories of how badly I have treated my self in the past, how much time and energy I have wasted in self-defeating attitudes and behavior, how much I have neglected to take care of my self in ways that were life-giving and appropriate.

This affirmation stings a bit because I am learning how much I have hurt others. I have hurt others because I have not loved my self enough. In defending a sensitive and damaged self-image, I have lashed out at others, assigning blame to them for the negative ways I was feeling about my self. I was a porcupine who learned to use my quills skillfully to protect my tender skin inside.

I forgive myself, however, for acting in hurtful ways to anyone, especially my self. The past is past. I have learned to let go. Loving my self now as I need will make me more relaxed and compassionate.

I FORGIVE MYSELF FOR LETTING OTHERS HURT ME

I was often bothered when I thought of what I have put up with by letting others violate my personal boundaries, how often I set myself up for getting "burned." In my desperation to be noticed or approved or loved, I have allowed my self to be used and abused. I have tried to live up to everybody's expectations for me but my own. It never helped, but rather made me more and more dependent on everyone else but my self. I was losing my soul.

I thank my Higher Power for bringing me back to my own senses. The past is past. I have learned to let go. I forgive myself for being so open to abuse. In learning to love my self adequately, I no longer need to be at the mercy of others. With the help of my Higher Power, I will learn to take care of my self.

I FORGIVE MYSELF FOR ACCEPTING SEX WHEN I WANTED LOVE

If you cannot afford an original, why not get a copy? If you cannot get the real thing, why not settle for an imitation? The problem with love, however, is that there is no "copy," there is no imitation or substitute. You either have it or you don't.

As strong as our drives are, what we all want is love. The hole we feel in our souls is a hunger for love. That emptiness, that hollow we are so anxious to fill with distractions, is nothing more than a hunger for real love. Using sex, or any other substitute, will never supply for the real thing.

I forgive myself for using substitutes when I should have been working for the real thing. As I learn to love my self more, I will not need the substitutes or imitations. I will have the real thing.

I AM WILLING TO ACCEPT LOVE

How different my expectations are when I come to appreciate how worthwhile and beautiful I am. I can accept love. It is the most natural thing in the world. In the past, when I was so ashamed of my self, I was not open to love. I mistrusted love. I mistrusted those who may have offered love. I didn't feel that I was worthy of love, and therefore I often figured that those who offered love to me must have had "an angle." I often threw love right back into the faces of those who offered it to me.

As I come to appreciate and love my self more, I see how deserving of love I am. I am willing to accept love without questioning the motives of those who are offering it to me.

I AM NOT ALONE; I AM ONE WITH GOD AND THE UNIVERSE

The greatest fear a child experiences is that of abandonment. I think that fear stays with us all our lives. To feel isolated and abandoned is certainly one of our most painful experiences. But I am learning that I am never alone. I accept that there is a Higher Power that creates and governs all that is, a Power that is in, and expresses itself through, everything that is, including me. I am one with God. This universe is an extension of God and me. It is my home.

The more I contemplate the infinite superiority of a Loving Intelligence in this universe, the more I acknowledge that there is a loving plan for all that is and transpires in life, the more I am willing to surrender my self with abandonment to God and his will. In surrender, I become one with God. In surrender, I no longer keep him at a distance. In surrender, I no longer doubt him. There is no better way that I could love and care for my self more.

I AM WHOLE AND GOOD

In the past I always looked outside of my self for what could heal me, what could make me feel good about my self, what could satisfy me and make me whole. I gave my power to take care of my self over to others. I am now learning that everything I need to feel good about myself and to feel worthwhile is right here inside me. What is truly needed is all already within. The great spiritual masters have always taught this. Jesus stated firmly that "the kingdom is already within you."

I am whole and good in myself. As God looked out upon his creation and found it good, I look upon my self and find it good too. I continually create my self by loving myself adequately and appropriately. As I advance toward reaching my fullest potential, I will continue to find my self very good.

I AM CAPABLE OF CHANGING

It has been such a relief to discover that I can become "unstuck." Nothing about me is cast in stone. I am as flexible and pliable as soft clay. True, I carry my past, but my past does not carry me. Only my Higher Power carries me. As I come to love myself, I discover my freedom to choose to be what I want to be.

Life is full of infinite potential. I am full of infinite potential. What else would we expect from a "child of God." Every day presents me with countless opportunities for change and growth.

I am changing already. I am learning to "live." I am learning to get into my life assertively. I am learning to live life, actively and positively. I am no longer content just to survive in quiet desperation, to react as a mindless bobber on stormy ocean waves. The more I "get into" my life, the more involved I am in my own living, the more I will change—for the better. I am not only alive; I am *living*. To live is to change; to live well is to change often.

THE PAIN THAT I MIGHT FEEL BY REMEMBERING CAN'T BE ANY WORSE THAN THE PAIN I FEEL BY KNOWING AND NOT REMEMBERING

One of the most self-damaging coping devices I have used when I was hurt or in pain was to "stuff it." In coming to love my self as I need, I am rediscovering just how much I have stuffed, how much I have repressed. I have repressed my honest needs. I have repressed my pain and most of the feelings that accompany it. It is painful to re-experience what I have stuffed, but only in re-experiencing it can I let it go. When I let it go, it loses its power over me, and I am free of it—free to be the self I want to be.

It is important that I remember. Without remembering and letting go, my past continues to rule my present. Without remembering and letting go, my past continues to keep me in chains with attitudes and behaviors that work against my best interests. I take care of my self, and show love for my self, by remembering, and then letting go.

I AM ENOUGH

This concluding affirmation says it all. I am enough. All that is required is inside, not outside. All that I need, I already have. I am adequate. I am adequate to handle life. I am adequate to give my self all those things which will make me happy. All that I need to be happy, I already possess within.

I am not ashamed of who or what I am. I am lovable and loving. The love that I need to carry on may be buried within, but it is there, waiting to empower me to be all that I can be. I surrender to that love. I will grow with that love in wisdom and in grace. It is enough for me. I am adequate. I am enough.

One Hundred Helpful Self-Affirmations

Self-affirmations are most helpful when they are said out loud, with a vigorous, assertive voice. They are also effective when said internally, especially in combination with an imaginative scene in which you see your self acting out the affirmation.

The biggest rule about self-affirmations, however, is that they must be repeated again and again. They must be especially repeated when King Baby or our self-critical tapes are trying to impose a negative message on us.

It is worthwhile that we compose our own set of self-affirmations to deal with our own particular needs in self-love recovery. It is good to jot down these self-affirmations on index cards or slips of paper and put them in a spot that we tend to frequent. The following list is offered as another start to get us into the habit of affirming our selves as they need.

1. I am lovable.

2. I need help but I can take care of my self.

3. I make mistakes but that is OK. I am only human. I love my self, mistakes and all.

4. I like myself as I am.

5. Life has a plan for me. It is good for me to be here.

6. I will live in the present moment. I have no control of the past or the future.

7. I am a responsible person.

8. I have all that I need to be happy right now.

9. I will not compare myself with anyone else. My dignity is my own.

10. I am a unique and valuable person.

11. I take one day at a time.

12. The sky is the limit for me.

13. I respect my own company. I am not afraid to be alone.

14. I take charge of my life. I accept the consequences of my behavior.

15. I am sorry for hurting others and do my best to make amends.

16. What I am is more important than what I do.

17. I have something to offer this life before I leave it.

18. I am worthwhile because I am a child of God.

19. I am worthy of the love of others whether they give it to me or not.

20. I am proud of my achievements.

21. I make no apologies for enjoying my life.

22. I generally do my best, and that is the best I can do.

23. I do what I can, and that's enough.

24. I can laugh at my self!

25. I care about others and wish them the best.

26. I can afford to be as generous as I can.

27. I am capable of being one with God.

28. There is no limit to how much I can grow.

29. I am beautiful.

30. My body is worth care and attention.

31. I do not confuse shame with guilt.

32. I can dare to be "average."

33. I do not need approval to feel good about my self.

34. All my feelings are valid.

35. My life is my own.

36. I cannot assume responsibility for the lives of others.

37. It is good to be alive.

38. There are no guarantees in life. I go with the flow.

39. I am always willing to learn.

40. It pays to listen.

41. I have a right to ask for what I need and want, even if I don't get it.

42. I will not tolerate being put-down.

43. I can forgive and forget.

44. I can endure what must be endured. I have what I need to do it.

45. I am powerless but not helpless.

46. I make mistakes but I am not a failure.

47. I accept the mysteries and paradoxes of life. They make life exciting.

48. In birth and death we are all equal.

49. I respect and enjoy the success of others.

50. I accept that no one has "final" answers.

51. Everyone has a right to their tastes, even me.

52. Resistance never changes reality. I accept what I need to accept.

53. Life is good.

54. I deserve love and respect.

55. I refuse to get over-serious about anything.

56. I cannot read anyone else's mind. I can only ask for what I want to know.

57. There are few things I cannot accomplish if I put my mind to it.

58. I no longer blame my parents for who and what I am today.

59. I take first things first.

60. It will all work out for my good.

61. I deserve to be happy.

62. I value my freedom.

63. I am comfortable with my weaknesses and failings. I will try to improve, but they do not reflect on my worth.

64. I believe in me.

65. I am not afraid to be myself.

66. I deserve time for my self. I can relax when I need to.

67. I deserve sufficient rest and recreation.

68. I take pride in my achievements, no matter how small they are.

69. I try, and that's what's important.

70. Compliments are nice, but not necessary for my self-esteem.

71. I do not identify with my short-comings.

72. I will not blame or complain. I will always take appropriate action on my behalf.

73. I'm OK as I am.

74. I deserve to enjoy myself.

75. I am willing to take risks to better myself.

76. I will not be anybody's victim.

77. I acknowledge a Power greater than myself who loves and cares for me.

78. I look forward to what tomorrow will bring.

79. I appreciate advice when I want it, but I will make decisions about my welfare on my own.

80. I live and let live.

81. I will always be gentle with my self.

82. I will keep it simple.

83. I stand up for my self.

84. Before everything, I will be true to my self.

85. I can set goals for my self.

86. I love my self.

87. It's easy if I take it one step at a time.

88. I have good memories.

89. I will fight for what is right.

90. I have needs that need to be respected and fulfilled.

91. I am free to make mistakes. I am willing to pay the price.

92. I am aware.

93. I am worthy because I exist.

94. Only I know what I really need.

95. I have compassion for my self.

96. Nothing is ever totally hopeless.

97. Good comes out of evil.

98. I am grateful to be alive.

99. I don't know it all, but I know enough to take care of my self.

100. I am good.

12

Developing Detachment of the Observing "I"

Throughout this book I have made a special point of separating "self" from the observing "I." Rather than myself or ourselves, I have divided the word into my self or our selves to emphasize that the "self" is to be treated by the observing "I" in a quasi dualistic fashion as a friend and companion.

To love our selves as we need, it can be productive for us to learn to "detach" from our selves. It can be productive for us to learn how to be detached observers, more aware and more conscious, of what is going on within us.

We have already seen what an important step it is in self-love recovery to "detach" and not identify (personalize) with our old tapes, problems, and issues. Keeping a more neutral and impartial stance toward our selves and our issues helps bring more moderation and balance into our lives. Any preoccupation that we have indicates that we have become identified with whatever holds our attention. Depression is directly connected with negative pre-occupation. Depression is indicative of over-identification with a problem. Any obsession that we have indicates that we have "personalized" with a person or object of our desire. Learning how to "detach", therefore, can be a great source of freedom for us and can allow us to take care of our selves in a more flexible and effective manner.

Detachment can also be beneficial in stress reduction. Stress also indicates that we are identifying with our issues. Our bodies and emotions are tensed for a "fight or flee" reaction to a perceived threat. Fighting or fleeing may be appropriate reactions to a perceived threat, but most often we neither fight nor flee. Rather we sit with a stressful situation, awaiting adverse conditions to change on their own. Detachment allows us to "pull back" from our issues, and even from our stress, and see things more objectively as going in and out of the natural flow of our lives. Not personalizing stress actually dissipates it. As stress continues to dissipate, we have more energy to work through our issues.

Self-love recovery depends a great deal on self-knowledge. "Pulling back" in detachment allows us to come to know our selves more objectively. When we become so over-identified with our selves and our issues, it is difficult to "see the forest for the trees." Learning to become more neutral "observers," watching our behavior, listening to our internal self-talk, noticing the influence of our old tapes, observing our spontaneous reactions, can help us understand our selves and how we "tick."

OUT OF YOUR MIND

Marta has recently celebrated her ninety-second birthday. Stooped over and severely crippled by arthritis, she cannot walk nor can she hold a spoon in her hand. Tears come to her eyes as she laments that this was the first year she was unable to blow out the candles on her birthday cake. Her dresser is cluttered with memorabilia, including photos of herself in graceful poses as a professional skater and dancer. "The problem," she relates to me, "is not that I am so crippled, but that inside I feel as young as a teenager. I don't feel old inside, and I'm locked in this old, crippled body."

Three year old Mickey has just taken a fall from his scooter. With two bad scrapes on his tender knees he is wailing bloody murder. His father comes running down the driveway and observes immediately that the damage is minor. He picks up his son and gently rocks him back and forth while offering soothing words. They have no effect and Mickey wails louder than ever. With a sudden "Look at that!" his father directs

Mickey's attention to a neighbor's Doberman who is leaping into the air retrieving a frisbee. Mickey's crying stops abruptly as he concentrates on the antics of the playful animal.

Chrisey has had chronic back pain for almost seven years. Conventional therapy has been ineffective and her prescription drugs leave her so dopey that she cannot concentrate on her work. She has refused a risky operation that holds a low percentage chance of correcting a spinal disc disorder. She has tried every remedy from chiropractic to acupuncture, with limited results. Recently however, she has found substantial relief with the use of biofeedback. She says she has learned to "disengage myself from my body and my pain." She affirms that the pain is still there, but somehow she is separated from it.

What Marta, Mickey and Chrisey have in common, together with people documented in studies of higher meditation states and out-of-body experiences, is an observing "I" that is detached, and detachable, from the self and the self's experiences.

There is something about us that is ageless and formless. There is something about us that is detached and separate from our bodies, from our emotions and mental functioning, from our feelings and imaginations. It takes some intensive reflection to become aware of it, but there is in us a primary consciousness that is above and beyond the self-talk that goes on within us most of the time.

This primary consciousness is the very center of our being. It is the "I" speaking at our deepest level. It is the "I" at our deepest spiritual center. It is the "I" which is connected to eternity. It is the "I" which for Marta (and for all of us) feels ageless and timeless, which for Mickey (and for all of us) is easily distracted to focus attention on something else, which for Chrisey (and for all of us) can detach from her physical self and "observe" the pain rather than personalize or identify with it.

The observing "I" is connected to, and yet at the same time detached from, our selves and all that comprises our selves. While there is self-talk going on in us with every conscious moment, the observing "I" knows everything as detachable.

Except when we are caught up in an "ecstatic" (ek-stasis: standing "out") moment, we normally identify with this self-talk. We normally identify with our selves and with all the complex parts, levels, functions and experiences of our selves. With awareness, skill, and practice, we can learn to detach from our selves. As an observing "I," we can become observers of the great life drama going on, in, and around us.

Becoming detached means that we go "out of our minds." We become detached and neutral observers of what goes on in our bodies, our emotions, our feelings, our imagination. We don't judge or go into dialogue with our selves. We don't enter the action of an experience. We simply observe. We notice what is going on. We don't identify with our experiences, we simply observe what is happening.

SEE FOR YOUR SELF

There are many good books and exercises on developing a sense of detachment of the observing "I." As I mentioned before, all religious systems have provisions for individual mystical development, which include exercises for achieving the deepest experiences of one's fundamental identity. Buddhism, for example, incorporates specialized techniques for detachment. According to Buddhism, happiness is found as we progress through higher and higher stages of detachment, until the "I" experiences nothing, no object, no thing, anymore. This state of "nirvana" is complete detachment, a complete "letting go." It is a state of pure consciousness, without connection to any object or thought process. It is a state of seeing, without seeing any thing.

A good way for us beginners to experience our observing "I" as detached from our selves can be found in a simple exercise. Sit in a quiet and relaxed space. Sitting back with eyes closed, simply note sensations your body is picking up. Make note of any tension in your neck, back, or stomach. Notice any itches or irritations on your skin. Stay with this exercise for a

few minutes. Then observe what is going on in your own imagination and thought processes. Calmly listen to the jabber that
goes on inside all the time. Notice and listen to thoughts coming in and going out. Without judging or talking back, listen to
all the self-talk going on. Watch and observe as one thought
after another runs through your mind. Allow it to happen spon-
taneously. Let it all flow. Watch it flow. While you will always
have the impulse to identify with what you are observing
(notice how difficult it is to stay detached), little by little you
will become more aware that you, in your observing "I," are
more than, are different from, are above and beyond, all these
thoughts and thought processes going on within you. Your
observing "I" seems to have a life and identity all its own—
which, of course, it does.

Practice observing your feelings, especially when you are
under stress of any kind. Watch those feelings come and go,
along with their accompanying images and physical sensations,
in and out of your consciousness. Don't challenge them. Don't
confront them. Let them pass without comment or judgment.
Take anger, for example. The next time you are angry with
someone, make it a point to stand back for a moment and watch
how anger operates in you. Notice how anger grows and increases in intensity as your thoughts about the person who offended
you come and go. Play with it a little. Stop the thoughts.
Deliberately think of something pleasant and watch the chem-
istry of your anger change. Then bring the thoughts back of how
you were hurt and watch the angry feelings come back again.
Soon it will become like a game. And it is a game—a game that
fools us every time if we are not aware of how detached we are.

The internal I, the observing "I" at the center of our being,
is never directly affected by what goes on in and about us. "I,"
at our deepest center, is changeless, formless and ageless. "I"
cannot be directly hurt or insulted. "I" cannot be offended
directly. We can watch offenses being offered and taken. We
can watch insults being tendered and considered. We can
observe our bodies in pain or discomfort. But, deep down, the
"I" within us is untouchable in its own sacred space.

Whenever you are in bad space or whenever you are upset with fear and anxiety, practice detachment. Put your self in quiet space, step back and watch the drama unfold on the screen of your own mind. Observe the tension in your body. Notice the feelings grow in intensity and then ebb away as your thoughts change from one minute to the next. Notice how fear works on your body, your feelings. Notice, most especially, that "you" are different from your body, thoughts and feelings. You "have" a body, thoughts and feelings. You are not identified with your body, thoughts and feelings. You are detached and increasingly detachable.

OPEN DOORS

What does all this have to do with self-love? How can developing a detached observing "I" help us come to love our selves as we need?

Again, by experiencing detachment of the observing "I," we become aware of the fact that "we," in the roots of our consciousness, are not identified with our selves or our experiences. We can detach and separate ourselves from what we observe going on within us. We are not identified with our memories, habits and mind-sets. We are not identified with our emotions and feelings. We are not identified with our moods. We are not identified with our depressions and loneliness. We are not identified with our old tapes.

All our memories, habits, mind-sets, emotions, feelings, moods and old tapes need not be personalized. They "belong" to us, and we can use or not use them according to what is in our best interest. They do not own us. We are not bound to them. We can disengage from them to change or modify their effect on us.

There is a great sense of release and freedom in this awareness—a freedom that can open many doors for us. It can help convince us that nothing is set in stone. We are not bound by our past or future. No fate holds us. As a detached observing "I," we are fundamentally timeless, formless and free.

As detached observers of the melodramas that go on within us, we can remain "above it all." We can watch our old tapes plug in. We can follow King Baby in operation. We can note how our resistance to change works. We can observe the dialogue that takes place between our proactive and reactive selves. We can watch how different levels of our selves interact with each other. We can watch how we operate. We can see what makes us tick. All in all, quite a show.

Being detached, we can be more objective in our own favor. We don't have to take everything so personally. We don't need to embrace shame because we are above it. When we are "above it all," we can entertain more options about what will serve our best interests. We can observe and make freer decisions, saying yes to what will benefit us, and no to what will not.

Being less identified with our selves and our experiences, we can extend our radar to pick up messages from our Higher Power. We ask our Higher Power for insights, guidance, correction, to know his will for us, and for clues to how we might reach our highest potential. And then, forsaking the chatter of our inner self-talk, we can truly listen for responses. Our Higher Power can speak to us in many ways, but often responds to our requests through our "inner voices." We are not crazy for listening to inner voices. We listen to self-talk going on all the time anyway and it doesn't mean we're crazy. Opening the door to our Higher Power by actively listening for his voice gives him the opportunity to be heard. God's "voice" is found through the discernment made by the observing "I."

TALK TO YOUR SELF

Throughout this book we have been encouraged to treat our selves as special friends, to love our selves as our most treasured companion through life. We have learned the importance of affirming our selves on a daily basis. We affirm our selves by speaking positively and supportively to our selves. Our selves will hear us as they would hear any supportive (or destructive) outside voice. We, in our observing "I," can do wonderful things for our selves in the very way we talk to our selves.

Talk to your self throughout the day. Tell your self, "I love you." Tell your self, "I will take care of you and protect you." Tell your self, "I will be your champion and you are safe with me around." Tell your self, "You are beautiful and I would pick you out of all the other selves in the universe to be my friend." Tell your self, "You are most worthy, and I am grateful to be your companion." The self cannot but feel upheld and loved by these "strokes" of approval and caring.

HIGHER CONSCIOUSNESS

Without question, developing awareness of yourself as an observing "I" is part of a great spiritual quest. When spiritual masters teach that the "kingdom is within," they are speaking of the observing "I" being already in eternity, already eternally united to the Creator Self, sharing its being. Heightened awareness of this unity is "enlightenment." This enlightenment is living in "the kingdom." This is a kingdom of absolute freedom because the observing "I" is detached from all that would weigh it down, imprison it, manipulate it, or cause it pain.

The higher we climb a mountain, the more surrounding country we are able to see. The higher we go in levels of our own consciousness, the more we will see and appreciate the relativity of everything in life. The closer we are to the absolute Self, the better perspective we will have of how all things fall into place, of how all things fall into a magnificent plan of which we are a part.

The higher our consciousness, the closer we feel to the Creator Conscious, and the more united we feel with all others in life, with everything in life, past, present and to come. When we perceive from our highest awareness, everything makes sense, everything is beautiful, and everything is lovable.

13

Use Your Imagination

Janet is a recovering alcoholic and drug addict. She has not been able to hold a steady job since she graduated from high school fifteen years ago. She has been through two failed marriages and has survived three miscarriages. When I spoke to her as she was coming to the end of four months of hospitalization in a psychiatric ward after her second suicide attempt, she reminisced about the highlights of her thirty-three years of life.

She was born and raised in a rural Wisconsin town. Her affluent farming parents were of hard-working German stock and had some very definite ideas on child-rearing. She had one brother, whom she idolized and envied. He was not only a handsome, popular, all-American athlete, but a brilliant and resourceful student. He was encouraged by their parents to go the full limit with his education. He eventually became a Rhodes scholar and launched into a lucrative career.

Janet was, and is, strikingly pretty. According to her grammar and high school teachers she was as brilliant as her older brother Kurt. Janet had as many dreams as her brother, but came upon one significant impasse to her ambitions. Her parents did not believe that girls need be intelligent or have "worldly ambitions." Janet had all kinds of dreams and ambitions in her childhood and early teen years, but when she would speak about them, her parents would severely reprimand her, call her a "dreamer," and solemnly assure her that they had no intention of sending her off to college.

Eventually Janet replaced her own dreams with the negative images imposed on her by her strong-willed and domineering parents. After high school graduation she began working in

256

the town grocery store. Her dreams for herself had become so severely down-graded that, in a short period of time, the life of this exceptionally talented girl unfolded like a nightmare.

A POWERFUL TOOL

One of the most powerful faculties we possess as human beings is our imagination. We are not only intelligent, we are imaginative. We not only think, we can fantasize. We not only reason, we can dream.

Imagination is not viewed by most of us for the significant and powerful resource it is. We readily use our imaginations. We picture ourselves on beaches enjoying a splendid vacation. A housewife imagines herself winning the lottery. The salesman on the road imagines the face of his young wife and feels love in his loneliness. I have a friend with advanced musical talent who can entertain himself by hearing a whole Beethoven symphony run through his imagination. I can change my mood in a minute by imagining fall weather, cool and damp, with the smell of fresh apple pie and burning leaves. We use our imaginations but rarely give them much thought as an important tool in self-love recovery.

In the evolution of human consciousness imagination developed because it obviously provided a significant and irreplaceable service for the well-being and development of the species. Our minds are wonderful in the way they can process data, but it is our imagination which opens the door to promise and creativity.

Imagination is not a quirk or superficial adjunct of our rational powers. It is not simply a creative mental toy that has given people like George Lucas and Steven Spielberg very successful careers in the motion picture industry. It is imagination which leads us into fulfillment of our innate potential. It is imagination which allows us to advance into higher and higher states of awareness and love. Imagination gives us horizons and goals. Imagination pulls us to our limits. Imagination is a powerful force—A force powerful enough to turn a Kurt into a Rhodes scholar or a Janet into a drug addict.

"When you wish upon a star, your dreams come true." What we imagine most often about ourselves eventually comes true. We become what we imagine ourselves to be. That is the purpose and plan for the imagination: to help us become all we are meant to be.

The hitch, however, is that the imagination can work just as powerfully in the negative. Imagination is only a tool. Like the mind, it has no mind of its own. As it can raise us, it can also tear us down. If what goes through our imagination most of the day is negative and down-playing, we become the negative and down-played person we imagine.

Life is fall-out from our imaginations. Life is imagination fulfilled. For better or worse, we become what we imagine for our selves.

Imagination is a powerful faculty for self-love recovery and enhancement. Imagination can be managed. Imagination can be creatively used. Imagination can be guided and directed for our personal benefit. Just as imagining negative things about ourselves has robbed us of self-love and esteem, so imagining positive things about ourselves will help to restore self-love and esteem. We become and perform what we imagine ourselves being and doing.

What imagination does is start wheels in motion. That is why we are wise to be extremely cautious about what images, especially self-images, we allow to run through our minds. *Imagination always triggers a "follow up."* Imagination begins a process to make an image a reality. Imagination begins a process to flesh itself out, or, as Jean Luc Picard of the starship Enterprise would order: "Make it so."

HOW DO YOU PICTURE YOURSELF?

Imagination is of enormous importance for our growth and development. It is unfortunate that we cannot treat the subject with the amplification it deserves in our limited space. Readers are encouraged to explore the power of imagination and visualization techniques with authors such as Shakti Gawain, who has made an art of the subject in her book *Creative Visualization*. Matthew McKay and Patrick Fanning, in their book *Self-Esteem*, have an excellent chapter on visualization techniques for building up a positive self-image. In this chapter, however, we are limited to more general principles of the power and use of the imagination.

As part of our program of self-love recovery, we need to be aware of the imagination and its power to trigger positive or negative consequences for self-love. We need to de-program our imagination of negative and hostile self-images, and to re-program it with positive and supportive self-images. And we can best begin with our self-image itself.

All of us have ways that we "picture" ourselves. Deep in our imagination there is a fundamental way that we see ourselves. This picture has been built up from years of input and experience. This picture may be positive or negative. This picture, however, is also relative, negotiable and changeable. As we have seen, nothing about us is ever set in stone. We need to examine, therefore, whether or not the way we picture ourselves is in our favor and best interests.

In general, then, how do you picture yourself? Take a few minutes and relax. Clear your mind of all distractions. Put yourself in a quiet space. Take some deep breaths. Ask yourself, "How *do* I picture myself?" Let ideas come forth without pushing them. Take a good look at yourself. Do you see yourself as attractive, reasonably adequate to meet the challenges of day-to-day living, wholesome, well put-together, loving, friendly, assertive when you need to be, having your needs met adequately, easy to approach and get along with, calm and self-confident? Or do you see yourself in general as a flop in your job, nervous and always on edge about something, always fearful about what tomorrow will bring, wishy-washy, insecure about your talents and abilities, frightfully dependent on the good will of others, basically afraid of authority figures, unable to ask for what you want, and very often shy and withdrawn? Or are you right in the middle of these extremes, inclined to go one way or another as various situations arise?

Be aware that this fundamental image you have of yourself invariably triggers a variety of chain reactions in every situation you experience. Whether you are conscious of it or not, your basic self-image is helping you fly, or it's beating you to the ground. The imagination has no morals or code of ethics by which it operates. It does not know whether it is helping you or hurting you. It simply works according to its blueprint to entertain images and trigger a chain of operations to bring those images to life in every experience you have. No faculty you have wants to "fulfill" your basic image more than your imagination.

If you find that your self-imaging is more negative than positive, stay in your relaxed state and use your imagination to conjure up images of yourself that would show you in a better light. What self-image would you *like* to have? Think out what qualities you would like to have and picture yourself *as actually having those qualities*. Think about yourself as positively as possible. See yourself to your best advantage. See yourself as well-dressed, full of life and spontaneity, popular and attractive, at ease in social relationships, confident in your job, assertive and independent. Imagine whatever you need.

Keep seeing yourself in this new light for up to ten minutes of concentration. Repeat the exercise twice a day, most profitably upon awakening or when you are about to fall asleep. Your mind will start working on new attitudes and behaviors while you are in dreamland or busy with your daily routine. Continue the exercise daily for a month and see if you don't notice a difference in the way you feel about yourself.

THINK AND ACT "AS IF"

Imagination is not "fantasy." Imagination is a powerful tool. Imagination works. Your imagination has been working all your life to make things happen for you. Like your mind, your imagination operates on data—data that comes from what you experience, from how you interpret experience, from what you consciously choose to focus on, and from what wells up from the recesses of your subconscious. The imagination is not self-conscious. Your imagination does not know if you are "faking it" out or not. (At the moment I am hungry for lunch and am imagining a Chicago-style hot dog with all the trimmings, and my mouth is watering.) It handles the data being offered and begins to trigger operations to fulfill the dream. Needless to say, this can work to our advantage in self-love recovery.

One of the axioms of the Twelve-Step program states, "Act 'as if'." If you really want to achieve a goal, *act "as if" you already have it.* If you want to develop a more positive attitude toward your self, act as if you already possess it. If you wish your self more respect and admiration from others, act as if you are receiving it already. If you wish more happiness in your life, act as if you have all you need already. If you wish you had more confidence in speaking to authority figures, act as if you already had that confidence.

Thinking and acting "as if" makes use of the power of our imagination. It is true that acting "as if" is an attempt to "fake out" our minds and feelings, but that faking out is perfectly legitimate in working on our self-love recovery. Is it any more legitimate faking our selves out with the old negative tapes that tell us we are inadequate and unlovable?

Psychologists have always known that when feelings can't determine appropriate behavior, deliberate changes in behavior can often create new and better feelings. I may feel in the dumps, and negative feelings seem to prevent me from doing the simplest of tasks. If I take some action anyway, despite my feelings (acting as if the feelings weren't present), those negative feelings often change in the process.

Thinking and acting "as if" is a tool of self-love recovery. It is not "delusional" any more than our self-defeating thinking and acting is. Used for positive purposes, it can be one of the most fruitful ways we can take care of our selves as we need. The mind, in response to our expectations, is triggered to call forth from its resources the ways and means to "flesh out" our imaginative thinking. It has no other choice. And it's amazing what resources our selves can find to make our "as if" thinking a reality.

In an interview, an Olympic skater commented that she "believed" herself into making an extremely difficult double set of triple axles. She said that if she doubted herself for a moment, she would have fallen. She acted "as if" it were easy, and it became so. Thinking and acting "as if" allowed her mind and body to draw on the resources they needed to make this very difficult maneuver.

A young friend of mine was going for an interview for a job he sorely wanted. The job had many applicants and he was nervous and almost totally lacking in self-confidence. There was little doubt that his negative attitude would prove disastrous for securing the job. However, with a little coaching, he learned a few stress-relaxing techniques and then began to imagine himself breezing through the interview. He saw himself answering questions confidently and assertively. He walked into the interview acting "as if" the job was already his. His "imaginative" attitude balanced out his nervousness and self-doubt, and he landed the job.

IMAGINATIVE DIALOGUE WITH YOUR SELF

Another powerful exercise in self-knowledge and self-love is to carry on an active, imaginative dialogue with our selves. We can imagine ourselves into greater degrees of self-love. I have found it best to do this in the following fashion.

Find a room where you can be alone and quiet. Place two chairs facing each other in the center of the room. Sit in one of the chairs and imagine yourself sitting in the chair opposite you. Look at your self sitting there. Concentrate on your features. Do you like what you see? Look at your self. Concentrate on your qualities. Would you pick that self for your best friend and constant companion? Again, do you like what you see? Talk to your self sitting in the opposite chair. Tell your self what you like about what you see, and what you don't like.

Take your time and keep the engine of your imagination running. Tell your self that you are going to be there for it, for now and forever. Tell your self what changes you intend to make to bring it more happiness and fulfillment. Tell your self about the negative images you won't have time for anymore. Tell your self how you are looking forward to new adventures together. Tell your self you will never allow it to be abused again. You will be its champion. Above all, you will never abuse it again. Finish the exercise by imagining yourself embracing your self, with full acceptance and love. Notice the good feelings that come about from this exercise.

Some people find great success in this exercise by imaging, and talking to, their "inner child." There has been much psychological literature of late promoting awareness and care of the inner child—an inner child which is very often insecure, frightened, and much abused.

The inner child, I think, is someone whose presence we sense, and never outgrow. For as old as we get, there is still a little boy or a little girl still alive within us. The inner child is us when we were the most vulnerable to input to our self-image. The inner child affects our thinking, feelings, and behavior in more ways than we might want to acknowledge. Nonetheless, this inner child, which is very much part of us, can be talked to in the same imaginative fashion that we talk to our selves in this exercise. We can speak lovingly to this inner child. We can assure our inner child of our concern and care. We can assure our inner child that we will do our best to protect and support his or her best interests.

Try visualizing yourself at four years old, seven, nine, thirteen. Try to see yourself at that age as clearly as you can. Observe how you are dressed. Look at the expression on your face. Try to get in touch with your feelings at that age. Visualize yourself embracing that child. Tell that child how much you admire it and how much you intend to care for its needs.

These exercises are best performed daily for a month. You

may notice that more positive behaviors on your own behalf become triggered, even without much effort on your part. Thank your imagination and encourage it to keep up the good work on your behalf.

REFUTING OUR INNER CRITIC

An effective exercise in refurbishing our self-image and in showing love for ourselves is to imaginatively confront King Baby, our old negative tapes, and the voice of our inner critic. Try to imagine what your King Baby or Queen Baby looks like sitting on the throne. When King Baby begins demanding, "This is what I want, and I want it now!," *talk back* and tell King Baby that it can't have what it wants. Tell King Baby to get off the throne, because you are replacing it there with your Higher Power. In the strongest terms warn King Baby that he will not be allowed to play havoc with your life anymore.

When you feel fearful and hopeless, when you feel in the dumps with self-doubt, when old negative tapes begin playing of how incompetent and unreliable you are—*talk back*. Imagine your inner critic talking. Put some flesh and blood on it to give it features. Talk back. Tell your inner critic that you are not going to listen to its ramblings anymore. Tell your inner critic that it is wrong in its assessment of you and that in no uncertain terms you want it to "lay off."

We have already learned that part of our program of self-love recovery was to de-program our negative and self-defeating tapes. Imagination can be a useful tool to accelerate this de-programming. Again, in a relaxed and quiet space, direct your imagination to bring forth from your memory some of the negative messages that control so much of your life—messages like "You can't do anything right," "You're a loser," "Everybody's out to get you," etc. Let one of these messages sit in your imagination. Take a good look at it. Then take an affirmative stand for your self and tell the message that it is no longer acceptable. Tell the message that you are going to delete it from you internal memory banks. Issue a command, "Let it be so," and see "DELETE" flashing in your mind. The stronger you mean it, the more effective the delete command will work. If you are new to this type of internal computer work, you may have to repeat the exercise daily for some weeks.

Any time a negative or put-down thought about your self comes to mind, perform the same exercise. See it on the screen of your imagination. Then command your imagination to delete the entry. You will not tolerate its presence anymore, because it is untrue and causes you nothing but distress. See "DELETE" flash across your mental screen.

Again, this may seem like mind games to a cynic, but they work. They *are* mind games—the same kind of mind games that were played on us when we were too young to know the difference, the same kind of games in which we absorbed "commands" and messages from our parents and significant others that have been causing dysfunctional thinking and behaving in our lives since the time they were entered.

McKay and Fanning in *Self-Esteem* offer many solid techniques for disarming our old negative tapes and disposing of our inner critic, which they call the "pathological critic" (pp. 43-56). Just knowing we have such a critic is a giant step in self-knowledge. McKay and Fanning suggest that we get angry and indignant with our inner critic for the damage it has done to us. They advise that we shout back to our inner critic with "howitzer mantras" of "Shut up!," "Stop this shit!," "Get off my back," etc. They also advise that we dialogue with our inner critic, showing it the price it makes us pay for its inappropriate stands, and affirming our selves in direct contradiction to its indictments and defamations of us.

This exercise should be performed anytime we observe our selves sliding into a defensive posture caused by a put-down or by feeling that we are inadequate to take care of our selves as we need. It is an effective tool for negating our self-negating tapes.

USING MODELS

Models for children, for youth, for all of us, have always been considered important in society. Models provide an indispensable service for helping us to grow and develop our potential. We hear top educators lamenting today that appropriate models are not available for emulation by our children. The media finds chinks in the armor of all public figures. We are becoming a nation without heroes.

Heroic models are powerful precisely because they strongly stimulate the imagination. The imagination in turn stimulates a chain reaction to copy-cat a style or a behavior. An aspiring young basketball player keeps a life-size poster of Michael Jordan in his bedroom. His idol resides in his imagination, day and night. The imagination energizes his ambitions and activates energies to do whatever it takes to make those ambitions come true.

We can use imaginative modeling to stimulate our self-love recovery. Try this exercise, especially when you are confronted with an exasperating problem or with something that is depressing you and getting you down. Relax yourself for a few minutes and clear your mind of distractions. Picture someone you admire and have great respect for. Visualize him or her as clearly as you can. Ask your self: What would (N.) do if he or she were in my shoes? How would he face my issue? How would she handle this? What would his attitude be to this problem? What steps would she take to bring this to a conclusion? See the look on your heroic figure's face. Hear that person talk in his or her own words about an issue you are facing. Watch the actions they take.

You will be surprised not only with the ideas you come up with, but with how much your imagination will stimulate you to "copy-cat."

THE GOOD OLD DAYS

No matter how down and depressed we get, no matter how bad our luck seems to be running, no matter how poorly we are currently getting along in life, we can all recall happy times, days of joy, moments of ecstasy, in our past. Joyful memories may be buried deep in our unconscious, but they are there and can be recalled and used imaginatively for our benefit. Whatever we allow to linger in our imaginations will have a ripple effect on our feelings, our emotions, our moods, and our physical well-being.

If I sit and ponder all the "garbage" that has gone on in my life, I can make myself physically ill. If I sit and stew over the terrible things that could happen in the future, I can literally immobilize myself with fear. On the other hand, if I vividly remember some of the "good old days," some of the "best of times" I have enjoyed, I can bring a sense of renewed joy to my self. Remember that the imagination has no sense of discretion. It operates on whatever data it is asked to access. We can show love for our selves by being vigilant about what we allow to be accessed by our imagination. We can take care of our selves by prompting images into our imagination that can give our selves a lift.

When negative and threatening images flood your imagination, take a break with this exercise. Use a little discipline to clear the "screen" and keep away distractions. Recall times past when things were wonderful for you—scenes of great joy, experiences of intense pleasure, serenity, and peace, times you were praised, applauded, and affirmed. Bring those scenes clearly in focus. Relive the sights, smells and sounds. Stay with the image as long as you can. Stay with the good feelings that accompany the scene. Observe the changes that take place in your emotions and body as you work your scene.

Remember, these pleasant memories are just as "real" for you as the unpleasant ones. Whatever you "put your mind to" becomes "reality" in any given situation. It may seem to be a mind game, and it is. It *is* a mind game. Most of what goes on in our lives is a mind game. Most of our feelings, good and bad, are results of our mind games. We live in our heads and in our feelings. We are never directly in touch with "reality" outside. *We are only in touch with our perceptions.* If we want to feel better about our selves, we need some discipline to access better images of, and for, our selves.

VANITY OF VANITIES

By now it should be clear what an enormous power we have in our imagination. It can pick us up and energize us for action, or lay us low with paralysis. Imagination, however, is only a tool at our disposal. We can use it to our best interests. We can use it as a means of assuring our selves that we are taking care of them. We can use it to keep balance in our lives and to keep us in perspective.

Ash Wednesday begins the solemn season of Lent for Roman Catholics. Lent is a season for helping Catholics to renew their faith and get back into "perspective" with fasting and liturgical observances. Perhaps nothing generates perspective better than the ceremony of receiving ashes upon one's forehead as the minister reminds the faithful, "You are dust and into dust you will return."

Without trying to be morbid, use your imagination to picture yourself at the end of your life. Imagine your grave-site, your tombstone, perhaps yourself lying in a casket being viewed by relatives and friends. It did wonders for Scrooge. It may do wonders for you also. "Vanity of vanities," the book of Ecclesiastes exhorts. What are all your worries, anxieties, emotional upsets, fears, when seen from the perspective of your own funeral?

Images of our death are forbidding but applicable because death is absolutely predictable. It can be a healthful exercise for balance and perspective to imagine our own death every now and then. We can get on with our lives, make the most of them, and not be tied down forever with the little daily deaths caused by being overly-serious, overly-anxious, overly-desperate, overly-depressed, about anything. In the long run, what does it really matter?

YOUR INNER VOICES

Some terrible offenses have been inflicted on individuals and society by people claiming that their criminal acts were inspired by inner voices: "God told me to do it." Without excusing or condoning such unacceptable behavior, we can once again see the enormous power of the imagination at work. It can get us to do things we might consider "unimaginable."

We do have "inner voices," however. And we do have minds that can discern and validate those voices ethically. Our Higher Power can speak to us through inner voices, especially in reply to our requests for guidance and inspiration.

Artists for ages have tried to describe and paint God as God was understood in any given era. Whether we picture God as a grandfatherly old man or as a blinding creative "Force," we can have a healthy and soul-enriching dialogue with our Higher Power, however the way we understand that Higher Power.

Imagine the presence of God within you, God as you understand him. This Presence is loving, caring, and wants to be there for you. In "prayer," speak to this Presence, using words of praise, thanksgiving, asking for forgiveness or favors. In "meditation," be silent and give your Higher Power a chance to speak back. Simply listen in peace and tranquility for whatever message your Higher Power wishes to give. Trusting your Higher Power's real presence and unconditional loving care, you will hear a response. Give it time. Let it come. Express gratitude. Over a period of time, the responses will become louder and clearer.

Many find great spiritual growth in performing this same exercise with the imaging of saints, heroes, departed relatives or friends, who were much loved and respected. Asking for what they need, they listen as responses are given in the voices of those they love.

SEEING YOUR SELF IN ACTION

Imagination can be effectively used to put us "into a scene" and see how it "works out." Rather than risk our selves in a potentially threatening or dangerous experience, we can visualize it ahead of time and ascertain what we might or might not do to keep our selves safe.

Try an exercise in which you watch your self be brave in

some threatening situation. If you are shy about asking for a raise, imagine yourself confronting your boss, being assertive, expressing your deservingness, and feeling confident that you are worth what you are asking for. Imagine yourself making difficult decisions with confidence and a degree of toughness. Imagine yourself taking a stand in your favor against someone who might be giving you unwanted advice or criticism. Picture yourself in actual dialogue and see yourself acting with self-assurance.

Picture yourself in a stress-filled situation. Watch yourself handling it appropriately, and affirm your self in the process. See yourself taking pride in your self and your work. Work out a scene in your mind where you are demonstrating your artistry to the people you work with. Picture yourself in social settings, being charming and approachable. If you are shy, see yourself taking the initiative and making introductions on your own.

Even if you feel you do not possess these qualities naturally, do not let that stop you from performing the imaginative exercises. Negative qualities which are now holding you back were themselves at one time generated in your imagination. Realize that you can just as well generate others more in your best interest. Imagination is a tool to use on your own behalf.

It is also a good practice to affirm your self in your imagination while you visualize yourself in a variety of situations. Combining a "scene" with an internalized affirmation about yourself can have double impact. If you imagine yourself surrounded by a group of people and you are entertaining them with your anecdotes, simultaneously say to yourself: "I am lovable," or "People enjoy my company," or "I am able to relate effectively." The following guide can provide more examples of how this can be done.

Scene

I see myself introducing myself to a group of strangers.

I see myself sitting at my desk at work. My boss' hand is on my shoulder.

I see myself jogging in the park.

I see myself speaking before a large audience. Hands are up to ask me questions.

I see myself buying a new home in a much more affluent neighborhood.

I see myself controlling my temper and patiently listening to what my children are telling me.

I see myself assertively telling my parents that I am old enough to make decisions on my own.

I see myself apologizing to someone I have hurt.

Affirmation

"I am comfortable with people. I am acceptable to them."

"I am worthy of respect for the work I do. I am good at what I do."

"I take care of myself because I am worth it. My health is important to me."

"I have worthwhile opinions. I have something to say. I can be assertive."

"I deserve good things in life that I work for. I take pride in what I can achieve."

"I have control over my behavior. I decide how I will act or react. I am a good listener."

"I take full responsibility for my actions. I make mistakes and it is all right to do so."

"I own the consequences of my behavior. I am mature enough to make amends."

I see myself in a restaurant having an enjoyable meal with someone I have been wanting to date for some time.

I see myself writing out a check for a worthy cause.

"I like myself. I deserve a good time with someone I like."

"I can be generous because I am doing well."

14

Loving Your Self Through Times of Crisis

The first of the "Four Noble Truths" of Buddhism begins with the recognition that "Life Is Suffering." To live is to suffer. To live is to experience pain. To live is to endure hardship. There is no escaping pain and suffering as long as we are part of life. To acknowledge this and accept this is the beginning of sanity and wisdom. Not to acknowledge and accept this is the beginning of all illusion and frustration.

That life is full of pain and suffering is hardly a revelation to any of us. We see it all around us every day. The news media daily document every kind of human misery. Our own lives are full of hardships and stress. There are minor physical ailments that our bodies endure, from cold sores to bunions. There are hundreds of little things that wear and tear at us—anything from the car battery going dead just when we are in a hurry, to having to work with someone who has offensive body odor.

Then there are traumatic upsets that cause us enormous stress—the loss of a job, a failing marriage, a son or daughter involved in criminal activity, the sudden death of a loved one, contracting a serious disease, getting sued, dealing with a spouse who has a serious addiction, dealing with one's own addictions. Sooner or later each of us is hit by a tragedy that can "try one's soul."

Self-love recovery is never more threatened than when we are facing a serious reversal of fortune. One's self-esteem is literally put on trial with each calamity we have to face. When misfortune hits, we are immediately inclined to feel that we are

273

failures because we have not been able to keep our selves out of harm's way. "There must be something wrong with me. No matter how hard I try, something always goes terribly wrong. I guess I'm just no good."

Whenever we face a crisis, heavy clouds of despondency and anxiety begin to gather. We enter a "dark night of the soul." The more sensitive the soul, the darker the night. The more self-aware we are, the greater the pain. Imagine the torment of the promising football star who suddenly finds himself paralyzed from the neck down, due to a freak fall from a routine tackle. Imagine the daily stress on the hostages who never knew for years if the next hour would bring the bullet that would end their senseless imprisonment. Imagine the anxiety of loving parents who discover that their only daughter has less than a 50-50 chance of recovering from leukemia. Imagine the fear in a mother of four who has just learned that her addict husband has lost the house, the car, and all the family savings in gambling. Imagine the strain on anyone who has been diagnosed as HIV positive.

Any crisis we face calls upon us to take particularly good care of our selves. It is in times of intense emotional turmoil that we need to love and take care of our selves the most. If ever we need to monitor what is happening to us and to provide for our selves what we need to pull our selves through, it is in times of personal calamity.

Tragically, it is often in such times of calamity and crisis that we tend to love and take care of our selves the least. We tend to shift into a semi-comatose state. We slide into the quicksand of depression and self-pity. When we most need to take care of our selves, we tend to forget the important lessons we have learned about taking care of our needs.

Our first response in any calamity is to expect, even demand, that something outside of us will make it go away. We may beg God to work a miracle for us. We don't want the pain. We don't want the stress. And the more we fight it, the more the pain and stress increases.

Our task in the face of crisis is to continue to love our

selves. Our task in the face of something personally traumatic is to continue to take loving actions on our behalf. Our task is to accept "what is," to endure what needs to be endured, while taking care of our selves in the process.

There are ways of "seeing it through." There are ways of handling a crisis when it overtakes us. There are ways of getting through and actually growing by the personal traumas we endure. Before we look at specific actions we need to take on our behalf in a crisis, there are some preliminary issues we need to be clear about.

OPTIMISTS VS. PESSIMISTS

There are die-hard optimists who think that we never left the garden of Eden and that somehow everyone and everything is just jolly good and wonderful. Crisis is to be handled and pain is to be deflected by always "looking on the bright side."

On the other hand there are die-hard pessimists who think that life is a living hell created by a demi-god who gets particular pleasure out of seeing human beings suffer. Crises and pain are to be anticipated daily. We live in a "valley of tears," and there is nothing we can do about it. Grin and bear it.

Neither optimist nor pessimist has ever resolved the blunt contradictions that riddle life. There is good and bad. Both are very real. There is joy and sorrow. There is sweet and sour. There are highs and lows. Life is full of paradox and contradiction. Life is a mix, and we get our share of both.

Life is full of pleasant surprises, but it is also true that tragedies happen. There are times we are flying high, and there are times we fall in the pit or get blown out of the water. That's life! That is what it means to be human. To expect life to be an endless bed of roses is simply unrealistic and sets us up for inevitable let-downs. To expect life to be one misery after another, however, is a logical invitation to suicide.

Buddha started off his noble path to enlightenment by acknowledging that life is suffering. Life is not fair. If we cannot accept that, we are living in unreality. If we can accept that, we already have a good head start in taking care of our selves during times of crisis. When a hockey player goes into a game, he expects some rough action. He does not come out of the game feeling "devastated" in mind and spirit because he sustained a few body checks.

WHY ME?

"This can't be happening to me." "It's unreal—I just want to wake up and realize I've had a nightmare." We may accept the fact that life is painful, but the next big step is to accept that we are part of that life and therefore life will be painful for *us*.

My inclination when I am confronted with a personally painful situation is to exclaim, "Why me?" Why should I have contracted pneumonia? Why should I have lost my job? Why should I have a troubled marriage? Why should I not be able to make ends meet? Life may be suffering, but why should I be the one who has to undergo it? Why me?

"Why me?" is obviously King Baby talking. King Baby is affronted and outraged that the suffering and pain which are part of life should be part of his life. King Baby assures us that we don't deserve what we are enduring.

A major part of the suffering we endure in any calamity comes from insisting that we don't "deserve" what is happening to us. Resistance doubles distress. And the point is: Of course we don't deserve calamities. Why me?...Why anybody? Normally calamities happen without our leave or expectation. That is precisely why they become "crises." Whether we "deserve" calamities or not, therefore, is not the question. The crisis we face is simply "what is."

Denying a crisis or denying that it should be our crisis will not make the crisis go away. Feeling that we don't deserve it does not make pain go away. Resisting pain does not decrease it. Insisting that it should not be happening to us only makes it worse.

This doesn't mean that we passively sit around and feel completely helpless. We need to take care of ourselves, especially in times of crisis. But we don't adopt the illusionary and totally unproductive attitude that "I don't deserve this." It only makes the situation worse. We live in a life where calamities happen.

POWERLESSNESS AND SURRENDER

Admitting we are powerless over life, people, conditions, and outcomes is a monumental step in the recovery of balance, composure, and serenity, even in the midst of profound suffering and extreme distress. Suffering is always exacerbated by insisting we should have control over what we endure. But it won't work! Suffering cannot be controlled by control. Control, and attempts at control, only mean more suffering. Control is a flexing of mental muscle—a flexing that inevitably becomes a cramp.

John and Anne have just learned that their eighteen year old daughter Marcie is planning to elope with her boyfriend of six months. John and Anne are beside themselves with grief and anger. They have met the boyfriend and disapprove of him heartily. John and Anne know that their daughter is headstrong, and that once she makes up her mind to do something, she does it. They know she will elope. But the knowledge that Marcie is headstrong and determined only make John and Anne more obsessed with trying to stop her. They threaten her, demean her, call her names. They point out how "irrational" it is to elope. They point out to her that they have no jobs, no financial resources, and that statistics prove such marriages never work out. They scream and threaten even more. They cry and lament how much pain she is causing them.

John and Anne are in a crisis. They are suffering over Marcie's decision to elope. Their attempts in the past of controlling Marcie have only succeeded in making Marcie more headstrong than ever. Further attempts at control only confirm

Marcie in her resolve "to get away from this madhouse." It's a no-win situation. Control, as a means of handling a stressful situation, will not change the situation. It will only make the stress worse.

To admit that we are powerless brings us to the next step of "surrender." We are willing to "let go." To be willing to surrender means that we are content to "hand it over." We hand over our powerlessness to a power greater than ourselves.

Surrender, which is such an important part of our self-love recovery, is an especially powerful spiritual discipline in loving our selves through a crisis. Addicts, in their Twelve-Step programs, learn this to their bliss. "I am powerless over this addiction, and I hand it over to a power greater than myself to have it removed." Surrender relieves us of our non-productive resistance and allows our Higher Power freedom to take over. Surrender also frees up our positive energy to work with our Higher Power to help bring the crisis to a satisfactory conclusion.

If our faith is strong enough, we can even embrace the crisis itself as our Higher Power's will for us at the moment. We can embrace God's plan to help us grow into greater self-awareness, higher consciousness, and a better and happier life through the trials we endure. There is a reason for everything that happens in this world. Nothing happens by chance. Our Higher Power is working something out for us in the sufferings we undergo. Our Higher Power has a plan that lovingly includes us, no matter how unappealing suffering may be. We normally only grow through suffering. And our Higher Power will never allow us to bear more than we can handle. In our willingness to surrender we accept suffering as part of "the Plan" and we look forward to whatever growth our Higher Power has in mind for us. Surrender, therefore, does not eliminate suffering; it makes suffering meaningful.

In the Christian view, suffering's sharp edge can be blunted by "embracing the cross" as God's will—not denying the cross, not deflecting the cross, not blaming our crosses on someone else, not shifting our crosses onto someone else, but "embracing" our crosses in life. A cross that is "embraced" is a cross that is accepted. Once accepted, it can be worked through. Denial, blame, anger make the cross a crucifixion.

We are not called to crucifixion. From the Christian viewpoint, Christ was crucified once and for all. Christ is the heroic figure because he accepted actual crucifixion so that those who believe in him wouldn't have to be crucified. Accepting our cross is not the same as accepting crucifixion. We are not being asked to be crucified. We are called to embrace the inevitable condition of living and growing in the real world—a real world full of joys and crosses.

POWERLESS BUT NOT HELPLESS

Our acceptance of the crisis, our admission of powerlessness, our willingness to surrender, does not mean that we just sit back and suffer in silence, or wait to see what happens. The first part of the serenity prayer of Alcoholics Anonymous begins: "God, grant me the serenity to accept the things I cannot change," but continues immediately: *"(Grant me) the courage to change the things that I can."*

We are equipped with instincts, inner movements, healthy impulses, and the resources of our minds and wills to come to our own assistance in any trauma. We have these instincts, movements, impulses and resources for good reason. In allowing that "God's will be done," we do not become wet dish rags. Surrendering to the will of a Higher Power does not mean that we become passive. Surrender means that we become *responsive* to the movements of a Higher Power that will lovingly work on our behalf.

If we surrender to our Higher Power, we need to listen for a response. We have already spoken before about the validity of our "inner voices." Our Higher Power speaks to us in the voices of others, but also through our inner voices. We have inner resources for our own healing within that are beyond our imaginations. Spiritual masters have consistently told us that

"Everything you need is already within." All that we need, we already have inside of our selves. We need to learn to listen. We need to learn to trust our inner resources.

We are not in control of events and their consequences. We are not able to guarantee results, but we are not doormats. We can do our part to make sure that we are responsive to the impulses of our Higher Power. Our Higher Power expects us to work with our minds and wills to do what is good for us. We are expected to nurture and take care of our selves.

It is never more necessary that we perform the affirmative actions we have learned than in times of personal crisis. Some of those loving actions are of special importance to carry us through a calamity. It is to those loving actions that we now specifically turn.

DON'T DENY FEELINGS

Jim loves to be considered a macho man. He loves to give the impression that nothing bothers him. The bigger the challenge, the bigger his shoulders are to handle it. Big and strong outside, Jim is little and weak inside. If it weren't for his daily doses of Tagamet, his ulcers would be eating him alive.

"King Baby" does not want us to appear as the fragile human beings we are. How can a god be hurt? How can a god appear weak and vulnerable?

There are millions of people walking around with smiles on their faces who are full of tension and stress and somehow feel obliged to hide it. We are a nation of people consumed with what kind of appearance we are making. "What will the neighbors think?" We not only hide our honest feelings; we feel obligated to hide them. Somewhere, somehow, someone taught us to be ashamed of our feelings, to be reluctant to appear weak in front of others, to be embarrassed about being a human being with obvious limitations. Rather than simply name and admit our limitations, we are geared to put on a show, to pretend, to make believe that "nothing bothers us," or that there is "nothing I can't handle."

Loving your self means being honest and open about your feelings. If you feel bad, down, sad, hopeless, depressed, anxious, mortified, crucified, it's OK. It's OK to feel those feelings, because they are real. It's OK to verbalize those feelings. Feelings are nothing to be ashamed of. They simply are. To put on a performance that "I'm all right," when you aren't, takes enormous energy that would be better spent on solving your problems. To claim that "No, nothing's bothering me," when something is, is a lie and destructive of your integrity. It also cuts you off from the very help you need, from people who are willing to give it.

Taking care of your self in times of crisis means that you fully acknowledge exactly how you are feeling. "I feel rotten." "I feel terribly vulnerable." "I'm scared!" It's the truth. Let it out. Pretending that those feelings do not exist, or that they are unworthy of you, will only make a crisis worse.

Don't be reluctant to express your feelings to your Higher Power. Don't be afraid to tell your Higher Power that you are angry with him. If someone told you that he or she loved you very much and then neglected you or treated you badly, wouldn't you complain? "How can you treat me this way?" "If you love me, this a bad way of showing it." You have a right to expect your Higher Power to watch over and protect you. You have a right to protest to your Higher Power that you feel disappointed. Our Higher Power wants us to be honest and authentic.

Presume to speak to God. Presume to be angry with God. God is not vindictive and petty. He will accept an honest prayer in the manner it is given. And, as a lover, he will respond.

TALK ABOUT IT

As we have noted before, wounded animals, if they do not go on the attack, will most often crawl into a dark space, alone and cringing, waiting for the inevitable. All of us in self-love recovery have the same inclination when disaster strikes. "I just wanted to crawl into a hole and die." As many people as these are who end up in the hospital and wish for visitors, just as many, if not more, prefer that no one even know. Misery only sometimes loves company. Most of us prefer to lick our wounds in solitude, to bear the pain alone. We don't even want to talk about it.

We are social animals, designed to aid and support each other. Most people love to be needed. That's the nature of human nature. But not everyone wants to be noticed and helped. It's almost as though we are ashamed of being in need, ashamed of being weak and needing healing, ashamed of being human. King Baby does not want to admit weakness or defeat.

One of the best disciplines for taking care of our selves during a crisis is to talk about it. If we ever need to talk about it, it is precisely when we are undergoing a trauma. We need to share. We need to give others the gift of letting them help us bear our burdens.

Our need to share stems from the fact that we are often our own worst advisors. We are too narrow-minded to see the whole picture. A crisis can make us exceptionally myopic. We become too focused on our pain and loss to see the forest for the trees. We are too clouded in our vision by the dark mood that grips us. We are too obsessed with the ramifications of the crisis we are undergoing. The way to care for our selves is to share, so that we can be open to others and to other more balanced perspectives.

Talk about it. Talk about what you are feeling. Ask for what you need. Get the help you need to make it through. Talk to family, friends, anybody who will not judge you. See a therapist if you feel you need one. Let it out. Allow your self the release that comes from talking about your pain. Suffering shared is suffering diminished. Keeping it bottled up is like covering a boil with a tight, rough bandage. When we talk it out with others, we get the benefit of their compassion and wisdom. Our issues become clarified and focused as we see them reflected in the eyes of a supportive partner. "Calamity" is seen in another perspective. We might find some our presumptions challenged. We might discover solutions that would not have come to light as long as we remain slumped in depression and isolation.

DISCIPLINE CATASTROPHIC THINKING

When faced with a personal calamity, we feel overwhelmed by negative feelings. A cloud of doom and gloom overshadows us. We want to hide, "to crawl into a hole and die." The mood itself has power to generate even more negative thoughts and feelings. We feel grief over something good that is being taken away from us. We feel anger over "the injustice of it all." Fear builds as we begin to look at the wide range of disastrous consequences. We begin to project the most catastrophic results of our present circumstances. We feel that our "whole life is over." It's "the end of the world."

In a routine check-up, a tiny shadow is discovered on Dina's mammogram. She is asked to return to the clinic for more tests and a possible biopsy. She is struck with fear. Leaving the clinic, she enters her car shaking so badly that she is afraid she will never make it back home without an accident. She "knows" she has cancer. She "knows" it is terminal. While there is not yet any evidence that this is so, she "knows." Her imagination goes like wildfire. She begins to cry over what her husband and two young children will do when she is dead. She has been a good practicing Christian all her life. How could God take her at such a young age when she still has her whole life before her?

A negative mood breeds "catastrophic thinking." We tend to over-generalize our condition and think in terms of all-or-nothing. "I'm ruined!" "Everything I have ever worked for is destroyed." "I might as well be dead." "There is no hope." In the grip of a negative mood, our mental filter limits our perceptions only to what is negative about our situation. We cannot perceive the good that might come about as a result of our ordeal. The mental filter will not allow anything positive to come through. We jump to conclusions that have no basis in fact. "Only lucky people get over this disease, and I have never been lucky; I will succumb." We become experts at reading other people's minds. "She hasn't called in three days. She must hate me!" We become fortune tellers and become convinced that our predictions are already accomplished facts. "I bungled this assignment and I will be fired. I'm a complete failure."

While it is difficult to be cool-headed and emotionally sober upon hearing bad news or facing a calamity, every effort has to be made to break the catastrophic cycle. *Distortions need to be named and forcefully refuted.* "This is not the end of the world." "I have been in difficult situations before, and I survived. I can do it again." "Nothing is hopeless as long as I am alive and can surrender to a Higher Power." "Life has its ups and downs. I am now in a down state. I am hurt but not defeated." "All things pass sooner or later. This too will pass." "What good could come out of this?" "What is my Higher Power teaching me here?" "What new step of growth am I being called to?"

Loving our selves in times of crisis should bring out the best, not the worst, care for our selves. Taking care of our selves means discipline. Discipline is never more necessary and meaningful than in time of calamity. Discipline is a refusal to futurize or to live as if the future were already here. In all honesty, we just don't know what the future will bring.

The catastrophic thinking cycle can also be interrupted by *determined efforts to focus*, especially by our efforts to focus on NOW. What is the real problem we are facing? What is the real issue? What is really going on here? What am I dealing with here and now?

When we are facing a particular reversal of fortune, focus is easily lost and we revert to cataclysmic thinking. I sat with Evelyn in a hospital waiting room while her sixteen year old son was being X-rayed after being hit in the head with a baseball bat. The concussion was serious but the doctors assured us that it was not life-threatening. Evelyn was seriously upset and rambled for an hour on how this accident would forever change her life and her son's life, how he would be brain-damaged and most likely paralyzed. She claimed that she knew about "cases like this." How would she support him? How would he ever support himself? What would happen to him when she was dead? She then went on for another hour, vividly describing all the other misfortunes she had faced in recent years: her divorce, having to get a job, not being able to make car payments, the broken washing machine, the leaking roof, her best friend moving away, her alcoholic brother-in-law who was making life hell for his family, and so on. With every new description and analysis of another problem, Evelyn's intense sobbing increased, until finally a nurse had to be summoned to give her a sedative.

Focus! Refuse to multiply issues. Focus on the real problem and don't waste time and energy over other issues that are not immediately connected. Solving problems takes energy. Energy is used best when it is focused.

I find it particularly helpful in times of great stress to "put it in writing." There is something therapeutic about putting it in writing. Writing of itself helps us to focus. Make a list of all your feelings. Which feelings are appropriate to the issue at hand? Make a list of ways in which your current dilemma could turn out. What are the possible consequences? Cross off the ones that really don't make any sense. What is reality and what is fortune-telling? What catastrophic distortions are running rampant in your mind? How can they be refuted? Write it out. Is there anything positive on your list? Do you really believe that no other human being has gone through what you are enduring? What possible good results could come out of this conflict? In what ways can you grow and become a better human being? Write it out.

Don't even waste energy by wallowing in the self-pity normally associated with catastrophic thinking. Self-pity is not a means of caring for your self. Self-pity only causes more emotional damage. It has never been known to solve any problem. Our tendency when we are in our dark night is to conjure up all kinds of skeletons in our closets. "Where did I go wrong?" "I must have done something to deserve this." "Why is God angry with me?" "I can't do anything right." "Everything I do turns out bad." "My whole life is just one bad luck story after another." "If I only hadn't done this, or hadn't done that." We find ourselves in the fire and then proceed to pour fuel over our heads.

I am not saying we must try to fool our selves into thinking there is no problem, or that everything is going to be all right. We never know for sure what will happen. Dina's test did come up negative. Evelyn's son did recover completely. What has to be short-circuited is the automatic pattern that takes place once a cloud of depression sinks over us. We need to learn to talk back to our selves and to argue with our selves that catastrophic thinking solves no problem and only increases pain. It is invalid and illegitimate, and we need to reject it outright.

STICK TO A ROUTINE

One of the greatest factors that ended up saving the sanity of the men who were held hostages in the Middle East was their commitment to a daily routine. Confined in a tiny cell, over years of time, with the minimal of resources and social interaction, they managed to maintain mental health and emotional stability under circumstances that most of us would deem unimaginably devastating. Along with amazing internal fortitude, much of their survival depended on a personal daily schedule.

When Fred lost his job with a large advertising firm, he felt that his life was over. "Everything collapsed around me." He refused to talk to his friends. He made his wife a stranger, so ashamed was he of no longer being the primary provider for the family. He lay in bed all day. He couldn't sleep at night. He was a bundle of nerves. He had fearful headaches and pounding in his chest. "I just wanted to die." Worst of all, he had no energy to pick up the paper for job listings, much less to go out and search for a job. He languished in severe depression.

It took courage for him to finally leave the house and

begin walking three times a day. The walking turned into jogging three or four miles twice daily. He began to eat regular meals at fixed times. He devoted one-half hour a day to reading the want-ads in the daily paper. He began to set up one job interview a day. He began to pray and meditate one-half hour each morning. He did the dishes, and then began devoting one hour a day to refinishing the dining room table and chairs. He began to help his children with their homework nightly.

In one month's time, he was actually busy each day, and his negative mood lifted. He has no time for it anymore. He is in a routine that occupies a good deal of his waking moments. He is also energized and presentable as a candidate for employment. He is currently building up a list of potential positions from which he will make a choice. He owes a great part of his recovery from severe depression to setting up and sticking to a simple daily routine.

There is nothing worse than moping around and feeling depressed. There is nothing more beneficial to break the hold of depression—outside of drug therapy for those clinically depressed—than just plain doing something. Do something! Do anything! Just do it on a routine basis, every day. Perhaps simple exercise is the best way to start. When the body is exercised, chemicals, hormones, and adrenalin begin flowing again. The mind takes a cue from the energized body and thinks thoughts more appropriate for a "person on the go." Energy becomes available for use in a positive way. Options become clearer. Goals can be set, and attained.

BE VIGILANT ABOUT DIET

Our eating habits change, often radically, when we are in a crisis situation. Some of us lose weight because we lose our appetites. Others overeat to compensate for bad feelings. They eat all the wrong things and, with the weight gain, have something more to be depressed about. Some begin drinking too much. Alcohol is a depressant—which is just what someone who is already depressed doesn't need more of.

As part of the daily routine we set up, we need to eat our regular meals and supplement our diet with additional vitamins. Vitamin C and the B- complex vitamins are especially important. Stress literally depletes us of the nutrients we need. Getting its cues from depression and fear, the body presumes a life-threatening attack and takes measures to cope. Coping is very costly to our energy reserves. The body assumes that we are mortally endangered and uses vital nutrients in its system to prepare for an attack. Stress is being in a state of constant alert. It takes a great amount of energy. Imbalances in the body's chemical, hormonal, and vitamin levels are predictable and must be re-supplied for by additional healthful foods and vitamin supplements.

ONE DAY AT A TIME

One of the slogans of the Twelve-Step program encourages us to take life "one day at a time." This excellent advice is especially true when we are living through a crisis. We can't handle the whole future. Nobody can. We are fortunate to handle this day, this hour, this minute. Hence, one day at a time. That is all we can ask of our selves.

Depression and stress are only multiplied by considering how long our trauma will last or by trying to calculate how much more suffering will have to be endured. Crossing the ocean in a small craft seems insurmountable. To cross in a small sloop might seem madness—but not if it is taken one day at a time. Those who have done it claim that taking it just one day at a time was what it took. All those one-day-at-a-times add up. What was insurmountable when looked at as a whole is accomplished. It even looks easy, because it was taken one day at a time.

The simple truth about crisis is that it will pass. Everything passes. "This too will pass" is another slogan of the Twelve-Step program. We all can tell countless stories of "disasters" we confronted in the past. We can recall traumas we considered to be "the end of the world." There were problems we judged unsolvable. And yet we are here. We have survived. We go on, as we will go on. Life goes on. No matter what we are enduring, it will pass. A new day will dawn in the great rhythm and cycle of life. Acknowledging its inexorable flow can bring us the peace we need.

We need always remember that the key issue for us in times of personal crisis is to assure our selves that they are safe. Things will work out. We need not have a grand strategy. We need not know where we will get the strength to move on. Our only goal is to make it one day at a time. Our Higher Power will provide all we need to make it today, one day at a time—one day at a time to take care of our selves, one day at time to protect and nurture our selves as they need. The self can handle just about anything as long as it knows it is safe, loved and nurtured by us, one day at a time.

USE TECHNIQUES FOR HANDLING STRESS

There is enormous stress in every crisis we endure. Handling stress is part of any program to take care of our selves in times of trauma and calamity. In the following chapter we will discuss handling stress more specifically.

15

Managing Stress

A moderate amount of stress is healthful and desirable in our lives. As a matter of fact, life cannot go on without stress. Stress is the energy of life. Without some stress and tension, there would be no movement for us. We would die in our tracks. Death can be defined as "complete cessation of stress." There is tension, stress, wear and tear on our leg muscles every time we take a step. But without that stress we couldn't walk. Life implies stress. That is why this chapter entitled "managing," not "getting rid of" stress. Managing stress implies that it is up to us to take care of our selves so that the everyday tensions of living do not end up debilitating or incapacitating us.

Some stress is acceptable, but undue stress is a liability. Without managing stress effectively, our ability to function appropriately on our behalf is diminished. Chronic low-key stress can lead to inappropriate discharges of anger, general irritability, impulsiveness, inability to concentrate and deal with priorities, chronic fatigue, and/or dependency on medications. Unmanaged stress can lead to psychosomatic disorders such as chronic headaches, "nerves," back pain, gastro-intestinal disturbances, high blood pressure, inability to sleep, and overall despondency. Some of us have higher or lower tolerances for stress. It is important for us to be aware of what our stress tolerances are. Work will never kill us, but stress will—and does.

The pressures of everyday life occur often enough to stretch our stress tolerance to the maximum. Millions of Americans are under enormous stress from job pressures, family problems, financial worries, physical and emotional ills, and a generally fast-paced life that constantly challenges our adaptability. Undue stress results when we cannot cope with the pace of what is going on. Undue stress indicates that we are on overload. Undue stress means that we are confronted with more than we can handle.

Managing stress is essential to our well-being. Being able to recognize the sources of our stress and being knowledgeable of appropriate measures we can take to relieve undue stress is an indispensable part of our program in self-love recovery.

Adequate stress management for many of us will often imply need for a change in life style. Coming to love our selves as we need will most often require a "conversion," an "awakening," a new outlook about our selves and life around us. Loving our selves as we need means living a "new life" on our behalf. Living a more balanced, self-assured and self-confident life will mean a significant reduction of toxic stress. If we love and care for our selves enough, stress management will come naturally and effectively. However, for those who are in an early stage of self-love recovery, some principles and techniques for stress management are well in order. If we are to love our selves and give our selves the assurance they need that we are solicitous for their welfare, there are steps we need to take to make stress more manageable.

In stress management, we will recognize many of the principles we have already discussed at length in previous chapters. Stress management will mean that we consciously and specifically apply those principles to stressful situations.

ARE YOU STRESS-PRONE?

Stress is generally related to temperament and general life style. We do our selves no favor by gulping down Mylanta and writing off our stress with a glib disclaimer that "everybody's got stress." If our stress is debilitating us in some way, it needs to be addressed. Our goal is to take adequate care of our selves. A good beginning is simply to ascertain how stress prone we are. Our life styles and habits will give us a good indication.

● Do you feel you are living "on the edge"? Are you highly ambitious and competitive, "driven," compulsive, jittery, usually impatient with people, always in a hurry, always on the move? Are you always trying to kill two or three or four birds with one stone? Do you cringe at the thought of meditating? Do you talk a lot about "burn-out"? Do you feel that "life is serious, and nothing to laugh about"?

● Are you inclined to perfectionism, grieved if the job isn't done "right," highly judgmental of others' "incompetence"? Do you need work done, "like yesterday"? Do you feel you are the only one who can do a job adequately and that you have to be in charge to make things "work"? Is "winning" the "whole game" for you? Do you "identify" with your achievements (have no identity separate from what you do)?

● Do you think leisure is a waste of time? Do you always have to have a project going? Can you enjoy a quiet evening at home? Is it fun to watch your kids play? Do you have to have a drink to enjoy yourself or to calm down?

● Do you have a clear sense of your and others' boundaries? Are you able to say 'no' to an imposition?

If your answers are in the affirmative to most of these questions, it is likely you are stress prone. Taking care of your self in a loving way would suggest that you seriously examine your life style and what it is doing to your self. Some significant changes may well be in order.

WHAT IS STRESS TELLING YOU ABOUT YOUR SELF?

When we find ourselves under stress, the first strategy we need is to become *aware*. We need to acknowledge the stress we feel. We need to own up to it without denial or shunting it aside with distractions. We do well to admit our stress to another person. Sharing about our stress helps to keep our awareness acute and focused. Where is this stress coming from? What is it telling us about our selves?

Perhaps stress is our Higher Power's way of telling us that something needs to be changed, that something in our situation or environment needs to change or that something about our selves needs to change. The greater the stress, the more urgent the need for change. There is no need to fear stress. And we do not fear stress as long as we accept it as a sign or a message from our Higher Power that we are up against something we are not equipped to handle at the present moment and that "something has to give."

SURRENDER

In general, stress in caused by *uncertainty combined with feelings of loss of "control."* Stress is a form of panic about losing control over an unknown and threatening future. More than likely, in any stress we endure, King Baby will be standing there somewhere in the background. King Baby's imperious demands make for more stress than we can imagine. I am most under stress when my agenda is not being met or my time-table is not being honored. "I want what I want, and I want it now!"

If we want to avoid toxic stress in our lives, we do well to continue our efforts to keep King Baby off the throne. We keep King or Queen Baby off the throne by *surrendering the throne* again and again to our Higher Power, to God, as we understand him. Surrender takes the stress out of stress. The most serene and stressless people I know are those who have taken the first three steps of the Twelve-Step program very seriously. They daily make a decision to hand their wills and their lives over to a power greater than themselves. The harder we "hang on" to our agendas and our timing, the more tension we will have to endure. The more we can "let go," the greater our sense of freedom and peace. Surrender can turn stress into serenity.

So much depends, therefore, on general mental attitude.

The most effective way to manage stress is again a willingness to surrender. We neutralize stress by embracing it. We modify stress by accepting life as basically insecure and unpredictable. We diminish stress by placing it in the hands of our Higher Power. Our "power" over stress is precisely in our powerlessness. We manage life by accepting its fundamental unmanageability. It is resistance, and fighting "what is," that is the root of all stress.

DEAL WITH THE PROBLEM

Effective stress management techniques can be readily learned, but it is amazing how reluctant we are to effect those changes which could diminish or eliminate our stress. King Baby goes into a panic about any change that would threaten his life style. Better to paralyze us into inaction than lose the throne. I have known friends who sat with stress for years when solving a few minor problems would have put their stress to rest. It's amazing how tenacious we can be in sustaining our own misery.

We repeat again that surrender does not mean we sit back and watch our problems unfold. Stress is amplified by inaction. Stress is increased by listening to our old tapes telling us that we are incompetent to take care of our selves, as we need. We need to challenge those old tapes vigorously by actually dealing with our problems and issues.

There is nothing worse than simply sitting with stress. The longer we sit with it, the more paralysis sets in. Stress means that we are "keyed up" for action. Stress eats away at us if we remain keyed up and no action is taken. The hydrochloric acid that our stomachs produce will effectively digest the food we ingest. But when hydrochloric acid is present with no food to digest, it may begin eating away at the lining of our stomachs. That is how ulcers are formed.

Our Higher Power expects us to do our part to take care of our selves as we need. We take care of our selves by dealing with our problems. Stress tells us clearly that we have a problem.

Stress indicates to us that some issue needs examination. If some particular problem is causing us stress, we look at it and handle it the best we can. If we need help, advice, or professional counseling, we seek it out. If we need to change our selves by asking God to take away a character defect, we do so. If there is some change we need to make in our environment or living conditions, we do it.

The less we sit with stress and the more action we take to correct the problem that is causing our stress, the better off for our selves. *Action*, however small it might be, is an effective way to challenge an old tape that tells us we can't handle our lives adequately. Action does speak louder than any words from our old self-negating tapes. Action says, "Oh yes I can," and then proves it.

There is a lesson in handling problems that we learn as children but often forget as adults: breaking up problems into manageable pieces. A big problem is an occasion for a lot of stress; small problems are occasions for less. A good means of managing stress, therefore, will be found in breaking up our major problems into smaller, more manageable problems.

Whatever we do, we take action on our behalf. We do whatever we are equipped to do at any given moment, even if that means solving our problems in bite-size pieces. If I feel stress over a deadline to complete a particular chapter of this book, I can modify that stress by assigning myself smaller segments of the chapter to be completed on a day-by-day basis. Looking at a whole assignment might easily overwhelm me, but looking only at parts of the assignment, one day at a time, can be handled without undue stress. Break a problem down into smaller, more manageable pieces, and the accompanying stress is broken down also.

DISCIPLINE-DISTORTED THINKING

"Cognitive Therapy," popularized by Drs. Albert Ellis, Aaron Beck, and especially David Burns in his widely popular

Feeling Good, is training in changing the way we think, interpret, and look at things. Cognitive therapy is based on the premise that how we think will affect how we feel. Our feelings rather mindlessly follow along with whatever we allow to go through our minds. Stress, depression, and a host of related emotional disorders often find their way back to our old tapes, our mind-sets, our habitual patterns of distorted thinking. Change the way we think and we change the way we feel.

Thanks to King and Queen Baby, our thinking is easily distorted. We don't accept the fact that life is essentially "gray," and tend to see things in black and white categories, *"all or nothing"*: "You're either a winner or a loser!"

Or we *overgeneralize,* by taking one example and making universal statements about it: "I lost this contract, and I'll never get another one again."

Or we *over-focus* on the negative in a situation and overlook the positive, or we use a *mental filter* whereby we only see the negative: "My life is one bad luck story after another."

Or we *jump to conclusions,* with little rational support: "My life is over." Or we attempt *mind reading*: "She must hate my guts." Or we get into *fortune telling:* "I'm going to get fired for this."

Or we *catastrophize* by amplifying the seriousness of a situation: "If we move, we will never have good friends again."

Or we *reason with our emotions*: "I feel lousy, so something bad is coming down."

Or our freedom and self-respect is bound up with *"shoulds," "oughts," and "musts"*: "This should never have happened." "I ought to have known better." "I must be crazy."

Or we take *full responsibility* for something going wrong: "My son was arrested while driving under the influence...where did I go wrong?"

It is easy to see how stress can be linked to these cognitive distortions and how much stress could be relieved if we fought back with self-loving (and more honest) affirmations:

"I'm neither a winner nor loser, I'm a player, and that's what counts."

"I may have lost this contract, but life goes on and there will be others."

"I've had some bad luck in my life, but there have been some good times too."

"My life is never over, until it's over!"

"Maybe she does hate my guts; I'll find out and face it."

"I really don't know for sure if I will get fired or not, and if I do, I have talents that can be used elsewhere."

"We've made friends here and we can make them again."

"I feel lousy and I'd better check into it."

"Funny how things happen in life. I make mistakes. I'll correct them where I can."

"If my son got arrested for drunken driving, he will have to face the charges."

Sounds a lot different from the distorted thinking that can cause us so much unnecessary distress, doesn't it? And it is more honest and rational. We need to confront and challenge our distorted thinking tapes, again and again. We need to confront King Baby's grandiose forbodings about "reality." Stress and distorted thinking walk hand in hand down the path of despair. The sooner we catch them at it, the better.

CHANGE A STRESS-PRONE LIFE STYLE TO ITS OPPOSITE

Loving our selves as we need will mean making a conscious decision to manage stress. And that will mean making a conscious decision to change habits which contribute to a stressful life style. Developing new habits will include:

1. Get your life goals in order. Be clear and rational about what counts and what doesn't. Come to terms with how stress is damaging your self. Keep your identity separate from your achievements.

2. Take time for your self. Seek some solitude for quiet reading, prayer, and meditation. Make sure you take ample

time for vacation and recreation. Make time for exercise and "smelling the roses." Slow down your pace of talking, eating, and walking.

3. Allow your self to be human, to be imperfect. Allow that life will go on whether the job is done perfectly or not. Allow for ambiguity and "loose ends." Allow your self a daily quota of mistakes.

4. Be direct and assertive about what you need and want, rather than passive or aggressive. Being passive makes others think you are not serious; being aggressive turns them off. Ask for what you need, assertively.

5. Pick up with people who are more spontaneous and carefree. Talk about "stress" with others. Utilize the company of people who are supportive, and avoid the company of people who might be "toxic" to you.

6. Know your limits. Set up your personal boundaries. Say "no" when a request goes against your established priorities. Focus on doing one thing at a time at a non-rush pace. Stop pretending that undue stress is just a part of modern life.

7. Set aside time every day to develop your spiritual/religious life.

8. Make sure your ideals and values are not too inflexible. Make allowances for, and expect, failings.

9. Do some things for pure enjoyment. Visit art galleries and public museums. Have a body massage. Take a long bath. Walk in the woods after a spring rain. Raise a pet. Have a leisurely dinner at a fine restaurant. Explore the varieties of sexual experience that can be found in *The Joy of Sex*. Play sports. Develop a hobby, especially one that can keep

you in contact with nature. Attend cultural events, the theater, and the movies (especially comedies).

10. Know that you are "enough" and be grateful.

PRACTICE DIRECT STRESS-RELIEVING TECHNIQUES

The are hundreds of stress reduction techniques on the market. They all work, if they are used. If I am working my self-love recovery program, I find that stress is significantly diminished. However, whenever I feel that stress has increased to such a degree that I am conscious of it, it is time to use a stress reduction technique to at least clear my mind for the inner work I need to do. For my self, I have found a combination of some of the more popular techniques to be most beneficial.

Sit in a comfortable chair, with your eyes closed. In your imagination, picture a place of great beauty for you: a favorite vacation spot, a sunset, a mountain view, looking out on an ocean or a canyon, the face of someone you love. Smile, whether you feel like smiling or not. (Research shows that smiling itself has physiological effects in stress reduction.) Breathe slowly and deeply, imagining the breath coming from the soles of your feet up through your whole body and up through the top of your head. Whisper to your inner self, slowly, but over and over again: "Let go, let go, let go."

Bibliography

Beattie, Melody. *Codependent No More*. San Francisco: Harper/Hazelden, 1987.

_____ *Beyond Codependency*. San Francisco: Harper/Hazeldon, 1989.

_____ *Codependents' Guide to the Twelve Steps*. New York: Prentice Hall/Parkside, 1990.

Borysenko, Joan. *Guilt is the Teacher, Love is the Lesson*. New York: Warner Books, 1990.

Bradshaw, John. *Healing the Shame That Binds You*. Deerfield Beach: Health Communications, Inc., 1988.

_____ *Home Coming*. New York: Bantam, 1990.

Branden, Nathaniel. *Honoring the Self.* New York: Bantam, 1989.

Bristol, Claude M. *The Magic of Believing*. New York: Pocket Books, 1969.

Burns, David D. *Feeling Good*. New York: Signet, 1981.

Cunningham, Tom. *King Baby*. Minnesota: Hazelden, 1986.

De Mello, Anthony. *Awareness*. New York: Doubleday, 1990.

Dyer, Dr.Wayne W. *You'll See It When You Believe It*. New York: Avon, 1990.

Ferguson, Marilyn. *The Aquarian Conspiracy*. New York: St. Martin's Press, 1980.

Fromm, Eric. *To Have or To Be*. New York: Bantam, 1981.

Gawain, Shakti. *Creative Visualization*. New York: Bantam, 1982.

Gendlin, Eugene. *Focusing*. New York: Bantam, 1982.

Heschel, Abraham Joshua. *God in Search of Man: A Philosophy of Judaism*. New York: Farrar, Straus and Giroux: Noonday, 1976.

Hitchcock, John. *The Web of the Universe.* New York: Paulist, 1991.

Johnson, Robert A. *Inner Work.* San Francisco: Harper & Row, 1986.

Kreeft, Peter. *Making Sense out of Suffering.* Ann Arbor: Servant Books, 1986.

Maslow, Abraham H. *Toward a Psychology of Being (2nd Ed.).* New York: Van Nostrand Reinhold, 1968.

May, Gerald G. *Will & Spirit.* San Francisco: Harper & Row, 1982.

McKay, Matthew & Fanning, Patrick. *Self-Esteem.* New York: St. Martin's Press, 1987.

O'Brien, George Dennis. *God and the New Haven Railway.* Boston: Beacon Press, 1986.

Paul, Jordan and Paul, Margaret. *Do I Have To Give Up Me To Be Loved by You?* Minnesota: CompCare Publications, 1983.

Peck, M. Scott. *The Road Less Traveled.* New York: Simon and Schuster, 1978.

Percy, Walker. *Lost In the Cosmos: The Last Self-Help Book.* New York: Washington Square Press, 1984.

Schuller, Robert H. *Self-Love.* New Jersey: Spire Books, 1975.

_____ *Self-Esteem.* Waco: Word Books, 1982.

Sinetar, Marsha. *Do What You Love, The Money Will Follow.* New York: Dell, 1987.

_____ *Living Happily Ever After.* New York: Dell, 1990.

Slater, Philip. *The Pursuit of Loneliness.* Boston: Beacon, 1976.

The Twelve Steps for Everyone. Minnesota: CompCare Publishers, 1990.

Viorst, Judith. *Necessary Losses.* New York: Fawcett, 1986.

Viscott, David. *The Language of Feelings.* New York: Pocket Books, 1976.

Wilber, Ken. *No Boundary.* Boston: Shambala, 1985.

Yankelovich, Daniel. *New Rules.* New York: Bantam, 1982.